Yearbook of Comparative
and General Literature II

"... a clearing-house, a rallying point,
a source of information and of strength ..."

Yearbook of Comparative and General Literature / *Vol. II*

NEW YORK

RUSSELL & RUSSELL · INC

1965

THE UNIVERSITY OF NORTH CAROLINA

STUDIES IN COMPARATIVE LITERATURE

FIRST PUBLISHED IN 1953

REISSUED, 1965, BY RUSSELL & RUSSELL, INC.

L. C. CATALOG CARD NO: 53-62589

PRINTED IN THE U. S. A.

YEARBOOK OF COMPARATIVE
AND GENERAL LITERATURE II

published in collaboration with

The Comparative Literature Committee

of the National Council of Teachers of English

and

The Comparative Literature Section

of the Modern Language Association of America

W. P. Friederich, Editor
University of North Carolina

Horst Frenz, Associate Editor
Indiana University

TABLE OF CONTENTS

Part One

Part Two

Part Three

Part Four

Part Five

Bibliography of Comparative Literature, 1950-1952

Preface

The first issue of the *Yearbook of Comparative and General Literature* has been received favorably. Our conviction that a need exists for an annual publication of this kind has been confirmed. Encouraged by numerous expressions of interest and approval, we now present the second issue.

The functions of the *Yearbook* are manifold. Programs in comparative literature have become increasingly important as part of a liberal arts education. While only graduate programs are offered in a number of institutions, there is every indication that additional programs on the undergraduate level will soon be introduced and developed in large universities and small colleges where they do not now exist. It is therefore highly desirable to have a clearinghouse for information on comparative literary studies and their place and importance in American education, and a forum for the discussion of how such programs are organized, what type of courses are being offered, and how they are being taught. The *Yearbook* can acquaint the teaching profession with existing conditions and interest its active and prospective members in furthering and encouraging a comparative approach to the study of literature.

In increasing numbers, instructors in foreign language departments, in the departments of classics, English, philosophy, fine arts, and history are called upon to participate in the teaching of courses in general or world literature and the humanities on the freshman and sophomore level. The *Yearbook* can offer assistance to all of them by providing a channel through which the discussion of teaching methods, the evaluation of guides to useful histories of foreign literature and source books, and the presentation of approaches to various problems in the field can be expressed. For instance, the section on recent translations of foreign classics, which will appear in each issue of the *Yearbook*, should assist the instructor in selecting the better available translations. The importance of good translations cannot be overemphasized. Translations of foreign literary works can lead our students to the author and his total work and often to the language in which the work was originally written.

Another function of the *Yearbook* is that of providing a meeting ground for the scholar and the teacher. There is need for both of them to be able to express their ideas on the problms and methods of teaching literature, on the best textbooks available in the field, on the relationship between undergraduate and graduate studies, on the integration of literature and the arts. At present many liberal arts faculties are investigating ways and means of improving the instruction offered in their colleges. Through this publication we can discuss these and other matters of common interest and profit from each other by exchanging views and ideas. The current bibliography of comparative literature is of inestimable value to both scholars and teachers. Prepared for each issue of the *Yearbook* by Professor Werner

P. Friederich, it is a useful and convenient guide to the research that has been done in the broad fields of literature — literary themes, genres and forms, literary currents, international literary relations, the relationship to the other arts, and so on.

At a time when foundations and councils are supporting projects that will explore the relations between the various branches of the humanities, this publication can serve a useful purpose by demonstrating how the gap that has unfortunately widened between literature and the fine arts, let us say, can be bridged. We believe that the separation of the various fields of the humanities is harmful and we hope to encourage a lively discussion of ways in which closer collaboration can be achieved.

For several years the Committee on Comparative Literature in the National Council of Teachers of English has been investigating the various problems connected with comparative literature programs, with world literature and humanities courses, with the study of the "Great Books." The functions of this Committee are almost identical with those we have envisioned for the *Yearbook*. Aided by a publication like this, the work of the Committee can be strengthened and become more effective. Through the cooperation of the National Council of Teachers of English and of the Comparative Literature Section of the Modern Language Association, the *Yearbook* should receive the attention and the support of all those vitally interested in teaching and research in this field.

If the *Yearbook* is to achieve all that we envision for it and that we feel it can and should accomplish, it must not only reach the teachers who will use it but also become their means of expression. Toward this end we should like to see a spirit of cooperative enterprise prevail which will contribute to the development of the essential character of the *Yearbook*. Contributions of articles dealing with problems or methods of teaching general and comparative literature, suggestions for reviews of books and research in progress, notices of new or overlooked translations, and news items of general interest will be welcomed by the editors. The *Yearbook of Comparative and General Literature* can be meaningful only if it meets the needs and desires of the readers.

H. F.

PART ONE

THE CONCEPT OF COMPARATIVE LITERATURE

René Wellek
Yale University

Last year's *Yearbook of Comparative and General Literature* reprinted Jean-Marie Carré's short preface to M.-F. Guyard's *La littérature comparée* (Paris, 1951, in the series *Que sais-je?*). As M. Carré is the Professor of the Sorbonne who represents comparative literature in its ancient center, and as the Preface gives an almost official blessing to what one must regard as the authoritative program, it seems worthwhile to examine the concept of "comparative literature" advocated by M. Carré and his disciple.[1]

M. Carré defines "comparative literature" as a "branch of literary history," as the study of "spiritual international relations, of the factual contacts (*rapports de fait*) which existed between Byron and Pushkin, Goethe and Carlyle, Sir Walter Scott and Vigny, between the works, the inspirations and even the lives of writers belonging to several literatures." M. Carré rejects the view that "comparative literature" is literary comparison. He objects to the old rhetorical parallels between Corneille and Racine, Voltaire and Rousseau and warns against transferring them to foreign literatures. We should not dwell on the resemblances and differences between Tennyson and Musset, Dickens and Daudet, etc. "Comparative literature" rather studies sources and influences, but even these seem to him "difficult to manage, frequently deceptive," exposing us to weighing the imponderable. More certain is the history of the success of works, the fortune of a writer, the fate of a great figure, the reciprocal interpretations of peoples, of travels, of national myths (*mirages*). "Comparative literature", he asserts emphatically, is not general literature: the great parallelisms, (romanticism, symbolism, etc.) run the risk of being too systematic, too extensive in space and time, of landing us in abstraction, in arbitrariness and in verbal disputes (*nomenclature*).

Does this conception hold together? Has it a meaningful unity? Does it hold out a promise for the future? Are its exclusions and inclusions justified? It seems to me that, in every way, M. Carré's concept of "comparative literature" is obfuscating and, if it should become universal, destructive of a meaningful study of literature. It is both too narrow and too broad, falsely limited and falsely extended.

If we limit the study of comparative literature to the relationships between two or more literatures, if we think of it merely in terms of the "foreign trade" of literatures, no distinct subject can emerge, no distinct methodology, and we are simply left with fragments of literary history, cut out of the living process of literary development. There is no methodological distinction between a study of the influence of Ibsen on Shaw and

---

[1] For a review of M. Guyard's book turn to p. 60.

a study of the influence of Wordsworth on Shelley. There is no distinction between a study of the influence of Shakespeare in eighteenth-century England and of Shakespeare in eighteenth-century France. Comparative literature thus narrowly defined, never allows us to analyze an individual work of art, or even to explain its total genesis, as this will never be found merely in its foreign relations. Comparative literature in M. Carré's sense will always be concerned only with externals, with second-rate writers, with translations, periodicals, travelbooks, "intermediaries", all duly discussed in M. Guyard's handbook.

M. Carré is even wary of the study of influences and prefers as more certain, more factual, more positive, the study of reputations. He draws an untenable distinction between influences undergone by a writer and influences exercised by a writer. These are, after all, the same but only looked at from different sides. We arrive at exactly the same problem whether we study Goethe's *Werther* in relation to Rousseau or study Rousseau in Germany. The second subject seems to M. Carré different, easier and more certain because the student can start with externals, with translations, opinions of reviewers, etc., while with the first approach he would have to start with an actual work of art. But the two must inevitably come together and if the fame and reputation study deals with significant materials it must arrive at the analysis of a work of art which cannot be carried on without criticism, without weighing imponderables.

The consequences of the whole mechanical conception of scholarship underlying these recommendations come out almost naively in M. Guyard's little chart (on pp. 124-5) which lists the great figures of French literature in their chronological order and tabulates then, under the headings of the main countries: Germany, Great Britain, Holland, Italy, Spain and Russia, the books about the foreign reputation of the French writer. The space marked by an *a* indicates the existence of articles on the subject while a blank is left if no work has been done on this particular pigeonhole. Thus we can see at a glance that there are books about Voltaire in Italy and Russia, but only articles about Voltaire in Germany, Great Britain, Holland and Spain, and that, *horribile dictu*, there are blank spaces for Marot everywhere, for Ronsard in England, Bossuet in Germany, etc. One can readily imagine the glee of the students who see these blank spaces not yet covered by any investigator and rush to fill them with books about Fénelon in Spain or Pascal in Holland. Unluckily they might discover that there is a very good two-volume work, by H. A. Korff on *Voltaire im literarischen Deutschland des achtzehnten Jahrhunderts* (1918) and that there is even a book on Voltaire in England (by Bernard Schilling) and one on Rabelais in England (by Huntington Brown), just where M. Guyard has left blank spaces. Or are these books considered non-existent because they are not in French? It is hard to believe that these books are ignored deliberately, as elsewhere English books which were not written as Paris theses such as J. G. Robertson's *Studies in the Genesis of Romantic Theory* are freely referred to. Even if the chart were perfect it would show a mechanical conception of literary scholarship at its worst.

But can one accept even the restriction on "comparative literature" which forbids it to compare two figures such as Racine and Corneille, Voltaire and Rousseau or even Tennyson and Musset, Dickens and Daudet? In the first two cases, a historical relationship holds good: it has been investigated, and such investigations cannot dispense with comparisons and parallels. One can sympathize with M. Carré's dislike of rhetorical parallels in the usual schoolboy exercises, but this should not blind us to the fact that comparison is a process inevitable in all studies, not only literary, and that it should not be discouraged anywhere. The trouble with such parallels is that they have been carried out without method, without critical or analytical power, without system. But they are perfectly legitimate and even important topics of literary scholarship. Nor can comparisons between works and figures unrelated historically be excluded. It is a prejudice of the genetically minded nineteenth century that there is no cognitive value in confronting and contrasting objects which are in no historical relationship. Linguistics has shown that much can be accomplished when we give up this one-sided approach and compare languages which are not genetically related at all. The same is true of literature. For instance, we would certainly profit from a study of old Chinese or Korean or Burmese poetry if we dealt with texts not influenced by the West and would learn more from confronting them with Western poetry than from a study of the fortuitous and casual contacts which developed later. No inclusive conception of literary scholarship can dispense with comparisons of this sort even if they are not made expressly: we cannot help using our scheme of references. To forego the illumination of comparison between different literatures, periods, movements, figures, works, even when we cannot prove a causal relationship would mean foregoing the illumination which the present sheds on the past, theory on history, criticism on research.

While on the one hand, Mr. Carré wants us to limit comparative literature to the old factualism, he also suggests that the subject should be widened: that we should not only study sources, influences and reputations, but arrive at some kind of comparative national psychology. M. Guyard develops the theme at some length at the end of his book and sees the future of comparative literature in this expansion. We should study national illusions, fixed ideas which nations have of each other. A second chart tabulates the work devoted to the image of foreign countries in the mind of the French. M. Guyard himself is writing a book on the view the French held of Great Britain between 1914 and 1940. He will tell us about Maurois' war books, Morand's travel sketches, Céline's nightmares and so on. It will, one hopes, be an instructive parallel to M. Carré's book on *Les écrivains français et le mirage allemand*. But is this still literary scholarship? It is certainly a topical and useful subject. It may be valuable for the analyst in the Voice of America to know what image of the American is current in France, how and why this image arose, and so on. One may grant the share of literature in the formation of this image, though one should not overrate it. The actual behavior of American tourists and soldiers, the political events of our time were much more important than the images of the novelist. But granted the interest of seeing these images reflected in fiction, do these researches go much beyond the old *Stoffgeschichte*: the Irishman on the English stage, the Italian in Elizabethan drama? As Croce has long ago pointed out in reviewing a German thesis on the Mary Stuart theme there is no literary continuity between such works: there is only a social history of these images. Literary scholarship dissolves into psychology and sociology.

It would be ungracious to criticize M. Guyard's book too closely: on a small space he succeeds in conveying much information and in giving a clear description of many books and problems. As a matter of fact, he has a more catholic conception of comparative literature than his master, at least, as far as he expounds it in the *Préface*. M. Carré wards off the notion of "general literature" as dangerous. But M. Guyard, in practice, constantly oversteps fictitious frontiers between comparative and general literature. For what is it but "general literature" when he asks for a "European history of the historical novel" or when he suggests themes from the history of ideas and sensibility? M. Guyard even admits that reputation studies require undue attention to "mediocre translations, to plagiarists without greatness, to critics without intelligence." In contradiction to M. Carré, he seems to prefer the study of sources. In praising Paul Hazard—to whom he devotes an appreciative chapter—he inevitably praises work far transcending the narrow limits of his own definition. Hazard wrote wide-ranging intellectual histories, as did M. Baldensperger in his study of the French emigration during the Revolution. M. Carré's own work, on *Goethe in England*, is sensitive and subtle and contradicts the narrow positivism which he seems content to recommend today. Nothing seems accomplished by excluding general literature from comparative literature and narrowing down its field as sharply as M. Carré does in his *Préface*.

If we want to define the province of comparative literature, we must, it seems to me, start with a meaningful conception of the nature of literature and literary study. I have argued many times that " literature" must be interpreted as "imaginative literature" as otherwise we arrive at the study of all printed matter, of all cultural history. If we recognize this we must say that the comparative psychoanalysis of national myths demanded by MM. Carré and Guyard is not a part of literary scholarship, but a subject belonging to sociology or general history. It can, of course, and will draw on literary evidence, as the history of law or the sciences and of every other subject can draw on literary evidence. But we need not only an idea of the nature of literature but also of the nature of literary scholarship. In such a concept the divorce between theory and history, criticism and research must be abolished or replaced by collaboration and synthesis. The attempt to isolate fact from opinion, criticism from scholarship, will and must fail. There are no neutral facts in literature: we have to know and know how to use critical concepts if we want to write history, we have to apply a scale of values, unless we want to condemn ourselves to the most arid factualism. "Comparative literature" cannot be satisfied with being a sub-discipline investigating data about the foreign reputations of writers. The concept propounded by Messrs. Carré and Guyard carries us, on the one hand, back into the old days of positivistic fragmentations, and, on the other, abolishes the clear subject matter of our study in favor of sociology and national psychology.

The great argument for "comparative literature" is the obvious falsity of the idea of a self-enclosed national literature. Western literature, at least, forms a unity, a whole. Not only themes and motifs, forms and genres, ideas and symbols migrate, but there is a general European (and American) development of literature. Possibly, the name was badly chosen. Mr. Lane Cooper has ridiculed its English form: he says one could just as well speak of "comparative potatoes" or "comparative husks". But it is now an established and comprehensible term, while "general literature" is not. "General literature" used to mean poetics, theory of literature, and M. Van Tieghem has tried to give it a new special sense. Neither meaning is well established today. M. Van Tieghem drew a distinction between "comparative literature" which studies the interrelationships between two or more literatures and "general" literature which is concerned with international movements. But how can one determine whether e. g. Ossianism is a topic of "general" or "comparative" literature? One cannot make a valid distinction between the influence of Walter Scott abroad and the vogue of the historical novel. "Comparative" and "general" literature merge inevitably.

Possibly, it would be best to speak simply of "literature." M. Albert Thibaudet, no mean critic and a professor, has suggested that there should be professors of literature just as there are professors of philosophy and not professors of the history of English or French or German philosophy. But while we may not succeed in completely overcoming the departmentalization along national lines, as it is established by the tradition of nationalism and the inevitable limitations of our linguistic equipment, we can all work toward a conception of literature which transcends all provincialism, however respectable and hallowed by time: French, English, German, Spanish, American, and even Western. If we have to keep the term "comparative literature" it will mean simply the study of literature, independently of linguistic distinctions. Literature is one, as art and humanity are one: and in this conception lies the future of literary studies.

THE SPIRITUAL VALUES OF GREAT BOOKS[1]

Sister M. Beatrice, O.S.F.
College of St. Francis
Joliet (Illinois)

World events have turned many educators to a new search for fundamentals. They realize that society, nationwide, world-wide, will be no better than the individuals who compose it. They are increasingly aware that the college graduate should be an integrated human personality. Because all great literature reflects human personality in its various relationships— to man, to society, to God,—courses in world literature receive ever wider attention.

There are many problems and confusions in these courses as they are shaping themselves; these include the matter of title, the matter of scope and specific selections, the length of the selections (whole or partial), the underlying principle of organization, by nation, century, type, mood, or some other fundamental principle.

My contribution will be a few thoughts centered on the selections of the works and the manner of studying them. As I see the problem, the matter of selection rests on our objectives in such a course. The field is broad, the approaches many, and the objectives varied. We all agree, I am sure, that our chief objective should be to develop the intellect and to enrich human personality by bringing together the great literature of the past for the contemplation of our inquiring minds of the present. Whether we hold with Arnold that literature is a criticism of life, with Croce that it is vicarious experience, or with others that it is an interpretation of life ultimately affects our teaching. But our aim should be to unfold the great masterpieces of the past for the enjoyment and formation of the younger generation today. It is hoped that through a study of human nature here portrayed, in its strength and in its weakness, our students may grow mentally, morally, and spiritually. Admittedly, this is a broad objective, but it can and should be a goal even when more specific aims are being considered.

World Literature is as wide as the world's horizons. There are advocates for the great and lesser classics. It is well to remember that the course as drawn up by Hutchins and Adler in the Great Books Foundation is an adult reading program and covers *ten* semesters; whereas in most colleges the course is limited to two semesters, carried by students with a full schedule. Consequently, the problem facing every teacher in organizing such a course is chiefly that of selection; one will want to take those works that will yield the most value and delight in the time available and for the student level studying them.

A corollary of what to take is how to take it. Most of us hold for the complete text. It enables the student to see the work as a sustained whole and provides the only true basis for evaluation. The author conceived the

---

[1] Address delivered at the NCTE Meeting in Cincinnati in 1951.

work as a whole, and its true, full power is felt only when it comes in its entirety. Study of the whole text will discourage hasty and superficial teaching. The whole text forces close study of ideas, pattern, relationships. Moreover, the whole book offers a challenge to students—and we do not challenge students enough. Good translations of most of the great works are available today, as the Rinehart classics, the Modern Library editions, the Penguin classics, the new-type Everyman. They are inexpensive, easy to carry, easy to pencil, and they offer a stimulus to the student to build his own library.

Another problem is the basis of arrangement, the underlying principle for the selections. The simplest arrangements thus far have been by chronology, genre, and mood. However, because these bases of arrangement tend to separate mankind by centuries and nationalities there has been some criticism of them. In a paper read two years ago at the College Section of NCTE in Buffalo, Professor Roy Basler asked if there is not some other more fundamental basis than these for the study of world literature. He thought that cultural patterns, folk customs, religious and ethical concepts appear to be better bonds between works separated by centuries. This matter of arrangement suggests that I digress a minute or so to outline our course at the College of St. Francis, Joliet, before I present briefly two main questions for the consideration of this group.

Our course was introduced twelve years ago under the title of the World's Great Books. In the beginning it was handled as a special honors course in reading, for superior students only. There were no formal lectures. The students met the teacher once a week, reported and discussed their reading. After three years, at the requests of students, the course was changed to a 3-hour class for upper-division students. This year, for several reasons, we have moved the course to sophomore level.

From the beginning we called our course "Great Books" rather than World Literature, since we felt the latter was too ambitious a title, laying us under obligation to cover too wide an area. We used the complete classic wherever possible. The aim has been to interpret the work as a literary piece, to see what inherent values have kept it alive. The basis of organization for the whole course is the dichotomy of the natural and the supernatural man. Within this we follow the chronological pattern, a logical one for our main basis of division. The first semester is devoted to works of ancient Greece and Rome, illustrating man's reason, unenlightened by grace. The second semester, all too short, is devoted to works in the Christian tradition, in which man is raised to supernatural dignity by virtue of the grace of baptism. Thus far we have not included Oriental literature, chiefly because of time and teacher limitations. (I happen to conduct the course.)

More specifically, the first semester includes the *Iliad, Prometheus Bound, Oedipus Rex, Medea, Hippolytus,* Racine's *Phèdre,* Aristotle's *Poetics,* Plato's *Phaedo,* Horace's *Art of Poetry,* selections from Pliny and Tacitus, and Juvenal's satires 3 and 10—the latter included for the sake of eighteenth century English satire. In the second semester, if it happens that a majority of the group have not had the course in Sacred Scripture, we read St. Luke's Gospel, the *Acts*, the epistles of St. Paul. The *Confessions of St. Augustine* is taken next. Because we are in the Franciscan tradition, we include St. Francis' poem, *Canticle of the Sun*, a few legends from the *Fioretti*, and St. Bonaventure's inspiring mystical treatise, *De Itinerarium Mentis in Deum—The Journey of the Mind to God*, reprinted today under the title of *The Franciscan Vision*. Then follows the *Divine Comedy*, the sixth book of Vergil's *Aeneid*, and Milton's *Paradise Lost*. It is a heavy schedule. As it is, we must omit the Scandinavian Sagas, the *Nibelungenlied, Don Quixote, Faust*. How other colleges can pack more into a two-semester course (without risking mental indigestion or opening themselves to the charge of superficiality) is something of a mystery. Other courses in Drama and Fiction include works omitted here. We realize that we will have to make some changes in opening the Great Books to non-majors on the sophomore level.

Thus, we have been following a basis of organization other than time and type; we have chosen the fundamental concept of man—'What a piece of work is a man! how noble in reason, how infinite in faculty. . .''

May I assume that our readers represent people who accept the great heritage of Christian thought and morality? In our age of materialism one cannot always make this assumption. That one simple question, whether Jesus of Nazareth was God Incarnate, has been and still is the decisive issue among men. Dr. Karl Stern, in his *Pillar of Fire*, quotes Dostoievsky as once saying that it is the one question on which everything in the world depends. When time is lived out in the light of eternity, when merely human values are transmuted by supernatural and eternal values, all teaching, including the teaching of literature, takes on a more intense meaning. Perhaps the whole concept of Christian education has never been more succinctly epitomized than in these two sentences by Pope Pius XI in his *Encyclical on the Christian Education of Youth:*

> "Christian education takes in the whole aggregate of human life, physical and spiritual, intellectual and moral, individual, domestic and social, not with a view to reducing it in any way, but in order to elevate, regulate, and perfect it, in accordance with the example and teaching of Christ. Hence, the true Christian, product of Christian education, is the supernatural man who thinks, judges, and acts constantly and consistently in accordance with right reason illumined by the supernatural light of the example and teaching of Christ; in other words, to use the current term, the true and finished man of character. . ."

And how does World Literature fit into this pattern of Christian education? This question raises the first of two other questions I would like to present: Are we not expecting too much from literature? Are we not perhaps looking to it for answers and solutions it cannot give, hoping in some vague way that a world literature course will be a substitute for religious training? In a day when Divine Revelation is cast aside, there is a marked trend to look to literature for more than it can or should supply. We hope that a study of Homer will instill ideals of courage and nobility, and dispel pettiness, infidelity, chicanery; we hope that a study of Rousseau's work will insure ideals of equality and fraternity and all the natural virtues that society needs so greatly. Let it be said that literature cannot be a substitute for religion. For the checking of man's passions and injustices, for power to act in accordance with ideals, mere words, no matter how powerful, are not enough; only the grace of God received through the exercise of intelligence and will, through prayer, through the Sacraments, can avail. Newman's famous words come to mind:

> "Quarry the granite rock with razors, or moor the vessel with a thread of silk; then may you hope with such keen and delicate instruments as human knowledge and human reason to contend against these giants, the passion and the pride of man."

Perhaps you will agree with Thomas Merton, who says in his recent book, *The Ascent to Truth*, that "the only thing that can save the world from complete moral collapse is a spiritual revolution."

However, if literature alone cannot form the true Christian mind and heart, the full human personality, it can still be a powerful aid to right living. The great works of world literature are really a study of human nature in both its strength and its weakness. As has been pointed out, a great book is not necessarily a good book, anymore than a great man is necessarily a good man. The distinction is important. Most world literature offers human thought on human problems, and it is unfair to consider it as the supreme and final answer to our problems, especially our moral problems. What it can do is to give us a better understanding of man's relations to himself, to his fellowmen, and to God. Through enlightening the intellect and exercising the imagination literature can help to form ideals and attitudes; it can develop the artistic sense, refine tastes, and sublimate man's emotional life.

My second question is—Are we not betraying literature as a fine art when we emphasize the sociological, historical, and didactic values in it? The didactic intention has had a long life in literature, but even Horace held for *"dulce* et utile." As teachers of literature we must recognize that literature should be studied primarily as an art. Pleasure, enjoyment, is still the first objective in all art. And by this I do not advocate the "art for art's sake" principle. The artistic approach to literature is still the only valid and sane one. We ask in regard to a work: What is it? What does it mean? What unity of design does it have? What sustained power of inspiration, creation, and expression does it have? What does it reveal of the significance of life as seen by an author? For we must distinguish essentially between life and literature. The subject, the material of experience, is not as important as what the artist has done with it. His selection and interpretation are of first importance.

To take one illustration: Dante's express purpose in the *Divine Comedy* is to force men to reflect on the eternal issues of good and evil-doing in this life. His aim is to teach. But his work exists as a piece of literary art and this aspect is of primary importance. We do not study the *Divine Comedy* to learn scholastic philosophy or medieval society. We study it as an epic. The design and sustained power of execution of this great poem comes over even in a prose translation. What must the pleasure be for one who can read it in its Italian terza rima? And beyond the technical design is the tremendous power and beauty of it all, especially of the closing cantos, which for a T. S. Eliot represent the highest point that poetry has ever reached. As Professor Blackmur writes: "Poetry is life at the remove of form and meaning, not life lived but life framed and identified." Dante has framed his vision of the ultimate goal of the life of grace in the majesty of an epic. Surely it is one of the best illustrations of Spenser's line—"The soul is form and doth the body make." It is the imagination of the poet working upon Divine Revelation and bodying forth the forms of things unknown. The *Divine Comedy* is primarily art, not dogma.

In closing I put the question uppermost in many of our minds: In what ways may a world literature course help to mold a new generation? One answer is, by a wise selection of materials that will yield the most delight and the most value for the human personality. Again, by recognizing that literature is not religion, but a fine art. Since most of the Great Books, besides having significance as art, also have a moral and religious value, they have great power: they stir the imagination and the will, they ennoble and strengthen the human personality.

DEBASED STANDARDS IN WORLD-LITERATURE COURSES

Calvin S. Brown
University of Georgia

On January 31, 1827, Goethe told Eckermann that national literatures no longer had much meaning and that the era of "Weltliteratur" was beginning. This prophecy proved to be correct: Goethe's new word has been adopted into practically all civilized languages. In the course of its diffusion, the term *world literature* has, as Fritz Strich has pointed out, acquired a variety of meanings and emphases, yet, as generally used, it remains a clearly understood name for that small part of literature which has proved itself to be intensely alive and viable outside its own country and age. When this definition is understood, it becomes a matter of simple fact rather than mere opinion or personal taste to say that Shakespeare, Molière, and Goethe belong to world literature and that Herrick, Gérard de Nerval, and Wackenroder do not.

It is neither possible nor desirable to try to make an exact definition of world literature or to draw up an exclusive canon of its writers or works. Though changes are necessarily gradual, they do occur: almost any listing of the works of world literature made in 1350 would have included Statius, but today no one would nominate him. Then there are a great number of borderline cases in which the degree of life and viability which works exhibit might or might not justify their inclusion. Byron and Lessing are examples. Again, there is a question as to how broadly the term *literature* is to be interpreted. Most people would include Plato and Herodotus as literary figures, but Aristotle and Suetonius might find more opposition, and Hegel and Josephus would hardly be considered. Thus the general concept of world literature is both clear and simple, but in particular cases the application of the term is necessarily elastic.

During the present century, American universities have increasingly tended to offer—and frequently to require— a course in world literature, on the assumption that an educated man should have some first-hand familiarity with the literary works which have been most influential in shaping our tradition and which are still an integral part of our thought. Both the decline in the study of Latin and Greek and the decrease in the general habit of reading seemed to require that curricula specifically include certain reading which formerly could have been taken for granted among people of university education, and today a great many of our colleges have courses, usually for sophomores, in which a considerable number of the works of world literature are studied.

By accident rather than any particular design, these courses are largely administered and taught by departments of English. The principal reason is that in most institutions they were introduced as alternatives to the traditional survey of English literature, or as replacements of it, and the old staff went on with the new courses. There were at least some schools in which the departments of foreign languages and literatures either refused to help with the courses when asked, or entered into them half-heartedly and soon dropped out. Nor was this development especially unfortunate. Most students of one literature had some background of real study of other languages and a habit of intelligent general reading in several literatures. Few comparatists were available, and the English teacher was as competent to teach world literature as any of his colleagues in other departments. There was always the possibility of an interdepartmental course in which various experts lectured on their own specialties, but most such experiments lost in direction and continuity at least as much as they gained in the competence of their peripatetic faculties. Furthermore, when the course was a large one, such a system became impossible: the Spanish department could not supply good teachers for fifteen sections during three weeks devoted to *Don Quixote*.

This brief and extremely general account is sufficient to show how various more or less accidental considerations have combined to produce what can now be called the traditional course in world literature—a course which, while falling far short of the ideal, has at least proved reasonably adequate and has played a valuable part in the education of a good many people.

Recently, however, there have been signs of alarming changes. An organization of college English teachers embracing four states recently distributed to its members a "report-questionnaire" dealing with sophomore courses in literature. In this document sample courses were given, including two labeled as "world" literature, and the members were asked to indicate their opinions of these syllabi and to answer some other questions, such as the percentage of time which should be allotted to recent and contemporary literature in such courses. One of the world-literature courses was organized by types and listed thirty-five titles, not counting "one or two novels" to be inserted from time to time. The section dealing with the short biography included eight examples, seven by recent British or American writers, and the other by André Maurois. Out of the total of thirty-five works to be studied, twenty-six were originally written in English, and twenty-seven were written during the past hundred years. The only French work appearing in both world-literature courses was Rostand's *Cyrano de Bergerac*, and another recent Hollywood hit, Arthur Miller's *Death of a Salesman*, was similarly designated as an essential work of world literature. Dante appeared in one list, as an alternative to the King James Bible, but when the questionnaires were returned he was found to have been voted out. Among the writers missing from both courses were Vergil, Montaigne, Cervantes, Goethe, and Voltaire.

This particular "report-questionnaire" deserves no further comment, for the facts already given will characterize it sufficiently for anyone with even a rudimentary understanding of occidental literature. Though it represents an extreme case, however, it is unfortunately by no means an isolated one. It fits into a general trend which has developed to alarming proportions during the past few years.

This development naturally raises four important questions. What is the purpose of its advocates? What will be its educational effects? How has it become possible for such proposals as those already cited to be not merely made, but acclaimed? And what can serious teachers of literature do about it?

The purpose seems to be simple enough. The elaborate jargon of "education for life," "student participation," "democracy in education," "self-evaluation," etc., in which such proposals are couched all boils down to the argument that students are not interested in "heavy" reading, that it is our job to entertain them and give them what they want, and that we must therefore furnish them with some of the better class of light reading. (Actually, sophomores can be interested in Dante—but only by teachers who know and value him.) If this purpose were honestly and plainly stated, it might possibly be respected, but it is evident that labeling these farragoes as courses in world literature is a direct misrepresentation. An advertiser trying to sell a shoddy product always tries to give it an impressive name that will somehow imply a very high quality. The same motives are evident in the attempted justification that such courses are intended merely as an "introduction to literature," though their students have been allegedly studying literature for years, and the course is really the conclusion of literature for most of them.

The educational effects are disastrous from any point of view. The student necessarily finishes the course without that familiarity with the shaping forces of our civilization which he is supposed to get. Likewise, he misses the possiblity of learning to derive any aesthetic or intellectual stimulation from the more complex literary works—and he misses both the satisfaction of this achievement and the possibility of learning to understand a great many things which he will be constantly encountering for the rest of his life. Finally, he gets some strange ideas of our literary tradition: that the literature written in English since 1850 outweighs all other literature put together; that there is nothing of great value in German, Spanish, or Italian; that the French don't amount to much, though their outstanding writer, Rostand, did produce one of the great literary masterpieces, etc. These notions, fantastic as they are, would be quite literally accepted—for life—by the sophomore who was subjected to these courses under the title of world literature. In short, the chief educational result of such offerings would be to confirm the student's linguistic, geographical, and chronological provincialism.

The question of how such proposals have become possible is more complex. It is significant that of the 16% of "returns" on the questionnaire already mentioned, the majority were admitted to come from the younger—and probably minor—members of English departments. The language and the anti-intellectual bias immediately reveal that many of those concerned in the project were at least as strongly conditioned by the study of pedagogy ("education") as by the study of the literature. The forces which have nearly succeeded in emasculating our secondary education are now beginning to undermine the universities. But this is not a complete answer. With the decline of foreign-language study, ancient and modern, most of the younger members of our English departments have no longer even an amateur competence in literatures outside their own tongue. (It is significant that the "report-questionnaire" blandly assumed throughout all its discussions that English teachers are, by definition, to be considered as authorities in the field of world literature!) Those who take advanced degrees in English and American literature now usually emerge with only a "reading knowledge"—i.e., a slow and stumbling translating knowledge—of any foreign languages, and the literatures of these languages are a sealed book to them. They can even plan world-literature courses without proposing to break the seals. In short, the younger English teachers, as a group, are utterly incompetent to deal with world-literature courses, and those who have been exposed to our educationists for any considerable period of time are opposed to the very idea of such courses, though the label itself can still be retained to disguise the adulteration of the product.

A recent experience of mine will illustrate two further points about the nature of this trend. Not long ago I happened to hear a man who did not know a word of Greek expatiating to a group of high-school teachers on the relative merits of various translations of Homer. The primary criterion was that a good translation must sound "modern"—must be like what is being written today. In fact, it turned out that a translation of Homer is good if it sounds like Hemingway. It is obvious, of course, that Homer does not sound like Hemingway, but the significant thing is that this critic (assuming that he was at least honest) not only did not have any basis for a judgment, but did not even know enough about the problem to realize his own incompetence. The other point of interest is the obsession with the modern, the lack of historical perspective which explains many of the fallacies of our present education and leads to identifying change with progress and stability with stagnation. This bias explains why two-thirds of those who answered the "report-questionnaire" favored devoting from one third to one half of a world-literature course to works written since 1870, and this fact, in turn, explains why they were impelled to endorse works which cannot conceivably be included in the canon of world literature. Basically, what happened was that the courses grew out of non-literary *a priori* prejudices instead of being based on a broad familiarity with the great literary works.

These facts suggest some tentative answers to the question of what can be done. In the first place, comparatists and others who have a wide knowledge of world literature must make themselves heard. Only sixteen per cent of the questionnaires came back, and I know many a competent man who glanced at his copy, saw what it was, and tossed it into the wastebasket. Thus it was possible for a fringe of educationists, novices, and devotees of "fully experimental trends" to pile up a spurious statistical endorsement of some fantastic proposals. When a literary scholar receives a document of this sort, he should answer it fully and, if necessary, brutally, distasteful though the task may be. Only thus can the movement to debase the idea of world literature be stopped before it becomes entrenched behind the sanction of statistically gullible administrators. If our fathers had joined battle with the pedagogues of 1900 instead of dismissing them with contemptuous amusement, our children's education today would be in the hands of educated people rather than certified educational technicians.

Since competent comparatists are far more generally available today than they were twenty years ago, we must insist that, as far as possible, courses in world literature be at least planned by such scholars. If a state endorses the idea of world-literature courses in its junior colleges, its university should maintain a strong department of comparative literature so that these courses may be competently planned and taught.

Finally, in the battle for literary standards in education, the scholar must abandon the modesty appropriate to his dealings with his peers and enter the dust and shouting of public debate. The type of man who prescribes current Broadway hits as "education for the Atomic Age" does not hesitate to proclaim from the housetops that he is an educational expert, and as long as his claims are uncontested, the public can hardly be blamed for accepting them. It is the duty of the real scholar to deflate these claims by showing what real competence is and where it can be found.

LA LITTÉRATURE COMPARÉE EN POLOGNE

Z. L. Zaleski
Paris

Par sa position même au carrefour du Continent européen, la Pologne semble comme prédestinée aux recherches "comparatistes." La littérature subit la règle générale. Ainsi, depuis longtemps, les recherches dans le domaine des lettres impliquent des éléments comparatistes: sans négliger l'examen philologique ou esthétique des oeuvres, les chercheurs aiment mettre en valeur les rapports entre la production littéraire polonaise et celle des autres pays occidentaux avant tout. Le problème des sources et des influences étrangères, flux et reflux de mouvements d'idées les préoccupent vivement. Rappelons qu'au temps de l'humanisme les voyages en Italie, en France, en Allemagne ont joué un rôle important et si fécondant dans le développement de la littérature polonaise. N'oublions surtout que la grande génération des poètes et artistes romantiques polonais a vécu et a créé en exil.

C'est ainsi que bien avant la première guerre mondiale cet aspect comparatiste apparaît nettement chez un essayiste de grande envergure, Ignace Matuszewski (*Essai sur le Diable en poésie* et son *Slowacki et l'art nouveau*), chez M. Zdziechowski (*Byron et son siècle, Messianistes et Slavophiles*), chez Kawczynski, chec J. G. Pawlikowski (dans sa magistrale étude sur la *Mystique de Slowacki*) et presque avec excès dans le dépistage des sources chez Stanislas Windakiewicz. A un degré moindre les mêmes orientations se manifestent chez Ignace Chrzanowski, Bronislas Chlebowski, Joseph Kallenbach, Tadée Grabowski.

Après la première guerre mondiale les mêmes tendances persistent et se développent. Elles sont orientées et renforcées à la fois par l'incidence du comparatisme français: Baldensperger, Paul Van Tieghem que cite Chrzanowski, et Paul Hazard.

Sans parler de Zenon Przesmycki qui continue son activité d'infatigable convoyeur de valeurs esthétiques européennes, d'un Tadée Sinko dans ses études sur les influences classiques, d'un Eugène Kucharski, d'un Victor Hahn ou d'un Bernacki, une nouvelle génération de chercheurs apparaît. Citons Jules Kleiner avec sa grande monographie de Mickiewicz mais surtout avec celle consacrée à Jules Slowacki où il emploie méthodiquement et brillamment à la fois le procédé comparatiste, ou Ladislas Folkierski dont la thèse *Entre le classicisme et le romantisme*, publiée en français, n'a rien perdu de sa valeur et de sa vivante saveur et dont les nombreuses études polonaises du domaine franco-polonais ou hispano-polonais ont grandement enrichi le patrimoine du comparatisme littéraire en Pologne. Le rôle de Waclaw Borowy, l'un des plus subtiles parmi les érudits et les théoriciens de littérature, se dessine nettement déjà à partir de son étude suggestive *Les influences et interdépendances littéraires*, pour s'affirmer plus tard avant tout dans le domaine anglo-polonais. Wenceslas Lednicki déploie sa riche activité en étudiant surtout les relations littéraires polono-russes et polono-françaises (Pouchkine, Alfred de Vigny); Manfred Kridl étudie en comparatiste de stricte obédience Mickiewicz et Lamennais; Z. L. Zaleski les relations de Mickiewicz et Michelet, de Quinet et Cieszkowski, Flaubert et ses contacts avec la Pologne. Stanislas Pigon use dans ses très substantiels travaux sur Mickiewicz et son époque des procédés comparatistes, de même que Stanislas Szpotanski dans sa monographie de Mickiewicz, et Kolbuszewski dans ses études sur le théâtre romantique, ainsi que M. Szyjkowski dans ses études sur les influences polonaises dans la littérature tchèque. Notons encore les incursions dans la littérature comparée du grand poète Jean Kasprowicz et les nombreuses contributions à l'étude des relations littéraires franco-polonaises de Jean Lorentowicz, et n'oublions surtout pas une série d'explorations comparatistes rigoureuses dans le domaine polono-italien de Roman Pollak. A cette énumération déjà longue et pourtant bien incomplète il faudrait ajouter une série de travaux présentés sous forme de thèses de doctorat comme *Balzac et le monde slave* de Sophie Korwin-Piotrowska ou la *Fortune de Sienkiewicz en France* de Maria Kosko.

Cette activité des comparatistes polonais se reflétait incidemment aussi dans les Congrès périodiques organisés par les comparatistes—avant tout à ne citer que le Congrès de Lyon en mai 1939, présidé précisément par Ladislas Folkierski avec plusieurs communications polonaises, entre autres celles de Folkierski, T. Grabowski, M. Kridl, Z. L. Zaleski.

L'occupation allemande depuis octobre 1939, infiniment plus dure en Pologne qu'en France et en Belgique, amena la fermeture de tous les foyers d'enseignement supérieur. L'activité des Universités fut reprise, il est vrai — tant au point de vue de l'enseignement que du travail scientifique — dans la clandestinité. Grâce à une volonté indomptable et à des miracles d'audace et d'ingéniosité, ce double effort n'a jamais été complètement interrompu. Mal nourris, grelottant de froid, privés de tout confort, les nombreux savants s'adonnaient pourtant au travail, y découvrant peut-être de nouvelles sources d'énergie ou d'efficace consolation. Notons incidemment qu'en Pologne orientale occupée par les Russes, alliés des envahisseurs hitlériens, la situation était quelque peu différente, mais en pratique conduisit également à la suppression de tous les centres scientifiques polonais.

Dans le présent aperçu nous essayons de rappeler aussi bien l'activité poursuivie dans le pays sous l'occupation que l'effort des savants émigrés et dispersés dans les différentes contrées de l'Occident.

S'il s'agit de la Pologne même, distinguons deux périodes: 1939-1945 et 1945-1953, non pas tant d'ailleurs pour classer les travaux que pour indiquer un changement radical des conditions de travail scientifique. La première — durant l'invasion germano-russe — est caractérisée par l'état de stricte clandestinité de toute activité intellectuelle. L'actuelle occupation politique russe par contre ne vise point la suppression brutale du travail scientifique. Elle l'encourage même dans un certain sens comme pour vouloir submerger le passé sous le flot de la production qui doit en principe remplacer, "corriger," assimiler ou refaire l'héritage de la liberté suivant les directives impérieuses d'une double doctrine: *marxisme, panrussisme*. C'est pourquoi on assiste à une activité en apparence exubérante, fébrile et multiforme. Remarquons tout de suite (sans pouvoir pour des raisons faciles à comprendre citer les noms) que toute cette activité est loin d'être scientifiquement stérile. Certains savants, il est vrai, se plient totalement (parfois de bon gré s'il s'agit de communistes convaincus, parfois par un calcul mêlé d'anxiété) aux exigences rigides des maîtres. Il y a heureusement aussi des cas relativement nombreux où, grâce à une sorte de virtuosité d'adaptation, on arrive au prix de quelques concessions de forme à sauvegarder une certaine liberté dans la démarche scientifique et parvient ainsi à des résultats scientifiquement valables. Certaines matières facilitent cette dangereuse entreprise permettant de cotoyer avec succès les abîmes béants. Il s'agit ici par exemple du compartiment d'influences antiques sur les lettres polonaises, où sont à noter les trauvaux de W. Wasik sur *Aristote en Pologne*,[1] de G. Pianko sur *Mickiewicz et le monde antique*[2] et de K. Dombska sur la *Fortune de Platon en Pologne*.[3] D'autre part Konrad Gorski, chercheur original et consciencieux, s'occupe utilement du *Rayonnement de la pensée d'Erasme de Rotterdam en Pologne*.[4]

Dans le compartiment franco-polonais on peut citer de nombreux articles, notes et aperçus. Stanislas Pigon étudie les influences françaises dans le théâtre scolaire au XVIIIe siècle.[5] T. Mikulski démontre l'influence des *Apologues Orientaux* de Billardon de Sauvigny sur les *Contes Orientaux* de Krasicki. B. Kielski compare le *Jocelyn* de Lamartine et le poème de Slowacki *En Suisse*.[6] Mme Kulczycka esquisse la parallèle entre *La Poupée de Prus et l'oeuvre d'Alphonse Daudet*.[7] Dans le compartiment polono-italien soulignons avant tout l'activité soutenue et efficace de M. Brahmer dont l'étude sur l'histoire des relations culturelles italo-polonaises a vu le jour un mois avant l'explosion de la deuxième guerre mondiale. Roman Pollak aves sa compétence habituelle continue ses remarquables études sur l'*Orlando Furioso* d'Arioste en Pologne. La personnalité de Mickiewicz attire comme toujours l'attention des comparatistes. *Mickiewicz et Dante* de Z. Sitnicki, et quelques aperçus de Kubacki en font preuve. Dans le domaine polono-espagnol relevons une étude sur les sources de *El rey sin reino*, tragi-comédie de Lope de Vega, de Maria Malkiewicz-Strzalkowa,[8] puis une étude sur les destinées polonaises de Don Quijote de Z. Szmydtowa[9] et *Don Quijote dans l'art polonais* d'Hélène Blum.[10]

En dehors de W. Borowy, dont on déplore la disparition récente, signalons les études de W. Chwalewik sur les rapports de la renaissance et du moyen-âge en Angleterre, de T. Grabowski sur les *Relations entre la Pologne et l'Angleterre à l'époque de la Réforme et au XVIIIe siècle*,[11] de G. Sinko sur *Sheridan et Kotzebue*,[12] enfin des aperçus de A. Swiderska sur le polonisme de Conrad, sujet traité d'ailleurs avant la dernière guerre mondiale d'une façon approfondie et suggestive par Joseph Ujejski. En ce qui concerne l'Allemagne nommons les articles de Sophie Ciechanowska

---

[1] Comptes Rendus de l'Académie polonaise, 2, 1950.
[2] *Meander* (Varsovie), 1947.
[3] C.R. de l'Académie polonaise, 7, 1948 et *Meander*, 1947.
[4] Dans: *Essais sur l'histoire de la littérature anti-trinitaire polonaise au XVIe siècle*. Cracovie, 1949.
[5] "Le Jay en Pologne." C.R. de l'Académie polonaise, 2, 1949.
[6] *Prace Polonistyczne*, Lodz, 1948.
[7] ibid.
[8] *La question des sources de El rey sin reino de Lope de Vega*. Cracovie, 1950.
[9] "Don Quijote en Pologne pendant la première moitié du XIXe siècle." C.R. de l'Académie polonaise, 2, 1948.
[10] ibid. 9, 1950.
[11] C.R. de la Société des Amis des Sciences, Poznan, 1948.
[12] Wróclaw, 1949.

sur *Goethe en Pologne*[13] et une étude de Z. Zygulski sur *Krasinski et Hebbel*,[14] sujet neuf et captivant.

Les relations littéraires entre la Pologne et la Russie font l'objet d'une multitude de travaux et d'articles. Le nombre nécessairement limité de sondages ne me permet pas d'apprécier la valeur de cette production quantitativement imposante, mais entachée semble-t-il d'un esprit d'adulation de mauvais aloi.

Qu'il nous soit permis à la fin de ce "tour d'horizon" nécessairement incomplet de nous arrêter très brièvement sur le secteur occidental où, à l'abri des pressions et des persécutions, travaillent les savants et chercheurs indépendants émigrés. Ils poursuivent leur tâche en ordre dispersé. En Grande Bretagne Folkierski[15] continue ses prestigieuses études comparatistes et savantes explorations de théories littéraires. St. Stronski poursuit ses importantes études provençales. Pawlikowski,[16] Giergielewicz, Terlecki, Danilewiczowa déploient une activité riche et variée, où les préoccupations comparatistes apparaissent souvent. Citons spécialement les *Indian Elements in Slowacki's Thought* de Maryla Falkowna,[17] les études sur le théâtre de Slowacki de Ladislas Günther, ainsi que les travaux en cours de J. Bujnowski et de W. Kwiatkowski (*Kasprowicz et Chevtchenko*). En France travaillent Z. L. Zaleski,[18] Z. Markiewicz,[19] Irène Galezowska (études sur Norwid et sur le positivisme en Pologne). J. A. Teslar poursuit en France ses anciennes explorations polono-anglaises,[20] W. Godlewski prépare une thèse sur Kasprowicz et les grands courants de la pensée européenne. En Suisse A. Bronarski exerce sa débordante activité dans plusieurs compartiments de recherches littéraires, entre autres dans celui des relations polono-italiennes. En Belgique J. Korab-Brzozowski n'abandonne pas ses études comparatives sur Dostoiewski. M. Kridl et Maria Kosko continuent leurs études aux Etats Unis et W. Lednicki approfondit ses investigations suggestives et péné-

[13] *Tworczosc*, 7, 1949.
[14] *Pamietnik Literacki*, 1947.
[15] "Dante et l'Islam," Communication au IXe Congrès des Sciences historiques, Paris, 1950. — "Rapport sur l'histoire littéraire et les beaux arts," Ve Congrès de la Fédération Internationale des Langues et Littératures Modernes, Florence, 1951. — " 'Deux voix' de Victor Hugo et de Jules Slowacki." *Zycie* (Londres), 22.II.1952.
[16] "Le Roi-Esprit de Slowacki comme un monument de la civilisation latine." *Livre du Centenaire de Jules Slowacki*, Londres, 1951.
[17] ibid.
[18] "Adam Mickiewicz et le mouvement de 1848." *Revue des Travaux de l'Académie des Sciences Morales et Politiques*, 24.V.1948. — "Balzac entre la Pologne et la Russie," ibid. 6.XI.1950 et Londres, 1953. — "Le théâtre de Jules Slowacki et le problème des personnages étrangers." RLC, 1950. — "Victor Hugo et la Pologne." ibid. 1952. — "Victor Hugo et l'institution de l'exil." *Revue des Travaux de l'Académie des Sciences Morales et Politiques*. 12.I.1953.
[19] "Le monde polonais dans l'oeuvre et la vie de Prosper Mérimée." C.R. de l'Académie polonaise, 4, 1948. — "Les personnages polonais chez Gobineau." C.R. de la Société Historique et Littéraire Polonaise de Paris, 1951. — "Les influences françaises sur le théâtre de Jules Slowacki entre 1832-1842." *Livre du Centenaire de Jules Slowacki*, Londres, 1951.
[20] "Polonius et la Révolution anglaise." *Revue des Travaux de l'Académie des Sciences Morales et Politiques*, 24.V.1948.

trantes sur les relations littéraires russo-polonaises.[21]   Les mêmes problèmes préoccupent W. Weintraub (intéressante étude sur Bakounine et Mickiewicz) et Jadwiga Jurkszus prépare un vaste travail sur les aspects essentiels du roman familial contemporain.

Arrêtons cette austère énumération et constatons que l'effort dispersé sinon quelque peu désordonné des savants et chercheurs émigrés tend spontanément à compléter, à rectifier, parfois à remplacer, certaines positions de l'abondante production des savants restés dans le pays et obligés de travailler sous la pression implacable des directives officielles.   L'organisation de foyers libres d'activité scientifique à l'Occident comme l'Université Polonaise à l'Etranger, le Polish Research Centre à Londres, la Société Historique et Littéraire à Paris ainsi qu'une large hospitalité intellectuelle des universités et des institutions scientifiques occidentales rendent possible le recrutement de jeunes chercheurs et semblent pouvoir assurer une continuité de travail.

LA LITTÉRATURE COMPARÉE CHEZ LES ROUMAINS

B. Munteano
Paris

La Roumanie offre aux phénomènes de relation un champ éminemment fertile : voilà bientôt deux mille ans qu'à ce carrefour, Orient et Occident se croisent ou s'affrontent sans répit.   Pressée, depuis le VI-e siècle, par les flots de l'océan slave, la "Dacia felix" de Trajan figure une île de romanité tranchant sur son milieu.   Les Roumains n'en furent pas moins contraints de frayer tour à tour avec le slavisme, puis avec Byzance, puis avec l'hellénisme moderne, ce qui peupla leur culture d'étonnants hybrides sans vitalité et ternit pour un temps leur conscience latine.   Le triomphe de celle-ci, au XVIII-e siècle, marque le début d'une renaissance qui va transformer la nation de fond en comble.   Ce fut, dès lors, la ruée panique vers l'Occident latin, l'importation massive de ses idées, de ses formes, tout un vaste mouvement passionné pour la conquête de l'indépendance et de l'unité nationales, autant que pour la création d'une littérature.   Au bout d'un siècle d'efforts, ces objectifs étaient tous atteints, étape par étape, et la "Grande Roumanie" issue, en 1919, du Traité de Trianon, venait clore l'époque héroïque des ferveurs, rendre au pays son équilibre et ouvrir de nouvelles perspectives à une activité créatrice dont les quelque dix-huit millions de Roumains se sentaient redevables vis-à-vis de leur nouvelle position en Europe.

Le moment semblait propice, entre autres, à l'épanouissement d'un comparatisme s'appliquant de sang-froid à débrouiller l'enchevêtrement d'influences contradictoires dont le passé national était tissu.   Par malheur, le meilleur de l'effort savant dut porter sur des tâches préliminaires, in-

---

[21] "Thèmes russes dans l'oeuvre de Slowacki." *Livre du Centenaire de Jules Slowacki*, Londres, 1951. — "Goethe and the Russian and Polish Romantics."   CL, 4, 1952.

dispensables — établissement d'éditions critiques, publication d'inédits, recherches d'archives, bibliographies, biographies, reconstitutions de l'ambiance sociale, politique, idéologique. Parallèlement, le point de vue comparatiste faisait son apparition dans la plupart des monographies et des histoires littéraires nationales. Pour sa part, N.Iorga, qui avait tout lu, ou tout vu, multipliait un peu partout, dans son oeuvre prodigieuse, les détails et les suggestions. On s'attaquait enfin, plus systématique-ment, à nombre de questions partielles, dans autant d'articles, souvent introuvables à l'étranger. Dans cette masse éparse, quelques bons travaux de plus large envergure émergent qui donnent la mesure de ce que le com-paratisme roumain serait devenu s'il n'avait prématurément sombré, avec le reste, dans la catastrophe qui est en train de détruire le pays.

Depuis les trop ambitieux travaux d'ensemble de L. Saineanu (1900 et 1902), la difficile étude des influences orientales avait retenu peu de chercheurs sérieux. Turcologues et slavisants avaient trop à faire sur les terrains contigus de la philologie et de l'histoire pour qu'ils puissent se vouer à des recherches proprement littéraires. La littérature trouvait davantage son compte dans les travaux des byzantinologues et des spé-cialistes du grec moderne. Là-dessus, avec son précieux ouvrage de prospection sur l'*Hellénisme en Roumanie* (en roumain, 1912), D.Russo fit école.

C'est à N.Cartojan que l'on doit en ces matières l'ouvrage le plus considérable. Son ample synthèse des *Livres populaires dans la littéra-ture roumaine* (en roumain, 1929 et 1938) porte sur l'origine, les vicissi-tudes et l'adaptation d'un grand nombre de légendes bibliques et hagio-graphiques, de toute une littérature astrologique et fatidique, de plusieurs "romans" du type *Alexandre le Grand*, ou *Barlaam et Josaphat*, d'un traité de zoologie populaire comme le *Physiologue*, cet ancêtre des *Besti-arii* médiévaux, etc. Cette naïve littérature, qui circulait intensément en Europe, parvenait au Danube par le canal byzantin et slave et passion-nait, jusqu'à nos jours, une masse de lecteurs de toutes classes. Chargée de mirifiques visions orientales et de sagesse hindoue, égyptienne, chal-déenne ou antique, elle aura, durant des siècles, pétri l'âme populaire, enrichi le folklore, influé sur les plus grands.[1] Une mention spéciale méritent les travaux d'Emile Turdeanu, slavisant et byzantinologue, qui s'attaque depuis une dizaine d'années au difficile problème des apocryphes et de leur circulation dans les Balkans, ainsi qu'à l'étude méthodique des relations avec les Bulgares, les Grecs et les Russes, à partir du XIV-e siècle: le prochain volume du *Yearbook* fournira, d'autre part, la liste de ces travaux.

---

[1] Pour une analyse détaillée du I-er vol. de cet ouvrage, ainsi que pour des précisions bibliographiques sur *Les influences orientales en Roumanie*, cf. l'article de pure information que nous avons donné à la *RLC*, 1934, 166--80. — Afin d'épargner l'espace, et pour que ce bref exposé ne devienne pas une fastidieuse énumération de titres, on ne donnera ici les signale-ments des ouvrages relevés que dans les cas d'absolue nécessité. Que l'on veuille bien, pour le reste, se reporter aux articles d'accès facile que nous indiquons, ou bien aux Bibliographies courantes : celle de M.M.Balden-sperger et Friederich, celle de la *RLC*, et le *Yearbook* de 1954.

Les échanges littéraires avec les voisins immédiats — Serbes, Bulgares, Hongrois, Tchèques — dans les temps modernes, ont si peu retenu l'attention, qu'il est encore impossible d'en évaluer l'importance. Nous savons à peine davantage sur la Pologne et la Russie, grâce, notamment, aux travaux de P.P.Panaitescu, lesquels portent d'ailleurs, presque toujours, sur des faits et des personnages du XVII-e siècle.[2] Une Roumaine de Bessarabie—province aujourd'hui annexée par les Soviets—Mme. E. Dvoichenko-Markov, actuellement aux U.S.A., a traité, entre 1930-1940, de l'influence de Pouchkine, dans une série d'articles en roumain, qu'elle a complétés plus récemment par une étude en anglais.[2bis] Rien cependant, à notre connaissance, sinon des considérations occasionnelles, sur un Tourguéniev, un Dostoïevski, un Tolstoï, que les romanciers roumains ont pourtant beaucoup lus.

Les relations occidentales, autrement accessibles, sollicitent la curiosité d'un plus grand nombre de travailleurs. Cette fois encore, on s'applique de préférence à recueillir une information générale, le plus souvent extérieure à la littérature — voyages dans les deux sens, études et missions à l'étranger, impressions, jugements mutuels, différents contacts politiques, intellectuels et autres.[3]

Il existe sur l'ensemble de l'influence anglaise un aperçu de P. Grimm, en 1923. Mais les monographies tardent à venir, bien que la matière ne manque point. Signalons toutefois, d'E.Turdeanu, en 1944, l'étude très poussée de l'*Oscar of Alva* de Byron, copieusement adapté, jusque par Eminescu lui-même. Et notons que M.E.D.Tappe, professeur à l'Université de Londres, trouve dans les archives anglaises de curieuses précisions, dont nous ne connaissons pas encore l'ampleur, sur les contacts anglo-roumains au cours des siècles.[4]

En fait d'influence allemande, l'effort des comparatistes a porté tout particulièrement sur Goethe, comme émetteur — à preuve la substantielle monographie d'I. Gherghel, 1931 ; et en tant que récepteur, sur Eminescu, dont s'occupe un petit livre en allemand d'I. Sân-Giorgiu, 1934. Dans sa monographie de 1930, en roumain, sur *La Poésie d'Eminescu*, l'esthéticien T. Vianu reprend avec autorité l'importante question de l'influence de Schopenhauer sur le poète. Du même auteur un précieux *Mémoire* sur l'influence de Hegel. Relevons enfin d'utiles travaux d'approche, en alle-

---

[2] Cf. une brève analyse de ces travaux (en roumain ou en français, 1925-1930) dans l'article ci-dessus.

[2bis] *Pushkin and the Rumanian Historical Legend.* ASEER, April, 1948. — Du même auteur, une monographie en roumain, 1933, sur le poète bessarabien C. Stamati (1795-1869), fortement imprégné d'éléments russes.

[3] Les notes de ce genre, éparses dans un grand nombre d'articles ou d'ouvrages variés, font masse. Signalons toutefois, pour l'ampleur du plan, le recueil de textes d'Al.Cioranescu, *La Roumanie vue par les étrangers*. 274 p. in 8°. Bucarest, 1944.

[4] P.Grimm, in *Dacoromania*, III, Cluj, 1923. — Cf. l'analyse de l'article (en roumain) d'E.Turdeanu sur Byron, dans la *RLC*, 1951, 281-3. — Le *Yearbook* signalera, à l'occasion, les publications de M.Tappe.

mand et en roumain, sur la fortune roumaine de Heine, que l'on a beaucoup imité et traduit.[5]

Sur la culture italienne en Roumanie, il existe un excellent ouvrage, bien connu, de Ramiro Ortiz, 1916. Les relations des deux pays remontent à la Renaissance. Déjà, au XIII-e siècle, le pape Innocent III était au fait de la latinité des Roumains et, devenue familière aux humanistes italiens, cette idée finira par toucher, au XVII-e siècle, les historiographes roumains. Depuis, nombre de voyageurs et de diplomates italiens visitent les Principautés, ou bien y séjournent et prennent des emplois à la cour ; alors que les grammairiens, les historiens, les philologues, abondent en détails sur les pays et le peuple roumains, témoignages qui se succèdent à peu près sans interruption jusqu'à nos jours, que l'on a recueillis plus d'une fois et que l'on peut enrichir encore, sans grande conséquence, semble-t-il, pour la littérature elle-même. Inversement, les Roumains se rendent de plus en plus nombreux en Italie — en mission, pour des études, ou tout simplement pour leur plaisir — et les "amants" de l'Italie, comme les poètes Georges Asaki et Basil Alecsandri, ne se comptent plus au XIX-e siècle. Une catégorie à part doit être réservée aux jeunes Roumains qui, à la suite de l'union, en 1700, d'une partie du clergé transylvain avec le Vatican, achèvent leur formation dans les collèges jésuites de Pologne d'abord, puis à Rome même, où ils se plongent avec ravissement dans l'étude de leur passé ancestral. L'Ecole latiniste qui se constitue en Transylvanie vers 1750, et dont l'importance est capitale dans la culture roumaine, tirera grand parti de ce contact permanent avec la ville éternelle. Notons enfin que les exilés et les révolutionnaires roumains du XIX-e siècle ont partie liée avec l'Italie des Mazzini et des Cavour.[6]

Sur le terrain proprement littéraire, les rapports italo-roumains ont inspiré peu de travaux notables, dont celui de N.Cartojan (en roumain, 1924), qui reconstitue la fortune roumaine des *Fiore di virtù*, la célèbre compilation de récits et de sentences du vieux bénédictin T.Gozzadini. Dans *l'Idéologie littéraire d'Eliade-Radulescu* (en roumain, 1935), D.Popovici apporte d'abondantes précisions sur l'activité de cet italianisant passionné, véritable fondateur de la littérature roumaine moderne. Pour sa part, A.Cioranescu fournit une sérieuse contribution à l'histoire du théâtre

---

[5] Quelques précisions supplémentaires dans notre c.r. collectif, *La Littérature comparée en Roumanie*, in *RLC*, 1931, 515-35. — I.Gherghel, *Goethe în literatura română*. Mémoires de l'Académie. Bucarest, 1931. Nous avons analysé ce livre dans l'*Europe Centrale* de Prague, 20 et 27 janv. 1934. — Différentes publications de D.Caracostea sur les sources d'Eminescu, 1926. — I. Sân-Giorgiu, *Eminescu und der deutsche Geist*. Iéna-Leipzig, 1934. — T.Vianu, *Influenţa lui Hegel în cultura română*. *Mémoires* de l'Académie, 71 p. in-8°. Bucarest, 1933.

[6] Pour les prémices de ces relations, cf. N.Cartojan, in *RLC*, 1934, 12-29. — N.Iorga, *Ospiti romeni in Venezia*, 1570-1610. Bucarest, 1932. — Une analyse de différents ouvrages d'Al. Marcu, dont *Alecsandri e l'Italia*, Rome, 1929, dans l'article cité de la *RLC*, 1931, pp. 526 suiv. — M. C. Isopescu a noté d'autres contacts au cours des siècles, dans des articles dont la plupart ont été réunis sous le titre *Saggi romeno-italo-ispanici*. Rome, 1943. — Du même: *La stampa periodica romeno-italiana in Romania e in Italia*. Rome, 1937.

de Métastase et d'Alfieri en Roumanie. Enfin, on attendait beaucoup des recherches entreprises par D.Caracostes sur les sources de G.Asaki[7]

Purement accidentelles, les relations hispano-roumaines n'offrent à l'étude que des épisodes.[8] On sait, en revanche, quel aimant la France représente, depuis deux siècles, pour les Roumains, dont elle fut proprement l'institutrice en fait de civilisation, de politique et de littérature et dont elle favorisa si fort l'ascension et l'émancipation. On le sait moins cependant en bonne littérature comparée, où l'on attend encore les études décisives, touchant au vif du sujet. Là, comme ailleurs, on multiplia les travaux de reconnaissance et d'approche. La *Bibliographie franco-roumaine* de Rally qui vint, en 1930, refondre et enrichir celle de Georges Bengesco, est elle-même à reprendre. Dans les trois volumes de son *Influence française sur l'esprit public en Roumanie* (en français, 1898, 1905, 1914), où il retraçait les grandes lignes d'une histoire politique, sociale et, si l'on peut dire, humaine de la communauté franco-roumaine, P.Eliade s'occupait à peine de littérature. Il fit école : nombre de travaux vinrent s'inscrire dans son sillage, le retoucher, l'amplifier. On s'appliqua aussi à en représenter la contrepartie, tel Ch.Drouhet, avec son article *Le Roumain dans la littérature française* (*Mercure de France*, 1-er mai 1924), ou bien V.Hanes, avec la *Formation de l'opinion française sur la Roumanie au XIX-e siècle* (en roumain, Bucarest, 1929). Les grands philoroumains de 48 et de plus tard — Quinet, Michelet, Bataillard, Picot, etc.—, leur expérience, leur action et leurs relations roumaines, inspirèrent autant de travaux à double versant, où l'on mit à contribution les archives des deux pays.[9]

Abordant enfin un sujet proprement littéraire, N.Cartojan entreprit l'étude d'un certain nombre de "romans" français du moyen-âge qui parvinrent aux Roumains par le canal italien et grec et dont il découvrit des traductions manuscrites datant du XVIII-e siècle finissant : *Le Roman de Troie, Pierre de Provence et la Belle Maguelonne, Paris et Vienne* surtout, dont N.Cartojan a pu établir qu'il est à la base du fameux roman

---

[7] Quelques autres indications dans l'article cité de N.Cartojan, *RLC*, 1934. — Les études d'A.Cioranescu sur Métastase et Alfieri figurent dans son recueil roumain, *Literatura comparata*, Bucarest, 1944. — Le petit volume de D.Caracostea sur les *Sources* de G.Asaki (en roumain, Bucarest 1928), n'a pas eu, que nous sachions, de suite.

[8] A noter une traduction moldave, au XVII-e siècle, de l'*Horloge des Princes* de Guevara, d'après le latin, et la traduction, au XVIII-e siècle, d'après le grec, du *El Criticon* de Gracian ; cf. N.Cartojan, *ibid.*, pp. 19 et 23. — Quelques épisodes hispano-roumains du XIX-e siècle dans un article de C.Isopescu, repris dans les *Saggi* cités, pp. 137 suiv.

[9] Les travaux, en français, sur Picot, Quinet et Bataillard figurent dans les *Mélanges de l'Ecole roumaine en France*, 1925, 1927, 1930. — Sur Picot et Bataillard, on peut lire nos c.r. dans l'*Europe Centrale* de Prague, 28 mai 1927 et 22 nov. 1930. — L'auteur du Quinet ci-dessus donnera aussi un *Michelet si Românii*, Cluj, 1935. — A noter, de N.Iorga, *Les Voyageurs français dans l'Orient européen* . . . *RCC*, 1929. — Analogue à celui d'A.Cioranescu, un recueil de textes par P.Desfeuilles et J.Lassaigne, *Les Français et la Roumanie*. Bucarest, 1937.

crétois l'*Erotocrite*, de Vincent Kornaros.[10] D'autres oeuvres françaises
encore pénètrent à la même époque dans les pays roumains. On les lit en
grec d'abord, puis on les traduit, d'abord du grec, puis du français même,
et on les fait circuler en manuscrit — l'*Alcidalis* de Voiture, *Télémaque*,
le *Charles XII* de Voltaire, le *Narcisse* de J.-J.Rousseau.[11]

C'est à Ch.Drouhet que l'on doit l'ouvrage le plus spécifiquement "comparatiste" que cette discipline ait produit jusqu'à ce jour en Roumanie :
son *Alecsandri et les écrivains français* (en roumain, Bucarest, 1924). Le
même savant portait encore son attention sur des points plus particu-
liers —Alexandrescu, à l'école curieusement éclectique de Boileau, de Voltaire et des romantiques; Conaki, chantre moldave de "l'âme sensible" à
la grecque, mais aussi à la française.[12] Dans sa monographie, déjà
nommée, sur Eliade-Radulescu, D. Popovici dégage avec le même soin les
influences françaises que les italiennes. Sous le titre *Santa Cetate*, qui
est celui d'un poème biblico-social d'Eliade, le même auteur a relevé chez
maint Roumain de 1848 l'empreinte du mysticisme social des Fourier, des
Saint-Simon, des Louis Blanc (en roumain, Bucarest, 1935). Enfin, du
même, une remarquable reconstitution, en français cette fois, de *La Littérature roumaine à l'époque des Lumières*, Sibiu, 1945, où l'on voit le
rationalisme français de l'*Encyclopédie* et de ses collaborateurs, ainsi que
l'*Aufklärung* allemande, avec ce qu'ils comportent de corollaires révolutionnaires, pénétrer en Roumanie dès avant 1800.[13] Dans son recueil
déjà cité, A.Cioranescu captait au même moment des reflets de Musset,
de Coppée, de Rollinat et, plus récemment, dans une étude accessible à
chacun, il reprenait la question de la *Roumanie dans la nouvelle littérature provençale*.[14] Tout cela complète et retouche heureusement la vieille
thèse de N. Apostolescu, *L'influence française sur la poésie roumaine* (Paris,
1909, Préface d'E.Faguet), à laquelle, en attendant mieux, on est toujours
obligé de recourir pour le reste.

Quelques études de thèmes — D.Caracostea, sur *Lenore* (en roumain,
inachevé, Bucarest, 1928) ; N.Condéescou, sur *La Légende de Geneviève
de Brabant et ses versions roumaines* (en français, Bucarest, 1938) —

---

[10] Cf., sur l'*Erotocrite*, N.Cartojan, *RLC*, 1936, pp. 265 suiv. — Sur le
Roman de Troie, une monographie en roumain, dans les *Mémoires* de
l'Académie, Bucarest, 1925. — Cf. *RLC*, 1934, pp. 27 et 176-7.

[11] Nous avons présenté l'étude de N.Condéescou sur *Alcidalis* (en roumain) dans la *RLC*, 1934, 189-90. — C'est A.Cioranescu, dans son recueil
cité, pp. 107-119, qui a signalé la traduction de *Narcisse*.

[12] Tous ces travaux sont en roumain. Nous les avons analysés dans la
RLC, de 1926, 174-84 (*Alecsandri*) ; de 1928, 338-39 (*Alexandrescu*) ; et
de 1931, 473-74 (*Conaki*).

[13] Nous en avons rendu compte dans la *RLC* de 1948, 426-29. — Nous
avons également analysé, *ibid.*, 1927, 198-99, un *Eliade-Radulescu et la
France* de G.Oprescu, en roumain.

[14] *CL*, 2, 1950. — Notons, pour mémoire, M.Fotino, *L'influence française sur les grands orateurs politiques roumains* . . . Bucarest, 1928. —
Nous ne sachions pas que I. M. Rascu ait réuni en volume ses différents
articles des environs de 1930 sur Eminescu dans ses relations avec les
romantiques français — Gautier, Lamartine, etc.

achèvent de rendre compte, sommairement, de l'activité du comparatisme roumain depuis l'autre guerre.[15]

Ressortissant à une conception plus large de notre discipline, voici un rapide essai où N.Iorga marquait un certain parallélisme entre littérature et architecture religieuse.[16] Enfin, à peu près seul en Roumanie, D.Caracostea vint considérer la valeur expressive des sons et des rythmes dans le *Wortkunstwerk* et appliquer, au roumain en général et à Eminescu en particulier, les méthodes de la *Stilforschung*.[17]

Ce bref aperçu ne prétend pas épuiser la matière. J'en oublie, ou j'en passe : trop souvent — zèle immodéré ou facilité — on assimile à la littérature comparée, cette bonne à tout faire, des investigations étrangères à son objet réel, ou bien de simples énumérations stériles, qui donnent le change. Les Bibliographies courantes, accueillantes par définition, combleront nos lacunes.

La plupart des titres que nous avons retenus désignent, on l'a vu, des ouvrages de cadre. Nombre d'influences étrangères réellement fécondantes attendent leurs auteurs, un peu comme les personnages de Pirandello — Lamartine, Hugo, Baudelaire, Gautier, Gessner (malgré un vieil article de G.Bogdan-Duica, 1901), Ossian, Young, voire Verhaeren, Laforgue, Mallarmé, Valéry, Rilke, etc., dont on ne traite qu'incidemment, par allusion, à l'emporte-pièce. A étudier également, les grands courants européens — du romantisme au surréalisme — qui traversent la Roumanie, y entraînent ou imprègnent plus d'un poète original.[18]

La contre-partie de cette dette est bien modeste. Ecrite dans une langue de faible extension, la littérature roumaine ne rayonne guère. Mais le cas des écrivains roumains d'expression française — le conteur Panaït Istrati, par exemple, qui eut son heure de gloire, Hélène Vacaresco, Mme Marthe Bibesco, voire, à quelque degré, la Comtesse de Noailles, sans

---

[15] Cf. dans la *RLC*, de 1933, 134-35, l'analyse d'un ouvrage en roumain sur le thème *Carpe rosam* dans la Renaissance italienne et française. — A.Cioranescu, dans le recueil cité, 7-26, a suivi la légende du "paysan du Danube" en Roumanie et en France, depuis sa création par Guevara. — Du même, *ibid.*, 269-78, quelques notes sur Jésus dans la littérature dramatique.

[16] *Art et Littérature des Roumains. Synthèses parallèles*. 98 p. in-8° et 72 planches. Paris, 1929. — Au même moment, en étudiant les *Livres populaires*, N.Cartojan relevait dans la peinture d'église la transposition de certaines légendes religieuses et de certaines scènes de romans.

[17] D. Caracostea, *Arta cuvântului la Eminescu* [l'art du mot chez Eminescu], Bucarest, 1938; *Die Ausdruckswerte der rumänischen Sprache*. Iéna-Leipzig, 1939; etc. — A noter toutefois, dès 1934, sur l'esthétique du roumain, un travail d'I.Siadbey.

[18] Notons cependant, de N.Serban, un bref *Racine en Roumanie*, Bucarest 1940. — Nos quelques pages récentes sur *Victor Hugo en Roumanie*, *RLC*, 1952, 313-17, ne font qu'énoncer la question et en montrer à la fois l'importance et la difficulté. — Nous avons consacré, en 1945, un *Mémoire* académique à O.Densusianu en tant qu'introducteur et adaptateur du symbolisme; cf. le c.r. de cet ouvrage par A.Guillermou, *RLC*, 1949, pp. 157 suiv.

compter de plus jeunes, morts ou vivants — propose à notre discipline des problèmes d'une extrême finesse.[19]

Dans l'ensemble, trop de questions restent à élucider pour que l'on puisse songer à des véritables synthèses. Dans une série de conférences, *Idées et Formes littéraires françaises dans le Sud-Est de l'Europe*, Paris, 1924, N.Iorga dégageait certaines constantes très générales, valables pour plusieurs pays : il y a là une grande vue, dont la réalisation n'est pas pour demain. Dans d'autres conférences, *Influences étrangères sur la nation roumaine* (Paris, 1923), le même savant s'occupait davantage de la "nation" que de sa littérature.[20]

Dans une littérature comme la roumaine, toute en anachronismes, en contrastes, en solutions de continuité entraînant de brusques mutations de valeurs, le comparatisme se trouve plus qu'ailleurs dans l'obligation de *penser* sa matière et d'affiner ses méthodes. Se présentent alors à sa réflexion des problèmes comme celui de voir ce qu'un romantisme d'importation a pu donner dans un pays démuni de traditions classiques et humanistes, mais fortement armé de traditions locales — historiques, paysannes, folkloriques ; et comment le romantisme est parvenu à se greffer sur ce fonds autochtone, dont on connaît l'extrême vitalité. La même question se pose plus gravement encore à propos du symbolisme et de l'expressionnisme, qui vinrent à leur tour s'imprégner, très curieusement, de sèves locales. C'est au comparatisme bien compris qu'il appartient encore, en dernière analyse, d'expliquer l'essor extraordinaire de la littérature roumaine d'après guerre, cette poussée de fièvre collective qui prêta des ailes jusqu'aux médiocres : il y a là une foule de subtiles sollicitations étrangères, tout un jeu, infiniment complexe, de valeurs indigènes et hétérogènes, dont l'étude ramènerait la notion d'influence, que l'on défigure quelquefois si grossièrement, sur son vrai terrain, qui est celui de la création et de ses mystères. Enfin, la stylistique comparée trouverait en Roumanie un champ d'application illimité. Le rôle de la France — Lamartine, Hugo, etc. — dans la formation précipitée de la langue littéraire et du vers roumains, l'affinement progressif de leur harmonie, la merveilleuse efflorescence de l'imagerie poétique, si caractéristique du roumain, les délicats transvasements des substances romantiques, symbolistes et autres — autant de questions que l'étude des traductions et, mieux encore, celle des simples imprégnations inconscientes, permettrait d'éclairer efficacement. Ce sont là, en fin de compte, les *vrais* problèmes de notre discipline: plus qu'une érudition, si souvent fallacieuse, ils exigent du chercheur une sensibilité à la fois souple et rigoureuse, capable de se

---

[19] I.Haseganu, *La France dans l'oeuvre des écrivains roumains contemporains de langue française*, Paris, 1940, entame à peine le sujet.

[20] A noter: Ch.Drouhet, *La Culture française en Roumanie*, dans *La Minerve française*, 15 oct. 1920. — Notre propre étude sur *La Littérature roumaine et l'Europe* (Extrait du *Bulletin de l'Institut roumain de Sofia*, 1942) n'offre qu'un tableau synoptique où, sans produire de faits nouveaux, nous proposons quelques interprétations personnelles. C.r. par A.Guillermou, *RLC*, 1949, 155-57. — Quant à notre *Littérature roumaine moderne* (Paris, 1938; trad. anglaise et allemande; trad. italienne,Bari,Laterza, 1947), elle ne relève qu'incidemment les contacts étrangers.

mouler sur les phénomènes et de peser les impondérables. A défaut de quoi, le comparatisme roumain, par la richesse même et la disparité de la matière dont il dispose, risquerait plus qu'un autre de tomber dans un rabâchage dépourvu de signification intellectuelle.

A ces difficultés foncières, des difficultés de circonstance s'ajoutent qui rendent aujourd'hui nos études bien pénibles. A l'intérieur du pays, toute activité de ce genre a dû cesser ou se réduire à l'admiration béate de l'occupant et de son génie universel, ce qui relève de l'idolâtrie et nullement de l'étude. A force de pression et d'oppression, l'envahisseur s'applique systématiquement à dénaturer la langue, les traditions et jusqu'à l'âme d'une nation qu'il s'agit de détourner de sa route historique, d'assimiler et, pratiquement, de supprimer : le comparatisme de demain aura fort à faire pour mesurer les résultats de cette torture et de cette mutilation.

Pour des raisons différentes, la tâche des comparatistes roumains à l'étranger n'est guère aisée, non plus. Séparés des archives et des bibliothèques du pays, certains travaux leur sont désormais interdits. Il reste à voir, par exemple, dans quelle mesure telle thèse sur le symbolisme franco-roumain, en préparation à la Sorbonne, est réalisable avec les moyens du bord. Plus heureux, H.Radulescu, muni d'une documentation qu'il a réunie jadis sur place, poursuit à peu près normalement son enquête sur le théâtre français en Roumanie aux environs de 1840. Sans prétendre à des conclusions décisives, il est cependant permis de puiser aux sources étrangères une information que l'on fera valoir plus tard, de traiter un certain nombre d'aspects plus ou moins épisodiques et de s'atteler à des problèmes de stylistique comparée.

Quelque peu à l'étroit dans un domaine rétréci de la sorte, les comparatistes roumains s'orientent parfois vers d'autres horizons, tel A.Cioranescu, professeur aux Canaries, qui se consacre à des études franco-espagnoles; ou bien P.Ciureanu, professeur à Gênes, qui est en train de publier les inédits français de N.Tommaseo (1 vol., Genova, 1950, et différents articles récents) et songe à retracer l'influence de Sainte-Beuve en Italie.

Cependant, l'émigration roumaine, comme toute émigration, intéresse le comparatisme d'une manière autrement vivante et dramatique, par son existence même. Elle a ses bibliothèques, ses revues et ses publications polycopiées, ses écrivains. Par un effort désespéré, les quelques centaines d'intellectuels roumains dispersés dans le monde libre, s'efforcent d'y faire survivre une littérature qui a cessé de fleurir dans son climat naturel. Dans leur vision du monde, dans leur coeur, dans leur langue même, d'étonnants processus s'accomplissent, au gré des mille expériences sensorielles et spirituelles qu'ils contractent tous les jours aux latitudes ou ils habitent. Condamnés à vivre en permanence aux limites du souvenir et du réel — un souvenir que la distance et la durée transfigurent singulièrement ; un réel dont ils font péniblement l'apprentissage — leur production littéraire s'en ressent de bien des manières et, d'ores et déjà, s'offre à la méditation du comparatiste clairvoyant.

COMPARATIVE, GENERAL, AND WORLD LITERATURE IN JAPAN

Joseph K. Yamagiwa
University of Michigan

The Nihon Hikaku Bungakkai or Comparative Literature Society of Japan gathers together 200 Japanese students in the field of comparative literature. Organized in 1948 under the leadership of Kenzo Nakajima, free-lance critic and lecturer in French literature at Tokyo University, and Kinji Shimada, professor of English and American literature in the General College of the same university, the work of this society can best be evaluated in three recently published volumes: a special issue on comparative literature published in October, 1948, by the journal *Kokugo to kokubungaku* (Japanese Language and Literature)[1]; a book entitled *Hikaku bungaku nyumon* (Introduction to Comparative Literature), written by Tadashi Kobayashi[2]; and a volume edited by Nakajima and Yoshio Nakano, which is entitled *Hikaku bungaku josetsu* (Preface to Comparative Literature) and consists of a series of 17 essays written by nine different authors.[3]

The very appearance of titles like the last two suggests that the study of comparative literature is relatively new in Japan. Indeed, the introductory sections of all three volumes contain a discussion of the meaning, scope, methods, origins, course of development, and present status of comparative literature. In these discussions, the authors have followed men like Paul van Tieghem (whose *La littérature comparée* was translated into Japanese in 1943),[4] Jean-Marie Carré, and Fernand Baldensperger. Both the *Introduction* and *Preface* draw from various studies by Western scholars (e. g., from certain articles in the *Revue de Littérature Comparée* and the UNESCO volume on Balzac[5]) for summaries of such subjects as the history of translations in the West, Shakespeare on the European continent, Goethe in England and France, romanticism, Balzac throughout the world, Poe's influence on Baudelaire and Mallarmé, and Rilke in the present age. The special issue of *Kokugo to kokubungaku* contains an essay on the influence of the Chinese work entitled *Yu-hsien-k'u* in early Japanese

---

[1] *Kokugo to kokubungaku* (Japanese Language and Literature), v. 25, no. 10, Oct., 1948.

[2] Tadashi Kobayashi, *Hikaku bungaku nyumon* (Introduction to Comparative Literature), Tokyo, 1950. Kobayashi is junior professor of French literature at Tokyo University. He once studied under Professor Jean-Marie Carré. He has also translated Paul van Tieghem's *Histoire littéraire de l'Europe et de l'Amérique*, Paris, 1941, under the title *Kindai Yoroppa-Amerika bungakushi*, Tokyo, 1950-52, 2 vols.

[3] Kenzo Nakajima and Yoshio Nakano, ed., *Hikaku bungaku josetsu* (Preface to Comparative Literature), Tokyo, 1951. Nakano recently resigned his position as the ranking professor of English literature at Tokyo University in order to devote himself to journalism.

[4] Paul van Tieghem, *La littérature comparée*, Paris, 1931, trans. by S. Ota under the title *Hikaku bungaku*, Tokyo, 1943.

[5] United Nations Educational, Scientific and Cultural Organization *Hommage à Balzac*, Paris, 1950.

poetry and in the novels of Saikaku Ihara (1642-1693), and an article on the influence of the Chinese poet Po Chü-I in Japan. The *Preface* includes a series of articles on the following interrelationships of Western and Japanese literatures: the history of translations in Japan, the influence of Christianity in the literature of the Meiji period (1868-1912), the influence of Western poetry on the Japanese *shintaishi* or "poems of long form," European naturalism in Japan up to about 1905, and American literature in Japan. A final note discusses the bibliography of translations into Japanese.

These studies suggest that Japanese students still look to Western models for guidance in their work. They also show that the Japanese have accepted comparative literature as the study of influences and of the spreading of movements and ideas from one literature to another. Those trained in European literatures tend to feel that native literature of the Meiji period offers a particularly fruitful field of study. It is here that they believe they will make a special contribution and here that they even express a sense of mission.

Despite the articles in *Kokugo to kokubungaku*, Japanese scholars appear somewhat hesitant to discuss the influence of China and Buddhism on Japanese literature. Nakajima tells us that these influences are difficult to handle because they were first felt in material culture rather than in letters.[6] Yoshida, a lecturer in Japanese literature at two Tokyo schools, is more inclined to find values in the study of this influence, perhaps because he is well grounded in the older native literature in which Chinese and Buddhist influence is more apparent.[7] Yoshida thus lists among the major native contributions in this field Masayuki Okada's work on *Chinese Learning in the Omi and Nara Eras* (667 to 794);[8] the same author's more extensive *History of Chinese Learning in Japan*[9]; Jin'ichi Konishi's work on the influence of Po Chü-I on the kind of representation found in the poetic anthology *Kokinshu*[10]; and Isoji Aso's work on the influence of Chinese fiction in Japan during the Edo period (1603-1867).[11] A long list of articles dealing with the impact of Buddhism on Japanese literature is found in a bibliography published in 1931.[12] For Buddhist influence on medieval Japanese literature, Yoshida gives special praise to a

[6] Kenzo Nakajima, "Hikaku bungaku no igi (The Meaning of Comparative Literature)," in Nakajima and Nakano, 9 (see note 3 above).
[7] Seiichi Yoshida, "Hikaku bungaku to Nihon bungaku," *ibid.*, 51-65.
[8] *Omi-Naracho no kambungaku*, Tokyo, 1929.
[9] *Nihon kambungakushi*, Tokyo, 1929.
[10] "Kokinshu-teki hyogen no seiritsu (The Origins and Development of the Kind of Representation Found in the Kokinshu)," *Nihon Gakushuin kiyo* (Bulletin of the Japanese Peers' School), 7.5.
[11] *Edo bungaku to Shina bungaku* (Edo Literature and Chinese Literature), Tokyo, 1946.
[12] Ryukoku Daigaku Toshokan, *Bukkyogaku kankei zasshi rombun bunrui mokuroku* (A Classified Catalogue of Magazine Articles Relating to Buddhology), Kyoto, 1931.

work by Gensho Sakaguchi.[13] He might also have mentioned *The Ways of Thinking of Eastern Peoples*, a two-volume work published in 1948-49 by Professor Hajime Nakamura of Tokyo University.[14] This ambitious study traces the changes undergone by Buddhism as it spread from its home in India to China, Japan, and Tibet. According to Nakamura, these changes are traceable to differences in the ways of thinking in the several national cultures. Thus, among the Japanese, Buddhism was changed by such traits as the following: the importance attached to human relationships, the emphasis placed on the hierarchical relations of status, the supremacy accorded to the state, the absolute obedience rendered to particular persons such as the emperor, acceptance of the closed character of sects and cliques and of the right to protect by force the particular social nexus to which one belongs, emphasis on activity in society, sensitivity to moral introspection, and lack of self-consciousness in religious reverence.

Despite the importance attached to influence studies, some of the Japanese students have come to express doubts on their usefulness or validity. Nakajima's views are particularly interesting because he is the president of the Comparative Literature Society. The burden of his argument is as follows[15]: Speed of communication today is such that foreign works and ideas come into Japan, either in their original form or in translation, almost as soon as they become current in the countries of their origin. The exact identity of an original work or translation that connects a particular author or movement in Europe or America with one in Japan cannot always be known. Thus Ariake Kambara (1876-   ) is a symbolist poet greatly influenced by the West, but whether he derives mostly from the German symbolists or from the English or from others is almost impossible to determine. The situation in Japan is further complicated by the use of amanuenses who have ghost-written for many a supposed author. Another complication is the omission in translations of entire sections in the Western originals that belong to the realm of specific social criticism. Thus the novels of Dostoevsky have not always been completely rendered. The Japanese student, moreover, must face the fact that in the future each national literature will probably follow more nearly the main currents of world literature. The method of mutual illumination will be used more and more, and increased attention will be paid to the fact that similar results tend to arise as conditions everywhere in the world become more alike.

The difficulties which, according to Nakajima, hamper the successful prosecution of influence studies in Japan are essentially the same as those found elsewhere and are not in themselves a reason to forsake research.

---

[13] Gensho Sakaguchi, *Nihon Bukkyo bungaku josetsu* (Preface to Japanese Buddhist Literature), Tokyo, 1935.

[14] *Toyojin no shii-hoho*, Tokyo, 1948-49, 2 vols.

[15] The following material is a summary of Nakajima's opinions as expressed in a paper delivered at the Kyoto meeting of his society in October 1950, in two papers given at the December, 1950 and January, 1951 meetings in Tokyo, and in an article entitled "Hikaku bungaku" or "Comparative Literature" in Shinobu Origuchi and others, *Nihon bungaku koza* (Papers on Japanese Literature), v. 8, Tokyo, 1951, 87-97.

Unfortunately, Nakajima has not been able to spell out the details of the kind of work which students of comparative and world literature should now undertake. His lone suggestion is that something along the lines of Toynbee's theory of history should now be formulated for literature.

Yoshida, too, is attracted to general and world literature; but he goes for guidance not to Toynbee but to the "universal" sociological principles of Emile Durkheim.[16] Shimada expresses an interest in the role played by great books courses in American education.[17] Kobayashi, on the other hand, points to the kind of work Baldensperger and van Tieghem have published,[18] and states his belief that world literature cannot be studied except historically and inductively, that it must concern itself with all works, lesser or greater, produced in the various national literatures, and that it must eschew over-riding abstract concepts. He thus insists that such criteria as "universality" and "permanence in value" cannot be used in distinguishing works that belong to world literature. This leads him to reject the proposals of Goethe and Strich,[19] and to look askance at the theories of such native students as Yoshie Okazaki, professor of Japanese literature at Tohoku University in Sendai, and Jiro Abe, retired professor of philosophy at the same university, who have suggested that formal aesthetics and certain preconceived aesthetic principles be combined with historical methodology in discussing world literature.[20] As far as the comparison of unrelated literatures is concerned, Kobayashi as a strict comparatist insists that this type of study belongs not to comparative but to general literature.[21]

A long-standing controversy between Kochi Doi, retired professor of English literature at Tohoku University, and Okazaki is related to comparative and world literature. Doi's theory as to the order of development of the literary genres was first proposed in 1920 and published in convenient form in 1927 in two essays in the first edition of his book entitled

---

[16] His reference is apparently to Durkheim's *Les règles de la méthode sociologique*, Paris, 1895; 11e éd., 1950.

[17] Kinji Shimada, "Hikaku bungaku no seiritsu to genjo (The Origins, Development, and Present Status of Comparative Literature)," in Nakajima and Nakano, 46 (see footnote 3 above).

[18] Kobayashi, *Hikaku bungaku nyumon*, 76, mentions specifically Baldensperger, "Les Lettres au XVIIe siècle; au XVIIIe siècle," in Maxime Petit, *Histoire générale des peuples de l'antiquité à nos jours*, Paris, 1926, v. 2, and P. van Tieghem, *Histoire littéraire de l'Europe*.

[19] Kobayashi, 79, quotes from Junsuke Fukida, "Gēte to sekai bungaku (Goethe and World Literature)," *Riso* (Ideals), April, 1949. Kobayashi, 82-83, refers to Fritz Strich, "Weltliteratur und vergleichende Literatur," in E. Ermatinger, *Philosophie der Literaturwissenschaft*, Berlin, 1930.

[20] Kobayashi, 34, refers to Yoshie Okazaki, *Bungeigaku* (The Study of Literature), in *Kobundo Kyoyo bunko* (Kobundo Culture Library), Tokyo, 1949, "Sekai bungeigaku no koso (Plan for World Literature)," section 3, and Jiro Abe, *Hikaku bungaku* (Comparative Literature), Tokyo, 1932-33, 2 vols.

[21] Kobayashi (*Hikaku bungaku nyumon*, 45) takes Yoshida to task for his proposal, made in the special number of *Kokugo to kokubungaku* (see footnote 1), 17-18, 31-33, that Japanese comparatists consider the comparison of unrelated literatures. However, he is willing to include this type of study under general literature (72-73).

Preface to Literature.[22]   His theory was attacked in a work by Okazaki entitled *The Forms of Japanese Literature.* This volume appeared in 1939.[23] Doi's rejoinder was published in 1949 in the preface to the second edition of his *Preface to Literature.* This was followed by two books written by Okazaki,[24] and the controversy has continued on a widening range of fronts in four articles, two by each author, in the Journal *Bungaku* (Literature).[25]

In the first of his two articles in this journal, Doi has indicated four main points of disagreement between himself and his adversary, and Okazaki, in his two articles, has asked twenty questions calculated to involve his opponent in contradictions and difficulties or to embarrass him in the positions he has taken. A separate restatement of their differences, drawn up by an outsider, might run as follows: Doi believes that literature first began in songs, and that these are usually found as accompaniments of dances. The genres next developed in the following order: epic, lyric, narrative, and dramatic, with the miscellany and criticism appearing in conjunction with the drama. This order, he says, is almost universally found; in early France, for instance, it is illustrated by the saints' lives, the songs of love sung both in Provence and in northern France, the romances, the lays of Marie de France, *Aucassin et Nicolette,* and the forms of dramatic pageantry in which priests engaged. In Japan, many of the poems quoted in the earliest chronicle, the *Kojiki* or *Record of Ancient Matters* (712) are songs that accompanied dances. Doi believes that the *Kojiki* itself is an example of the epic. It was followed in succession by the lyric poetry of the *Manyoshu or Collection of Myriad Ages,* compiled in or after 759, and *Kokinshu or Collection Ancient and Present,* dated about 920; by fiction like the *Ise monogatari or Tales of Ise,* dated about 877, and the *Genji monogatari or Tales of Genji,* dated about 1000-1020; and by the *no* drama, the miscellany *Tsurezuregusa or Idle Jottings* composed by Kenko Yoshida (1283-1350) and the writings of the priest Shinran

---

[22] Kochi Doi, "Nihon bungaku no tenkai (The Development of Japanese Literature)" and "Bungaku no yoshiki no tenkai ni tsuite (On the Development of the Forms of Literature)," in his *Bungaku josetsu* (Preface to Literature), Tokyo, 1927, 105-196 and 197-237. Doi's views on the relationship between national and world literature are found in a third essay entitled "Kokumin bungaku to sekai bungaku (National Literature and World Literature)," likewise included in *Bungaku josetsu,* 395-436.

[23] Yoshie Okazaki, *Nihon bungei no yoshiki* (The Forms of Japanese Literature), Tokyo, 1939.

[24] Yoshie Okazaki, *Nihon bungei to sekai bungei* (Japanese Literature and World Literature), Tokyo, 1950, and *Bungeigaku gairon* (Outline of Literary Study), Tokyo, 1951.

[25] Doi, "Nihon bungaku no jidai kubun (The Chronological Divisions of Japanese Literature)," January, 1952, 1-13; Okazaki, "Nihon bungei no jidai yoshiki (The Chronology of Japanese Literature)," March, 1952; Okazaki, "Bungei no Toyo-teki yoshiki to Seiyo-teki yoshiki: Nihon bungei no sekai-teki ichi (The Oriental and Western Forms of Literature: The Place of Japanese Literature in World Literature)," April, 1952, 306-315; and Doi, "Futatabi Nihon bungaku no jidai kubun ni tsuite (A Second Time on the Division of the Ages in Japanese Literature)," June, 1952, 52-65.

(1173-1262). Doi tells us moreover, that this order of development repeated itself twice more in Japan as it did in France and Italy.

Doi's thesis was attacked by Okazaki, who claimed that it does not apply to Greek literature and that in Japan it can hold only if the first and second sequences of development are permitted to overlap. Instead of studying literature as a constant repetition of the epic-lyric-narrative-dramatic cycle, Okazaki prefers to study Japanese literature as having gone through the classical, the medieval, and the modern period; indeed, he claims that these phases are approximately coeval in Europe and in Japan—an assertion which seems quite untenable. Doi, in rejecting this viewpoint, stresses that older Japanese literature, caught in a web of traditions and tastes peculiarly Japanese, can not enter into the currents of world literature. In ancient Greece and again in Dante, Shakespeare, and Goethe one can find aesthetic concepts of general validity, but older Japanese terms of beauty such as *aware, okashi, yugen, shibumi,* tentatively translated as *sympathy, fascination, profoundness,* and *chaste refinement,* are almost occult and essentially Japanese and do not evoke an echo in the world at large. With Doi national literatures would disappear and would tend to merge with the general trends of world literature—but Okazaki insists that rather than lose its identity Japanese literature should preserve its traits and seek its proper place in world literature. *Aware, okashi* and the other concepts which Okazaki has studied so profoundly, belong to the aspects of universal beauty and he insists that in his many writings he has explained them so well that foreigners will understand and respect them.

According to Doi, modern Japanese literature began to develop only in the second half of the nineteenth century when the Japanese abandoned their insularity and began to be influenced by currents of thought found elsewhere in the world. In becoming aware of their common humanity they are approaching world literature. It is only now that Japanese literature tries to reveal man directly, to unite reality and ideals, to pay attention to man's individuality and universality. Okazaki, however, retorts that the humanity which Doi is seeking is colorless, since national traits and traditions are lost. Okazaki is an apologist for the East and speaks in Buddhistic terms which to Westerners may seem obscure. To him Asia and Europe are complementary; their differences should not be blurred. The East, according to him, is characterized by a romantic, medieval civilization in which man is attracted by the limitless, seeks to transcend reality, adjusts his individuality to a pantheistic cosmos, tends to regard beauty as a supreme value, and endows nature with an emotional quality. Doi, however, prefers to define romanticism in a Western sense which is but rarely encountered in Japanese literature; he searches for a fresh and wondering individuality, a revolutionary spirit, a poetry intoxicated with the passions of youth and love, stressing the free and new, and paying little heed to traditions and rules—a disciple of Rousseau rather than of Buddha.

In this Japanese search for the essence of literature and for the place and the mission of Japanese literature within a larger framework, it is natural that both Okazaki and Doi envisage an ultimate world literature which is unified because it is based upon a common humanity. It is possible to study the literatures of the world for the features that they have in common (Doi) and for those that are peculiar to each of them (Okazaki). According to Okazaki the nature of world literature is found in the receptiveness and tolerance with which it welcomes, embraces and absorbs the several national literatures, each of which has its own special mission and qualities. He regards the literatures of the world as one, and each national literature is looked upon as a part or fragment of the whole. No one literature is dominant; each contributes to the harmony of the whole. In that sense we already possess a world literature. In Doi's view, however, if world literature is ever achieved it will be in the distant future. It transcends the concept of a medley of national literatures and may be expected to arise after the fullest development of regional contributions in form as well as in thought. Man's concept of humanity is developed as his experiences multiply and as the spirit of each age and each region affects him. World literature will develop as the most nearly complete expression of our common humanity; it will be a symbol of man completely freed from the prejudices of any age or region and from the dictates of national tastes. The Western reader will perhaps feel a closer sympathy with Doi than with Okazaki. The latter speaks about the inalienable cultural heritage of Japan in metaphysical terms which are probably losing currency and acceptance among the Japanese themselves. He seems to disregard the fact that in Japan, despite war and periods of nationalistic and anti-foreign feeling, the trend has been toward the adoption of Western ways and thought. Doi appears more willing to accept the idea that the Japanese individuality is being emancipated as it receives more and more stimuli from outside nations. The argumentation, especially in Okazaki's case, is long, personal, and heated. It suggests the need of time and understanding before a common world literature, equally understandable to all peoples, can emerge.

A stimulating attempt to compare Japanese and Western literature in their totalities is found in an essay by Professor Ryoichi Ikushima of Kyoto University entitled *Western Fiction and Japanese Fiction*.[26] Ikushima begins by telling us that in medieval Europe learned treatises were written in Latin, whereas the vernaculars were used for literature which ordinary men enjoyed. Similarly, in the Heian age in Japan (794-1185), Chinese was the language of government, law, and scholarship, whereas fiction was written in Japanese. The word *roman* was probably pejorative in meaning. This is true of the Japanese word for fiction, *shosetsu*, which means "a small statement, opinion, or view." On the other hand, the early *roman* and the earliest examples of fiction in Europe were often composed for the amusement of women and children, whereas such a work as the *Tale of Genji*, dealing with courtly life in Heian Japan, was quickly received as a masterpiece by the nobility, though it was virtually unknown to the illiterate people of the lower classes. The high recognition which the

---

[26] *Seiyo no shosetsu to Nihon no shosetsu*, Tokyo, 1950.

Tale of Genji received may even have retarded the further development of Japanese fiction. In any case, medieval fiction in Japan is unusually sophisticated as compared with the first Western novels. According to Ikushima, various influences were combined in the development of the realistic novel, both in the West and in Japan. But among these influences, those which made a study of man and of man's nature were more strongly felt in Europe than in Japan. In their place, in the Edo period (1603-1867), are found miscellanies that describe the physical and material aspects of the things, manners, and customs found in Japanese society of the day. It is frequently said of Japanese fiction that it lacks the kind of plot possessed by epic poetry, that it is deficient in imagination, that it is superior in the short story and not in the longer forms, and that it is weak in its grasp of human character.

More positively, Ikushima believes that Japanese fiction is characterized by a close relationship to poetry. The *Tale of Genji*, instead of telling facts or stating an idea, conveys a lyric feeling to its readers. In medieval times fiction declined when poetry declined, and flourished again when it came under the influence of the *haiku* or 17-syllable poem. It was training in the *haiku* which gave to the master writer of the realistic novel, Saikaku Ihara (1642-1693), his predilection for concrete imagery. A poetic rhythm is found in the writings of Bakin Kyokutei (1767-1848) and Tanehiko Ryutei (1783-1842), and persists in the works of Koyo Ozaki (1867-1903); Futabatei Shimei (1864-1909); Ryunosuke Akutagawa (1892-1927), who spoke of a "plot-less fiction" and "a poetic fiction"; and present-day writers like Naoya Shiga (1883-   ) and Kosaku Takii (1894-   ). Disregarding the lyrical novel, Ikushima tells us that only a few European writers like Flaubert have tried to add a poetic, artistic quality to fiction. He finds the fiction of the West centrally concerned with the exercise of reason and analysis and the presentation of ideas, while that of Japan is more a series of scenes and images. Moreover, in Japanese fiction there is much less preoccupation with the flow of time. The *Tale of Genji* is an exception, since every event in it may be given its place in a temporal scheme and each character ages in proper accord with time, but the Japanese author still seems to Ikushima to take a rather cavalier attitude toward chronology.

Ikushima's work persuades us to reconsider the problem raised by Nakajima, Yoshida, and Kobayashi, and to ask whether truly significant results would flow from comparisons between relatively unrelated literatures. Ikushima suggests that totally or almost totally disparate literatures may be compared or mutually illuminated in respect to the distinguishing characteristics of the forms or genres in which they appear; the historic range, course of development, and periods of greatest vogue of these genres; the ideas and subject-matters; the attitudes toward man, man's works, and nature; and the symbols, rhetoric devices, and special qualities in these literatures which natives who are practiced literary men consider to be of the highest aesthetic value. In comparing disparate literatures, the student will necessarily indicate the workings of great cultural movements, the influence of foreign ideas, and the social, economic, and political backgrounds from which particular writings arose. As Doi and

Okazaki have suggested, similarities between the literatures of East and West no doubt arise because man everywhere has common desires, urges, and ideas. The differences presumably come from differences in heredity and environment, both of individuals and cultures. At least two questions may be asked: whether the comparisons that might be attempted will lead to a richer understanding of peoples and literatures and of the role literature plays in the lives of men both in the East and West, and whether in studying Eastern and Western literatures in conjunction with each other we will arrive at a more comprehensive definition of literature itself than is furnished, let us say, by reference to European literature alone.

In comparing unrelated literatures, the student is beset by many problems. He needs to know at least two foreign languages and cultures. As he works, he finds himself confronted with the tenuous subject of national temperament. Perhaps he may decide that in each literature it is much safer to deal with individual authors and to describe their particular attitudes and techniques than to find common attitudes and techniques in the whole group of writers of the same nation or race. But traditional points of view and recurrent attitudes may be found, and some of these may be common to literary men everywhere. The student may begin with the assumption, found in Nakajima, Doi, and Okazaki, that men's minds are becoming more and more alike. He should expect, as he compares different literatures in the future, that more and more common themes will appear. Already Freudianism, Marxism, naturalism, and romanticism are found in Japanese as in Western literature, though it is probably true that they are differently revealed in accordance with differences in the native traditions. Faith in positivism and science, which has been a crucial force in the West, has spread to Japan and China if not to other areas of Asia. The student thus studies and compares the literatures of the world at a time when their ideas and techniques are still various, but are becoming more and more uniform.

The Western comparatist has in general deplored the pointing out of parallels and differences in literatures which have had no history of contact with each other. Students of general literature appear to be more lenient in this respect. Actually, Western students of Eastern literature have persistently pointed to parallels and differences between the East and West, in the sense that almost every statement made of a foreign culture or literature is by its very nature comparative. If, for instance, we read the *Tale of Genji*, the novels of Saikaku Ihara, or those of Seiichi Funahashi and say that Japanese fiction has a strong erotic strain, we may mean at the same time that English and American literature is less erotic. If we say that brief statements pregnant with many meanings are characteristic of Japanese poetry, we usually mean, or may mean, that longer statements, more completely stating the poet's feelings and ideas, are preferred in English poetry. If we observe that the writings of a modern Japanese author like Shohei Ooka are marked by his characters' almost intuitional perceptions of each other's attitudes and feelings, we are probably saying that many such intuitional perceptions would be obtrusive in Western writing. If we assert that the coincidental meeting of characters mars the plot of many Japanese novels, we are probably reasserting our belief that each action in a plot should be clearly motivated. Eroticism, the statement that suggests more than it states, and the role dreams and superstitions as well as coincidences play in motivating literature and life may all be more acceptable to the Japanese than to us. In these respects the Japanese reader and the English reader make different demands on their authors.

Comparatists may dispute whether a procedure which is at once rigorous, perceptive, and suggestive can be developed for the comparison of unrelated literatures. An absolute requirement would be the provision of a series of competent descriptions of the several national literatures both of the East and West. These descriptions, many of which are already available, may well be made the bases of comparative statements. If only two literatures are being compared, the student should probably first devote himself to discovering which are the elements that the literatures have in common and which are the ones in which they differ. If Japanese literature differs from a second literature, say English, in having a fiction that is more erotic, the possibility should not be overlooked that Japanese fiction may be closer in this respect to Chinese and Korean fiction than to English. But if a series of comparisons is stated between many pairs of literatures, an up-and-down gradation in terms of eroticism or of any number of other traits becomes possible.

Serious study of the relations between Eastern and Western literature would bring students of letters in line with scholars in other disciplines who have already ventured into work of this kind. A group of philosophers have recently collaborated in *Essays in East-West Philosophy: an Attempt at World Philosophical Synthesis*. Toynbee's *Study of History* is well-known. So is Northrop's *Meeting of East and West*.[27] For many suggestive comments on the relationship of Japanese to world history, one may turn to two works by Sir George B. Sansom, *The Western World and Japan*, and *Japan in World History*.[28] Parallels in the geography and history of Great Britain and Japan are given in a brief note by John K. Fairbank entitled "Insularity in Japanese History; a Comparison with England."[29] Fairbank warns us that many of the parallels are superficial, and that "in general the Japanese have been much less closely related to the continent than have the British." As Fairbank points out, the Straits of Tsushima, separating the Japanese islands from Korea, are, after all, 120 miles instead of 20 miles wide. The late John F. Embree, a social anthropologist, has told us that the Japanese "have developed, like the British, as an insular nation and have created their own characteristic culture."[30] The

---

[27] Charles A. Moore, ed., *Essays in East-West Philosophy: an Attempt at World Philosophical Synthesis*, Honolulu, 1951. Arnold J. Toynbee, *A Study of History*, London and New York, 1934-39. F. S. C. Northrop, The *Meeting of East and West*, New York, 1941.

[28] Sir George B. Sansom, *The Western World and Japan*, New York, 1950. *Japan in World History*, New York, 1951.

[29] *Far Eastern Leaflets*, no. 1-6, (Feb. 15, 1942), 3-5.

[30] John F. Embree, "The People," in H. Borton, ed., *Japan*, Ithaca, 1951, 18.

need for data from Eastern literature is voiced in Professor Harry Levin's introduction to the symposium on realism published by *Comparative Literature*: "It would be useful to verify our premises, which derive from a closely related group of cultures, by considering parallels among the Classics or in the Near and Far East."[31]

Important values flow from the study of any foreign literature, but when we examine a literature far removed from our own, we open up the possibility of studying and analyzing native literature under categories that are fresh and new. Values found important in relatively strange and "exotic" literary cultures may well be applied to one more familiar and result in new analyses of the several literatures. Thus the point of view taken by Cleanth Brooks in *The Well-wrought Urn*[32] might well stimulate Japanese students into making new analyses of their own poetry. Although there is probably nothing about the 17-syllable *haiku*, considered simply as a type of poem, to make it superior to the 31-syllable *tanka*, the emphasis which Brooks gives to wit, irony, and paradox would, if applied to Japanese poetry, probably result in the poets of the *haiku* being given a higher place than those who compose the *tanka*. The images in the *haiku* seem to be more tightly put together. Short as it is, the *haiku* has more the kind of tension Brooks finds in the best of English poetry, whereas the *tanka* tends to be more sentimental. Brooks' comments give rise to the question whether such qualities as *okashi* (interest or fascination), found in Japanese poetry by native students, do not have points in common with the wit, irony, and paradox which he finds in the best poetry of England, and whether such terms as *mono no aware* (the rapport or sympathy which beings and things have for each other) would not be descriptive of a triter type of poem.[33]

---

[31] "What is Realism?" *Comparative Literature*, 3, 1951.

[32] New York, 1947.

[33] Not only the precepts of criticism, but techniques too may be adopted. An interesting example of application in Japan of a technique used in the West is found in an article by Professor Takeo Kuwabara of Kyoto University entitled "Second-class Literature," (*Sekai*, Nov., 1946). In this article Kuwabara tries out for the *haiku* a procedure similar to the one which I. A. Richards employed in gathering data for his *Practical Criticism*. Taking 15 *haiku*, of which 10 came from well-known men and 5 from sheer amateurs, he showed them, without indication of authorship, to a group of colleagues and students who possessed more than average competence in literary matters, and asked them, first, to group the poems in an up-and-down order in terms of their relative excellence; second, to indicate the precise authorship of the poems coming from the better-known poets; and third, to separate out the ten poems from the better-known poets from the other five. The answers were almost helter-skelter; the poems of the best-known poets received no higher evaluation than those of the rankest amateurs. This, plus a consideration of the conditions and precepts under which the *haiku* is produced today, persuaded Kuwabara to conclude that literary ratings in the *haiku* depend more on the reputations of the authors than on the intrinsic worth of the poems they produce and that the *haiku* is probably a second-rate form to begin with.

Comparisons between East and West run the danger of being meaningless or fatuous. The parallels and differences drawn may be so obviously a matter of externals and of forms that fundamental differences in ways of thinking and expressing are lost, or overlooked and never discovered. But these comparisons may still help us gain a better world perspective, and suggest ways of dealing with the peoples of the East. The study of Eastern literatures will take us outside the known Western half of the world and into the lesser known Eastern half. Rich rewards may come from a comparison of the West, whose ways of thought and expression have largely developed out of the Hebraic-Christian and Graeco-Roman traditions, and the East, which is shaped mostly by ways of thought that are Hindic-Buddhist or Confucian-Taoist in origin.

CHILDREN'S LITERATURE[1]

Alison White
Indiana University

As one of the regular offerings of the English department, the course in children's literature may be as purely literary as any other.[2] It is not designed to repeat specialized work in child psychology, classroom and library activities, or problems in therapy. It is, rather, a belletristic, humanistic course, providing the undergraduates of various schools with the only study in world literature that is available to many of them. Clearly, it may some day have its practical applications, but the course itself presents its stock of readings in their guise as literary works of art. That is what they are: myths and folktales, romances and poetry of the world's great writers. Such a textbook as the widely-used *Anthology of Children's*

---

[1] This represents some findings from a year's study abroad, 1951-52, as Marion Talbot Fellow of the American Association of University Women.

[2] The average college course in children's literature offers an extensive body of readings in world literature. The inevitable anthology-textbook, a 1200-page tome of double columns, provides selections from every period and virtually all literatures, together with an illustrated account of the history of children's books. Bibliographies and appendices further classify books for various uses: to supply the parent, teacher, librarian, nurse, social worker, minister, and the author, illustrator, dramatist, choreographer, radio-television writer and artist with hints and admonitions. Such vocational diversity has pulled the study of children's literature away from the education and library schools into the general arena where its position amid other literary studies suggests its development as a part of the offerings in world literature. Even when this study was available solely in training courses for teachers and librarians, it sustained its literary orientation. This is owing to several men of letters whose work affected it from the start. All of the textbooks, anthologies, and college catalogue descriptions reveal their debt to F. J. Harvey Darton, son of the Darton publishing family and onetime scholar of St. John's College, Oxford. He contributed a chapter on children's books to the *Cambridge History of English Literature* and supplied the *Cambridge*

Literature by Johnson, Scott, Sickels, presents the usual categories: traditional verse, folk tales, myths, hero stories, literary fairy tales, Old Testament stories, fiction, and poetry. To each of these is affixed a critical analysis of the genres, an account of their histories, and a summary of scholarship available for the further study of each. The term "world literature" is no misnomer here, for the Orient and the Antipodes are represented, as are also the Arctic and Equatorial "literatures." Folklore aside, the main division is between the books annexed (to use Darton's term) by the young from general literature, of which *Robinson Crusoe* is an example, and those created directly for the child audience, as was *Alice in Wonderland.*

If "world literature" is ideally composed of books which are accepted abroad in their original languages, children's literature may have first claim to the title, in that the child's classic is what one reads in learning almost any foreign language. This was evident in Goethe's list of his boyhood favorites (in five languages)—a list familiar today to the student of children's literature as well as to learners of languages. Goethe's boyish favorites were "Ovid, Comenius' *Orbis Pictus,* Fénelon's *Télémaque, Robinson Crusoe, Eulenspiegel, Fortunatus.*" Other children's classics familiar to novices in language study are the tales of Grimm and Perrault, Fouqué, Kästner, Alain-Fournier, and Saint Exupéry.

As an aspect of world-literature study, the recognition of important translations is a part of the student's examination of children's literature. He acquaints himself with such epochal translations as the one celebrated in Wordsworth's *Prelude:* "the little yellow canvas-covered book/ A slender abstract of the Arabian Tales," which appeared in 1708, between English editions of D'Aulnoy and Perrault. Among other translations notable in children's literature is Edgar Taylor's rendition of the fairy-tales by the Grimm brothers (1823) with his perceptive analysis which was commended in the preface to Thomas Warton's *History of English Poetry.* One notes that the Howitts' translations of Andersen's tales and Chamisso's *Peter*

Bibliography of English Literature with substantial sections listing "books originally meant to be read, or in fact habitually read by young persons . . . in their leisure hours, for enjoyment." These items and his valuable *Children's Books in England* set the key for commentators and students. Algernon Tassin's chapter on children's books in the *Cambridge History of American Literature* maintained the standard set by Darton, as does some scholarship today—notably the work of Peter and Iona Opie whose *Oxford Dictionary of Nursery Rimes,* published last year, is to be followed soon by a history of children's literature. From France came Paul Hazard's *Books, Children, and Men,* published in Boston in 1944 by the *Horn Book.* In England Frank Eyre, Marghanita Laski, Roger Lancelyn Green, and Geoffrey Trease have written book-length criticism, mainly of children's books in the nineteenth and twentieth centuries. America has produced characteristically practical books: immense bibliographies, richly illustrated; anthologies for class use and for the "trade"; informal essays of book-length—the reminiscences of librarians. The textbooks used in children's literature classes bear the stamp of the authors named above, a stamp that is predominantly literary rather than pedagogical. Across them also falls the benignant shadow of McGuffey.

Schlemihl, and F. E. Paget's of Hauff and Fouqué, produced reverberations beyond those of nursery and school.

The student of children's literature is able to give himself a sense of literary traditions reaching into all directions, as he prepares himself to preserve for children the sense of the past that awaits them when they are led to read the books of their ancestors' youth. Our study includes such early testimony as Rousseau's praise of *Robinson Crusoe,* Addison's of *The Children in the Wood, Dick Whittington,* and *Child Rowland.* One reads Steele's account of his godson who thought Aesop's fables to be "untrue," but who approved Hickathrift, Bevis of Southampton, St. George—the pedlars' chapbooks. It is diverting to find Dr. Johnson's confession that when bored in company he thought about the adventures of Tom Thumb; also his confident declaration to Mrs. Thrale that "Babies do not want to hear about babies. They like to be told of giants and castles and of somewhat which can stretch and stimulate their little minds."

Children's literature puts the romantics under tribute, as we recall De Quincey's report of nursery debates on the merits of Sinbad, Coleridge's praise of Fouqué's *Undine,* and his marvelling at the "astonishing image of the whole rookery that flew out of the giant's beard, scared by the tremendous voice with which this monster answered the challenge of the heroic Tom Hickathrift." In its modern aspects, children's literature can be perceived as emerging from the Romantic Movement, turning away from the eighteenth century didacticism which had all but marked it for its own. Though the psychological and pedagogical considerations cannot be ignored as one studies children's literature, they must not take the dominant place, or the study becomes quickly speculative, and the body of literature which gives it its reason for being, is submerged.

As a field for literary inquiry, children's literature except for the undergraduate readings discussed here, has been virtually unseen or overlooked. It is a ghost literature: existing half below visibility as a stock of nebulous books once read, now recalled among ancient toys and lessons. As an entity it tends to lose itself in the general literatures from which it largely emerged. The items that Caxton chose to print and Locke in his day so approved—Malory, Aesop, Reynard—supply their permanent ballast to literature for the young. Before them there were riddles, colloquies, mild and monkish diversions amid the precepts. One forgets that such elements compose the beginning of children's literature even though antiquarian interest has been a mainspring to what scholarship there is in this subject. Before those bookish beginnings there were such beginnings in speech for the race as there are yet for every child. Children's literature came late into the libraries; for a longer time than did "adult" literature, it lived in the oral tradition. There it lives abundantly still, fed though it may be by the sub-literary publications that bridge oral to written tradition—the throw-aways of all eras, from broadsides to boxtops.

An oral literature is an invisible literature, and children's literature has been at times submerged in another way, caused to sink beneath the pressures of didacticism. Largely a body of lays, rimes, fables, travel-tales, *Märchen, Kunstmärchen,* it is accessible to the probe of the propagandist. There will always be an Aunt Agitate and a Cousin Cramchild, as Kingsley made so painfully clear, and they will try to deny to children's literature any life but that of mother lode for the memory gem.

In our study of genres and the history of books for children, observe that it is the scholars in comparative literature who have led the return to a primarily literary consideration of children's books. These have a special interest. Lina Eckenstein, in *Comparative Studies in Nursery Rhymes*, examined poetic effects in the intervals of her speculations upon Mother Goose derivations from Egyptian hieroglyphs, the rites of Sul in Bath, and Norse moon myths. This, with some of the speculations upon myths and folktales preserved in children's libraries, permits a natural correlation between the study of literature and aspects of anthropology, religions, the graphic and the ritual arts. The student is compelled to a consideration of literatures and cultures under comparison. In Hazards *Books, Children, and Men*, he reads Fernand Baldensperger's comparison of the modes of Asiatic fairy tales with those of the French, and his observation that "the fairies of Perrault are, in their way, Cartesian fairies . . .they work. . . .as if fancy were being governed by common sense. . .take care not to confuse appearances and analogies for the empty pleasure of displaying their authority, and. . .are willing to sacrifice some of their power for the subtle pleasure of showing respect for the logical concept of things."

As he reads historical and critical examinations of his subject, the student of children's literature will find scholars represented from several nations. Fanciulli's *Letterature per l'Infanzia* and H. L. Koester's *Geschichte der deutschen Jugendliteratur* are contemporary with Darton's *Children's Books in England*, which include literary importations. Seeking suggestions for his own research or critical writings on children's literature, the student may come upon "The Conscious Faerie Tale," in which Paul Rosenfeld urged genre study in the *Kunstmärchen*, or upon Robert Graves' analyses of the verse of Edward Lear and the traditional rimes. Other suggestions rise from William Empson's and Hubert Nicholson's illuminating studies of Lewis Carroll in which we find an account of the influence of Novalis and other German romantics. For diversion one might read, in *The Lost Childhood*, Graham Greene's engaging parody of the techniques of literary historians and critics. His subject is the works of Beatrix Potter: her empiricism, epic personalities (Peter Rabbit, Tom Kitten), and ironies.

As in general studies in folklore, the student in children's literature is encouraged to observe the persistence of themes, and their recurrence in various cultures. As he studies the *Kunstmärchen*, or literary fairy tales, he will move from them to the folktales and back again, to note the subjective, sophisticated, moralistic manipulations of folk-motifs. In Hans Christian Andersen he finds this instructive as he proceeds from Andersen's early, folklorish tales to his more contrived romances such as "The Little Mermaid" and "The Snow Queen." Ruskin's "King of the Golden River" affords an exhibit of *three brothers* kind of adventure folk tale turned into a sermon *cum* travelogue *qua* Gothic romance. Hawthorne's "Snow Image" precipitates the Baba Yaga snow witch from the steppes into a New England garden where she becomes the melancholy instructress of a commuting business man who has yet to learn the transcendental doctrine of reliance upon intuition.

In examining these as part of the stock of books written directly and especially for the young, the student finds that they compose a literature which invites scrutiny as a phenomenon in itself. He observes how the child audience enters into the fiction, collaborates, acting upon the author's intentions. He will perceive that sometimes, as in the fantasies of Andersen and Lewis Carroll, the child audience finds its image in the author. That the opposite may happen, appears in Thackeray's *The Rose and the Ring*. Such action exerted by child upon teller may so wrest the author's pen out of its accustomed track as to yield something wilder and, with luck, richer, than appears in his works for the adult world. Kingsley's *Water Babies* continues to attract the reflective student of Victorian literature or times. *Treasure Island* has the literary-psychological critics pondering. It is hardly necessary to mention the "boys' books" of Mark Twain, so clear it is that they feed some of the most sophisticated sensibilities of our time.

Students in the children's literature course might profitably make critical studies of the child's book as such, written, as it often was, with the direct collaboration of its audience. Celebrated novelists have used the child's book as a mask behind which they were sometimes able to attain to an abandon not available for their usual writings. Such books might well be studied together—not, as now, separately, each as an item in its author's general bibliography. By this the student might cast himself in the way of a proliferation of insights: literary, psychological, sociological.

The child's tale as a genre or group of genres, from *Kunstmärchen* to the inspired art of future cinema (may we hope?), is suggestive for intensive study in one aspect of world literature. Among practitioners of the child's tale are Tolstoy, Hawthorne, Spyri, Lewis Carroll, Lagerlöf, Maeterlinck, Kipling. It thrives today, engaging such distinguished writers as Walter de la Mare, John Masefield, James Thurber. Students interested in contemporary fiction may be able to spy out unsuspected resources in such fantasy as E. M. Forster's "The Celestial Omnibus" and in semiautobiographical writings such as William Faulkner's "The Bear." They may observe the continuous movement from "adult" to "children's" literature when, as in the recent experience of Ernest Hemingway, an author is discovered by the very young and taken as their own. The fan letters recently sent to Mr. Hemingway by his admirers in the seventh grade who had enjoyed *The Old Man and the Sea*, point us to that major part of children's literature: books annexed from the world's library. This particular encounter of books and very young readers awaits the pen of the literary-psychologist. The works of Homer, Malory, Cervantes, Swift, Defoe sped to the children as to a lodestone. When examined as a part of children's literature, even these books may reveal afresh what is their essential vitality: the core myth, with as much accrual of image as gets through to that universal touchstone, the mind of a keen child. Perhaps Juan Ramon Jimenéz said it all when he remarked of his *Platero y yo*: "My book went forth and met the children."

PART TWO

PAUL HAZARD   **par Fernand Baldensperger**

Rien de plus édifiant, ce me semble, et même de plus émouvant à sa manière, que le témoignage d'une grande amitié qui va naître—surtout si des affinités pratiques doivent au plus vite s'ajouter à la formule simple, mais vitale, de Montaigne : "Parce que c'était lui, parce que c'était moi."

L'auteur de ces lignes, docteur en Sorbonne l'année précédente, avait succédé en 1900 à Joseph Texte dans la seule chaire de littérature comparée existante en France, celle de l'université de Lyon. C'est là qu'il recevait une lettre qu'il n'a point manqué de conserver, à divers titres aisés à comprendre:

Le 24 mars 1902

Monsieur,

Sans avoir l'honneur d'être connu de vous, je me permets de vous écrire pour l'objet que voici.—Je suis élève de seconde année à l'Ecole Normale, et, délivré de mes obligations en grec et en latin, je compte consacrer les quatre mois qui restent avant la fin de l'année à un travail de français. Je serais très heureux de m'orienter vers la littérature comparée, spécialement pour ce qui concerne l'Allemagne. Je ne sais, en effet, que très peu d'italien, encore moins d'anglais, mais j'ai fait un peu d'allemand. Et voilà pourquoi, Monsieur, j'ai recours à vous : je voudrais trouver, en effet, un sujet de nature telle, qu'il me permît de le reprendre, de l'étendre plus tard, et, si c'était possible, d'en faire une thèse. Et je sais bien ce que ma demande a d'étrange et d'inattendu : mais je serais heureux si vous vouliez bien m'indiquer la route.

Nous avons comme professeur de français Monsieur Lanson, qui nous dirige excellemment, mais qui n'est pas "spécialiste" en littérature comparée, ni surtout pour les choses allemandes. J'ai pensé que le successeur de Monsieur Texte voudrait bien conseiller un élève de l'Ecole Normale, et lui indiquer des points sur lesquels un effort pourrait devenir fructueux.—Je vous prie de vouloir bien agréer, Monsieur, l'expression de mes sentiments respectueux.

P. HAZARD
45, rue d'Ulm, Paris.

Dès les vacances suivantes, et à Paris, la jonction personnelle fut aisée entre l'enfant des Flandres françaises et le Lorrain annexé provisoirement par Lyon. Mais ce dernier, qui publiait un peu plus tard son *Goethe en France* et sa réédition de la *Bibliographie* de Betz, orienta aisément le "comparatiste" *in spe* vers une région où notre italianisant H. Hauvette l'encouragea: *La Révolution française et les Lettres italiennes,* thèse soutenue à Lyon en 1910, fut à la fois le témoignage universitaire de mérites qui devaient trouver leur sanction suprême à l'Académie française, le début d'une spécialisation méridionale promise à bien des missions et des contacts féconds, et la désignation du jeune docteur à la chaire lyonnaise devenue vacante quand la Sorbonne appela à son tour un provincial à inaugurer l'enseignement des lettres modernes comparées.

Cela coïncidait avec la deuxième décade du siècle. Dès lors et jusqu'en 1914, début de la première guerre mondiale, l'affermissement d'une jeune

discipline fut le commun souci des quelques initiés, si l'on peut dire, qui s'efforçaient de lui mériter ses lettres de créance chez nous et au dehors. Des voyages, des cours de vacances, des publications d'articles de périodiques s'ajoutaient à l'enseignement régulier, et cette période "probatoire" coïncida avec bien des vocations d'historiens littéraires de marque. Chez Paul Hazard, qui maintenait le contact avec ses maîtres parisiens et aussi avec la *Revue des Deux Mondes*, un souci de publicité n'était point sans l'emporter peut-être sur la simple recherche et la démonstration de réalités intellectuelles dont ne s'avisait pas le grand public lettré.

Il y parut lorsque, en 1912, son *Discours sur la langue française*, présenté à un concours académique, reprit en les modernisant les fameuses données de Rivarol plutôt qu'il ne se préoccupait de vérifier les nouveaux obstacles à l'universalité." Par ailleurs, sans aller jusqu'à la poésie émancipatrice (même pour les *Sonnets de Michel-Ange*, en traduction de 1928) les excursions de Paul Darmentières et de P. de Saint-Maurice, témoignages émouvants de ses attachements de naissance, sont plutôt des hors-d'oeuvre que de libres propos.

Sa carrière n'en était que plus favorablement aidée: à une suppléance en Sorbonne (1919) devait succéder en 1925 son élection au Collège de France, et ses cours devaient se cristalliser en volumes, dont les derniers, hélas! suivraient sa mort le 12 avril 1944. En 1935 paraissait la *Crise de la Conscience européenne*, dont je lui disais qu'un titre plus exact eût été *la Conscience de la Crise européenne*, puisque dès la fin du moyen âge chrétien s'amorçaient des différenciations qui ne devaient point attendre l'ère des Fontenelle et des Bayle pour se manifester.

La fondation, en 1921, de la *Revue de Littérature comparée* créa entre nous un lien de plus. Mais mon acceptation, en 1935, d'une chaire à l'université Harvard allait enlever toute "unité de lieu," si je puis dire à des carrières parallèles qui doivent être jugées sur leurs résultats. M'excuserai-je, en mon amère qualité de survivant, d'avoir évoqué la noble destinée d'un cher cadet de cet angle plus fraternel que scolastique? Aux accomplissements communs de répondre.

Paris

IRVING BABBITT   By Austin Warren

Shortly before the turn of the century—and partly, at least, as protest against the older type of German philology, still dominant in the United States—a few American universities established Departments, chiefly titular, of Comparative Literature. The most notable, patently, were those at Columbia and at Harvard. The Chairman of the former, George Woodberry—a graduate of Harvard College, a minor poet, and a critic in the Romantic Tradition but of wide reading in the classics and modern European literature—exercised an influence beyond his brief period of formal teaching. In 1903, he founded the *Journal of Comparative Literature*, which produced four creditable issues; and he taught John Erskine, the inaugurator of courses in the 'Great Books' (tradition carried on by Mark Van Doren, Norman Foerster, St. John's College at

Annapolis, and R. M. Hutchins' University of Chicago), and J. E. Spingarn, whose *Literary Criticism in the* [Italian, French, and English] *Renaissance* pays him handsome prefatory tribute.

At Harvard, the Chairman was W. H. Schofield, a mediaevalist and more technically a scholar than Woodberry; yet the first volume in the 'Harvard Studies in Comparative Literature' (1910) was so 'literary' and ranging a work as Santayana's *Three Philosophical Poets* (Lucretius, Dante, Goethe). With the early death of Schofield and the early resignation of Woodberry, their Departments remained in the respective catalogues, and their publications continued, Columbia listing its as in "English and Comparative Literature," Harvard persisting in its initial title, but chiefly—till Volume XX (*Perspectives of Criticism*, 1950)—limiting itself to the mediaeval studies appropriately associated with the influences of Schofield and Kittredge.

Now, since the Second World War, the study of Comparative Literature has acquired a new impetus, and with it, a shift in the direction taken by the Departments surviving from the past and by those more recently founded. "Broadly speaking," says Harry Levin, first Chairman of the reoriented Department at Harvard, "the focus has shifted from mediaeval to modern culture, while the approach has shifted from philology to the history of ideas" and literary criticism—or, more closely to follow Levin's summary in the Preface to *Perspectives*—to the history of criticism. At Harvard, this shift was, as Levin acknowledges, chiefly due to the influence of Babbitt.

Irving Babbitt (1865-1933), born in Dayton, Ohio, attended high school in Cincinnati. A post-graduate year he devoted to the study of chemistry and civil engineering, anticipating his lifelong scope: his classroom examples from *Photoplay*; his close concern with both stock-market investments and Buddhism; his skill (achieved through his own methods) at tennis and golf.

He came to Harvard College at the ripe age of twenty,—already, thanks to his violent reaction against his father, a naive and belated Transcendentalist—both "over-prepared" (his own estimate) and sure of what he believed and what he wanted. By some academic arrangement (doubtless that of President Eliot, instigator of what Babbitt ever regarded as the *pernicious* 'elective system'), he was able to spend his junior year in Europe,—not pursuing university courses but walking, with a companion, through France, Italy, and Spain—to the advantage brilliantly witnessed by his early *Atlantic* essay on the Spanish character.

After graduating from Harvard, in 1889, he taught Greek and Latin for two years in the College of Montana. It was his desire to teach the Ancients as his permanent professional—and professorial—center; but he was unable to sell himself to the classical scholars at Harvard; so he turned to French, and was slowly promoted to a Professorship in 1912.

Babbitt published no book in the 'Harvard Studies'—partly, perhaps, because the series ran to mediaeval and philological themes—but doubtless still more because he wished to reach a wider public than that of other scholars. All of his books—except four school texts (Taine, Renan's

Souvenirs, Voltaire's *Zadig,* and Racine's *Phèdre*), done for the Boston firm of Heath and done to augment an instructor's pittance, yet endowed with introductions which do not 'talk down,' and are serious literary criticism—were published, upon his paying for the plates, by the 'trade' publisher, Houghton Mifflin.

It is an open secret that Babbitt's presence in the French Department was scarcely more acceptable to his Romance colleagues than it would have been to the Greek professors. Edwin Arlington Robinson used to urge that he was a poet because, try as he would, he couldn't do anything else—a confession which earlier and sounder civilizations would have taken as mark and seal of a man's being *called,* having a *vocation.* It was by such procedure that Babbitt became Professor of 'French and Comparative Literature.' By 1920, he gave two large courses: one in Romanticism as a European and American movement and another in the History of Criticism. He was, at minimum, certainly a 'comparativist'; but, as I think of the work of his successor in the Harvard chair, Baldensperger, or of Van Tieghem, author of a clear and useful monograph on *La littérature comparée* (1931), I am chiefly struck with Babbitt's transcendence of 'comparativist' transcendence.

Despite his admiration for French culture, he took a much less academic line than the French comparativists, who conceived of suitable studies as 'Goethe in France' or 'Richardson in Germany' or 'the influence of Corbière on T. S. Eliot'—or, more boldly, 'the influence of French Symbolism on American Poetry.' Already in his first book, published in 1908, when he was over forty, Babbitt had dispensed himself from dealing with the Influence of A^1 on B^2 or the Reputation of F^3 in G^4. His concern was with methodology, 'first principles,' 'main currents': Georg Brandes' work on nineteenth century literature was one which, justly, he commended to his students.

Babbitt was a scholar and an 'historian of ideas'; but he over-reached those expertnesses, for he was also a critic, also a philosopher, also—I would add—a theologian. Nor was he content to be descriptive or analytic: he had to evaluate what he described; and it is doubtful whether he would have bothered with books had he not, unlike most scholars, supposed them capable of changing men's thought and, consequently, their lives.

In his first book, *Literature and the American College* (published in 1908,—but far from obsolete today), he asserts: "Comparative Literature owes its sudden prosperity to the talismanic virtues that are supposed to belong to the historical and comparative methods. . . . But Comparative Literature may become positively pernicious if it is allowed to divert undergraduates [or—he would certainly have supposed—graduate students] from gaining a first-hand acquaintance with the great classics, to a study of interrelationships and interdependences either of individual authors or national literatures."

In the same book—in words applicable to himself—he praises Goethe for refusing "to treat Latin and Greek in a purely historical way, and affirming for them not only a *relative* but an *absolute* worth." Babbitt was in search of the aesthetic and spiritual constants and in search of the hierarchy of values. It follows, doubtless, that his brand of comparativism passed beyond literature to philosophy and religion, and that it included the Orient as well as the Occident: Confucianism as well as Aristotelianism; Buddhism—a strong interest from youth to age (his last work was a translation of the *Dhammapada*)—as well as Christianity (St. Augustine, Pascal, St. Francis of Sales, Niebuhr, Maritain).

Much of Babbitt's greatness as a teacher—a greatness present also in his books, notably *Masters of French Criticism* (1912) and *Rousseau and Romanticism* (1919), lay—only one cannot use so passive a verb of Babbitt—in his spontaneous, because personal, integration of all he had read and thought,—his spiritual integrity. This is best demonstrated by the Introductions and Conclusions to these two masterly books,—especially the long Conclusion to the *Masters*, chiefly devoted—surprising in anyone save Babbitt,—to an American,—Emerson.

The University of Michigan

DON MIGUEL ASÍN PALACIOS   por Francisco López Estrada

Entre las figuras más importantes de los estudios comparatistas en España tiene excepcional relieve don Miguel Asín Palacios (1871-1944). Nació en Zaragoza, hijo de modesta familia. Cursó en esta ciudad los estudios de la Facultad de Filosofía y Letras, al tiempo que los eclesiásticos en el Seminario Conciliar. En el año 1891 oyó en las aulas de la Universidad aragonesa a don Julián Ribera, y desde entonces quedó señalado el camino de su actividad erudita: los estudios árabes. En 1895 cantó su primera misa, y en 1896 se doctoró en Madrid con una tesis sobre Algazel. Asín Palacios reunió, pues, su vocación sacerdotal con el consciente y luminoso trabajo sobre los árabes, y esta doble dedicación pudo armonizarse en beneficio de una mejor obra erudita. Por su formación y por su activo e inquieto espíritu estuvo en condiciones de realizar su más importante contribución a la historia del comparatismo: establecer las relaciones entre la religiosidad árabe y la cristiana. A. J. Arberry pudo escribir: "The student of Sufism ought himself to be something of a Sufi" (*An Introduction to the History of Sufism*, Univ. of Calcutta, s.a., pág. 61). En 1901 publicó su tesis ampliada *Algazel: dogmática, moral y ascética* que le prologó don Marcelino Menéndez Pelayo. No había de abandonar luego el estudio de este escritor árabe, que constituye el tema de uno de sus más importantes libros: *La espiritualidad de Algazel y su sentido cristiano* (1934-1941). La monografía sobre *El averroísmo teológico de Santo Tomás de Aquino* apareció en el "Homenaje a don Francisco Codera" (1904). De esta manera comenzaba a tender la trama de su obra sucesiva. En 1914 ingresó en la Real Academia de Ciencias Morales y Políticas, y en su discurso trató de *Abenmasarra y su escuela. Orígenes de la filosofía hispano-musulmana*. Asín demostró en este estudio las peculiaridades espirituales del Islam andaluz. En sus estudios el sabio español buscaba sistemática e implacablemente las relaciones de la espiritualidad árabe con España, y consecuentemente con Europa, y en esta orientación llegó a la más im-

portante de sus tesis: *La escatología musulmana en la Divina Comedia*, primero discurso de ingreso en la Real Academia Española, y después, libro (1925; y 1943). Dante, la figura representativa de su tiempo en Europa, según Asín, debía parte de los elementos de su obra a los árabes: "De hoy más, ya no creemos que se pueda negar a la literatura islámica el puesto de honor que le corresponde en el solemnísimo cortejo de los precursores del poema dantesco. Ella, por sí sola, descifra, de la génesis de este poema, más enigmas que todos aquellos precursores separadamente y aun tomados en conjunto" (*La escatologia* . . ., 1943, pág. 419). Esta tesis se puede contar entre las más audaces concepciones del comparatismo moderno, y tuvo una viva repercusión mundial; la polémica que suscitó ha sido recogida por el proprio Asín en un largo apéndice de la edición de 1943. Estudió la vida y la doctrina y tradujo la obra de Ben Házam. También dedicó particular atención a Ben Arabí. En relación con estos trabajos publicó *El Islam cristianizado* (1931), un estudio del influjo del monacato cristiano oriental sobre el Islam, complementado por el libro sobre Algazel, antes señalado. En este ir y venir del mundo islámico al cristiano trató en 1933 de *Un precursor hispanomusulmán de San Juan de la Cruz*. La relación se establecía también con autores cumbres de los Siglos de Oro de España. En el libro *Huellas del Islam* (1941) reune varios trabajos en este sentido sobre Santo Tomás, Turmeda, Pascal y San Juan de la Cruz.

Tal es una breve relación de la obra más importante de Asín Palacios. Y en concordancia con ella, una actividad magistral que comienza en 1903 al ocupar la cátedra de lengua árabe de la Universidad de Madrid. Allí ejerció su magisterio con una probidad y disciplina admirables, y supo rodearse de un grupo de afanosos discípulos que continuaron y ramificaron los estudios por él emprendidos: Angel González Palencia, Pedro Longás, Emilio García Gómez y otros más.

A más de las mencionadas Academias, perteneció a la Real de la Historia, y desde su fundación (1916) al Instituto de Valencia de don Juan, y también desde su origen a la Escuela de Estudios Arabes (1932). Dirigió desde su primer número (1933) la revista *Al-Andalus*, la más importante que en España se dedica a los estudios árabes.

Universidad de Sevilla

FIDELINO DE FIGUEIREDO par Antônio Soares Amora

Né à Lisbonne en 1889, Fidelino de Figueiredo appartient à cette génération estudiantine agitée qui déclancha la grève universitaire de 1906 contre l'autoritarisme réactionnaire d'une monarchie en pleine crise et qui, quatre ans plus tard, prit une part décisive dans la révolution républicaine. Adhérent enthousiaste du mouvement général de renovation de la culture portugaise, Fidelino de Figueiredo aussitôt après le triomphe de la République commença son oeuvre de réforme de l'esprit historique. Contre les iconoclastes hostiles au passé il chercha à défendre et à mettre en évidence la "tradition vivante et les valeurs permanentes de l'âme nationale" (*O espírito histórico*, 1910; *Historiografia portuguêsa do Século XX*, 1941).

Ce n'était pas seulement l'historiographie qui, au Portugal, demandait des interprétations nouvelles et de nouvelles méthodes de travail, mais aussi la critique et l'histoire littéraires. Dans l'oeuvre de Fidelino de Figueiredo qui commença en 1910—oeuvre immense et systématique, dont l'influence se fit sentir au Portugal et à l'étranger—il y a trois aspects fondamentaux: la critique littéraire (*História da crítica literária em Portugal*, 1910; *A crítica literária como ciência*, 1912; *Aristarcos* [Méthodologie de la critique littéraire] 1939; *A luta pela expressão*, 1944), l'histoire de la littérature portugaise (*História da literatura romântica*, 1913; *História da literatura realista*, 1914; *História da literatura clássica*, 3 vols., 1917-24) et les essais d'interprétation des principaux thèmes et des individualités littéraires portugaises les plus significatives (*Estudos de literatura*, 5 séries, 1917, 1918, 1921, 1924, 1950). En chacun de ces domaines, la première préoccupation du grand critique a toujours été de diriger la culture portugaise dans le mouvement critique mondial et ainsi d'introduire au Portugal les conquêtes permanentes de la critique moderne et d'élever la discussion et l'étude de la littérature portugaise au niveau des intérêts de cet esprit universel. Il élabora une histoire de la littérature portugaise sur les bases de l'histoire littéraire comparée et d'un point de vue sévèrement esthétique. Il est aujourd'hui au Portugal le maître non seulement de la critique comparée, mais encore de la littérature comparée—comme l'atteste une foule de livres et d'articles sur Shakespeare et Garrett, sur les sources portugaises de Lope de Vega ou de Molière, sur les aspects du donjuanisme, etc.

Dans le domaine de l'essai d'interprétation des principaux thèmes, oeuvres et écrivains du Portugal il a écrit des livres décisifs comme *Pirene* (1935), qui étudie pour la première fois les problèmes essentiels de l'histoire comparée des littératures portugaise et espagnole; ou *A épica portuguêsa no Século XVI* (1931, 3e éd. 1950), où il expose et défend une thèse entièrement nouvelle sur la genèse des épopées et sur la signification des *Lusiadas* comme oeuvre de Renaissance. Intelligence inquiète face à la réalité et à la vie de l'esprit, il a construit aussi une oeuvre d'essais personnels qui sont parmi les plus importants de la culture ibérique moderne—soit en étudiant la vie tchèque (*Iniciação boêmia*, 1932) et la vie américaine (*Interpretações*, 1933), ou bien la dignité de l'esprit et les responsabilités de l'intellectuel devant la vie (*Menoridade da inteligência*, 1933; *O dever dos intelectuais*, 1936). Nous ne devons pas oublier son activité et son oeuvre de critique, d'essayiste et d'érudit dans le monde de la culture luso-brésilienne et de la culture ibéro-américaine. Constamment intégré au mouvement critique moderne, introducteur et maître de la critique comparée au Portugal, il a ouvert de larges horizons à la critique portugaise ainsi qu'à celle de l'Espagne et du Brésil, et il a attiré sur sa littérature l'attention de spécialistes étrangers de valeur.

Cette intégration des lettres portugaises ne s'est pas limitée au domaine d'études mémorables—elle s'est accompagnée de relations personnelles avec les spécialistes européens et américains, à l'Université centrale de Madrid l'Université de Santiago de Compostela, en France, en Angleterre, en Tchécoslovaquie, en Amérique du Nord (Universités de Berkeley, Harvard

Jolumbia), en Argentine et, surtout, pendant de longues années, au Brésil 1938-53). Professeur titulaire de la chaire de littérature portugaise à 'Université de São Paulo, il a créé et dirigé les études supérieures de cette ittérature. C'est avec justice qu'il est considéré aujourd'hui comme l'am-•assadeur principal de la culture portugaise moderne, un des esprits les •lus cultivés, un des critiques et essayistes les plus influents de la culture béro-américaine.

Jniversidade de São Paulo.

PART THREE

COMPARATIVE LITERATURE DEPARTMENTS IN AMERICAN UNIVERSITIES

COLUMBIA UNIVERSITY   By Roger S. Loomis

The following courses which were not given in 1951-52 were given in 1952-53:

English-German Literary Relationships in the Nineteenth Century (Nobbe)
History of the Novel (Nobbe)
Dante and Medieval Culture (de' Negri)

Doctoral dissertations completed in 1952:
Mabel Worthington: *Don Juan: Theme and Development.*
Edwin Conn: *The Vogue and Influence of Madame Bovary.*
Robert Wagner: *The Last Illusion: Examples of the Spiritual Life in Modern Literature.*
Ervin Gaines: *Mercantilism and Literature of the Later Seventeenth Century.*

Work in progress:
O. J. Campbell: Shakespeare's Italianate Comedies.
M. J. Valency: The Renaissance Lyric.
S. Nobbe: Germanism in Victorian England.
R. S. Loomis is acting as general editor of a collaborative work on the Arthurian Legend in the Middle Ages, to which some twenty-five European and American scholars are contributing.

HARVARD UNIVERSITY   By Renato Poggioli

In 1953-54 our Department will add the following undergraduate courses:
The Literary Epic (Lord)
Readings in European Humanism (Dieckmann)

and the following graduate courses:
American-European Literary Relations (Levin)
The Structure of a Poem (Singleton)

Ph.D. dissertation finished in 1952:
Bernardo Gicovate: *Herrera y Reissig, A Symbolist Poet.*

The following dissertations will be presented in 1953:
Claudio Guillén: *The Anatomies of Roguery: A Comparative Study in the Origin and the Nature of Picaresque Literature.*
John L. Bishop: *The San-yen Collections: A Study of the Colloquial Short Story in Seventeenth-Century China.*

Research finished or in progress by individual members of the Department:
Harry Levin: *The Overreacher: A Study of Christopher Marlowe.* Harvard U.P., 1952
Cantare della gesta di Igor (Slovo o polku Igoreve)—Introduction, translation and commentary by Renato Poggioli. Now in press (Einaudi, Torino)
Howard Hugo: a book on the Romantic Hero.

THE UNIVERSITY OF NORTH CAROLINA By Werner P. Friederich

The Department added a new requirement for Ph.D. candidates in Comparative Literature: besides giving proof of a thorough knowledge of two to three modern languages and literatures, they must also pass a reading examination in Latin (or Greek) before being accepted to candidacy.

In addition to the three titles listed last year, the Department has the following two Ph.D. dissertations and one master's thesis in progress:

William Heald: *Lope de Vega and Shakespeare.*
Venice Poulos: *Baudelaire in Germany.*
Loyal Gould: *The Conservative Social Attitude in the German and American Regional Novels in the Second Half of the Nineteenth Century.*

Among the research finished or in progress by individual professors in the Humanities (not necessarily members of the Department of Comparative Literature):

R. P. Bond: *Queen Anne's American Kings.* Oxford, 1952.
A. G. Engstrom: Balzac and English Literature.
    Criticism of Baudelaire in England and America.
W. P. Friederich (and D. H. Malone): *Introduction to Comparative Literature* (completed).
G. M. Harper: Platonism in Blake.
    The Dionysius Myth in Blake.
S. Stoudemire: The Relationships Between the Spanish Romantic Drama and the Italian Opera.
F. Stovall: Three articles on Whitman and Shakespeare (in PQ, SP and JEGP, 1952).
E. W. Talbert (and D. T. Starnes): *Classical Myth and Legend in Renaissance Dictionaries* (completed).
B. L. Ullman: "Renaissance—the Word and the Underlying Concept." SP, 1952.
    Studies in the Italian Renaissance (in press).
L. Wiley: *The Gentleman of Renaissance France* (in press).

YALE UNIVERSITY By René Wellek

The following new courses will be offered in 1953-54:
Literary Criticism in Europe: The Mid Nineteenth Century (Wellek).
The European Enlightenment (Wellek).
Dostoevski and Tolstoy (Wellek).
Baroque Poetry in the Latin Countries (Auerbach).
Existentialism in Denmark, Germany and France (Douglas).

Ph.D. dissertations to be completed in June 1953:
Konrad Bieber: *The Attitude of French Resistance Writers towards Germany.*
Ralph Freedman: *The Lyrical Novel in France, Germany and England.*
Geoffrey Hartman: *Poetry and Epistemology.*
Anthony Thorlby: *The Theme of Fatality in the Novels of Stifter, Turgenev, Flaubert, and Hardy.*
Frederick S. Will, Jr.: *The Aesthetics of Victor Cousin and its Sources.*

There are eight other students all working toward the Ph.D. in Comparative Literature. No M.A. is offered; no undergraduate major is offered.

Mr. Kenneth Douglas was made Associate Professor of French and

Comparative Literature and Mr. Wellek received the new title of Sterling Professor of Comparative Literature. The latter has also finished the manuscript of the first volume (1750-1830) of his *History of Modern Criticism* (dealing with Voltaire, Diderot, Dr. Johnson, Lessing, Herder, Goethe, Schiller, the Schlegels, Novalis, Mme de Staël, Chateaubriand, Hugo, Stendhal, Wordsworth, Coleridge, Hazlitt, Foscolo, Leopardi, Solger, Hegel et al) which will be published by the Oxford University Press.

INDIANA UNIVERSITY   By Horst Frenz

The Comparative Literature Program at Indiana University has added two new courses to its list of graduate offerings and revised the course in methods required of all majors. Formerly a course in problems and methods, this course is designed now only for an investigation of the diverse problems pertinent to a study and knowledge of comparative literature. The material relating to methods of research and bibliographical tools has been taken out, and a new required course intended to give the graduate student a more thorough training in the use and knowledge of these essential tools has been created. The second new course, Modern Fiction, is a study of English, European, and American fiction from French and Russian realism to the masters of the twentieth century.

Ph.D. Dissertations completed in 1952:
Brown, R. D.: *Joris-Karl Huysmans and the Bodley Head Decadents.*
Gaither, Mary E.: *Ancient and Modern Concepts of the Tragic Hero.*

New Ph.D. dissertations in progress:
Sheldon, James Gail: *The Relation of Nicholas Berdayev to Earlier European Thought.*
Spilka, Mark: *Myth in Modern Literature.*

M.A. thesis completed in 1952:
McLean, Robert C.: *Stephen Crane in England.*

M.A. theses in progress:
Gerkin, Barbara J.: *William Morris and the Saga of the Nibelungs.*
Whitfield, Joyce: *Occultism in Modern French and German Poetry.*

Research finished or in progress by individual members of the Program:
Francis Fergusson: Reprint of *The Idea of a Theatre.* Doubleday Co. 1952.
Horst Frenz: *Whitman-Rolleston, A Correspondence.* Dublin, 1952.
    "Bemerkungen über Thomas Wolfe" (Die neueren Sprachen, 1953).
    "Eugene O'Neill on the German Stage" (Theatre Annual, 1953).
    Eugene O'Neill—World Dramatist.
Norbert Fuerst: The International Emergence of R. M. Rilke.
Henry H. H. Remak: The German Reception of French Realism.
    Franco-German Literary Relations in the Eighteenth Century.
Eward D. Seeber: Literary History of English Spleen, French *mal du siècle*, and the Problem of Suicide in England and France.
A. Lytton Sells: Italian Influence in English Poetry.

UNIVERSITY OF CALIFORNIA   By Arnold H. Rowbotham

The University of California at Berkeley has no Department of Comparative Literature, as such. It is however making some progress in that direction. In 1948 we instituted the Master's Degree in Comparative Literature and have had a number of successful candidates. The work is under the control of a faculty group, chosen from the language departments (including the department of English). This group examines the competency of the proposed candidate in the field, as well as his record of prerequisite subjects taken. After the candidate, with the group's advice, has decided upon the particular aspect of the subject he wishes to choose for his thesis, he is turned over to a special committee who then takes over the task of directing his studies, including the writing of the thesis.

The administration and program of the group is, of course, under the general supervision of the Graduate Council of the University.

In the development of the program we have been feeling our way slowly, in order that any program of study outlined may be maintained on the high scholastic level of the graduate studies in general in the University. In a few years we hope to have progressed far enough to be able to offer the Doctor's Degree in Comparative Literature. In the meantime we are slowly adding Upper Division and Graduate courses to our offerings in the subject.

During the years 1950-52 the following M.A. theses have been presented and accepted:

Lamb, Jean Darling: *Gothic Novel and Roman Noir.*
Godkin, Ruth P.: *The Influence of Rabelais on the Satire of Thomas Love Peacock.*

The following are among the theses being prepared for the year 1952-53:

Collis, Harry: *René Ghil and the French Symbolist Aesthetic as reflected in The Balance.*
Uiti, Carl: *Conceptions of Pure Poetry in French and English, from Poe to Yeats and Valéry.*

CORNELL UNIVERSITY
By Victor Lange

We do not at Cornell have a specific departmental structure dealing with comparative literature. We have rather an Interdepartmental Committee, which is in the main devoted to a constant exchange of the problems both educational and critical with which all of us in the literatures have to deal. This committee also offers a considerable number of courses devoted to subjects and fields of study that are not normally provided for in the departmental programs. I am, for instance, this term lecturing on European fiction in the nineteenth century. There is a course in "Literary Criticism," another in "Humanisms and the Renaissance." All together there is a list of some twenty courses. This is, of course, only in the loosest sense of the term a program of "Comparative Literature." But it is important to recognize our willingness to relax departmental confinement and develop an awareness of historical and critical interdependence.

We have not as yet thought much about comparative literary studies on the graduate level. The reason for this is no unwillingness to enter into such teaching, but rather the peculiarly flexible and enviable structure of graduate instruction at Cornell, which does not depend on departmental offerings, but hinges a student's work almost entirely to two or three chosen professors, who can then easily meet the student's particular interests.

MUHLENBERG COLLEGE   By H. Meyer

Boys' Colleges are not a fertile field for comparatists, and poor church-related colleges have a large number of students who want to prepare for jobs in the recognized professions, among which that of a teacher of Comparative Literature can hardly be said to be pre-eminent. But since I felt that I could contribute something to the good of the school and do what I liked better than teaching elementary German, I convinced the Faculty that a Divisional Major in Comparative Literature might be a practical start. The Departments of English, Romance and Classical Languages joined in the project and a Major was set up. Students can distribute their interest in such a way that at least four of the following six fields are represented: Spanish, French, German, Greek, Latin, and English. At least four courses from the following group are required: *Literary Forms and Values, The Great Critics, Greek Literature in Translation, Latin Literature in Translation, Renaissance Literature in Italy, France and Spain, Mediaeval Literature,* and *World Drama.*

The success of a joint program depends on the ability of those responsible, to draw and to keep interested students. The weakness of such a program is inevitably that of the weakest contributor to the course offerings. Experience has shown that there is not going to be a great rush of students into Comparative Literature as a major subject; but that three of the courses, taught by several members of the staff, attract a wide variety of the best students in the College, who wish to broaden their experience in literature for the sake of literature rather than a life's work.

The course on *Literary Forms and Values* drew fifteen students. They were required to write two term papers per semester, and their topics had to be chosen from a list of about twenty names. Besides, a list of books available in inexpensive, paper-covered volumes had to be read. On those the tests were given in class. The books included the *Odyssey,* Vergil's *Eclogues,* Dante's *Divine Comedy* in the partial translation of Dorothy Sayers, Manzoni's *Betrothed,* Keller's *Romeo und Julia auf dem Dorfe,* and others. The class lectures represented a third field of interest and, though referring to the books read or assigned for later reading, not limited to them. As the stated aim of the course was not that of teaching history of literature, but the enjoyment of literature and an understanding of the writer, such topics as Symbolism, Realism, Expression and Convention in Poetry, or Suspense in Fiction came up.

The course in *Great Critics* was historically conceived and went through the history of theories with the help of a textbook. It was informative, but not inspiring and failed in the opinion of the students. *World Drama* on the other hand, and the mediaeval course are favorites. These courses may indicate that this is not meant to be a program for future graduate students, but rather aims at equipping men for life with a basis for enjoying literature. The historical outlook of the nineteenth century is fading away rapidly and has never been strong in this country to begin with. Unless the teachers of literature give up the history of literature in favor of literature itself, they will probably succeed in killing all literary interest. It is not necessary to give surveys and to be informed about all that has been designated as great; it is much better that some selected writers and poets, great and small, but interesting in themselves, can be made interesting to every new generation so that those who have gained something from such courses will go out and explore further for themselves. It is in this direction that the future development of our studies is likely to proceed. Those who want to be scholars can then continue to the great seats of learning and receive, if not the charisma, at least a Ph.D. in Comparative Literature.

NEW YORK UNIVERSITY SCHOOL OF COMMERCE

By Vincent F. Hopper

I am not at all sure that a description of our literature group set-up would be of general interest since we face the special problem of teaching the humanities in a technical school.

It may, however, be of interest to you to know that our "practical" students were unimpressed by the "practical" value of "a sense of conduct and a sense of beauty," but that we have been able to appeal to them with the promise of attempting to analyze the major components of Western civilization. Our freshman required course is therefore entitled "The Great Western Literary Heritage." We examine the classical tradition by study of the *Odyssey*, several Greek plays, a few Platonic Dialogues, and the *Aeneid*. We then turn to Hebraism with the assistance of the Pocket Bible, note the confluence of the two in Christianity, survey the Gothic invasions, and note the mingling of the three cultures in the Middle Ages through a study of the *Divine Comedy*. We conclude with Goethe's *Faust* which serves as an excellent springboard for a discussion of the problems of modern man and modern society—and which (Part II especially) is actually a review of the whole course. One of the attractive features of the course is its novelty to freshmen who have had touches of English literature in high school and who are made (delightedly or painfully) aware that this isn't "the same old stuff."

After this introduction to general literature, our students may elect from a modest number of offerings:

> American Literature to 1900
> Contemporary American Literature
> Masterpieces of British Literature
> Contemporary British and European Literature

Our offerings are necessarily limited because our students may also elect any of the literature courses offered in Washington Square College, which is the liberal arts school of N. Y. U.

UNIVERSITY OF WASHINGTON   By Jackson Mathews

The department of General Literature at the University of Washington was established in 1926 as an inter-departmental committee of four members: Professors Allen R. Benham (English), Eldon Griffin (Oriental Languages), Edward N. Stone (Classics), and Louis P. De Vries (Romance Languages). Two courses were offered: Introduction to the Theory of Literature, and a Conference course of individual reading. In 1936 Professor John H. Groth (Germanics) joined the committee, and two other courses were added: History of Literary Criticism and a Seminar in Comparative Literature. In 1941 Professor Benham took charge of the department and offered a two-year course in General European Literature. All these courses were for undergraduates.

Upon Professor Benham's retirement in 1949, the department of General Literature became the General and Comparative Literature section of the English department, under the direction of Professor Jackson Mathews. The program of courses was revised and requirements set up for the M.A. and Ph.D. degrees. The program is administered by the English department, but an inter-departmental committee of three members advises on the operation of the program as it affects the several departments.

The advanced degrees are in English (and American) and one or more foreign literatures, the assumption being that a serious interest in literature is founded on the literature of one's own language. For foreign students, we believe their interest in English and American literature may equally be assumed from their presence in an American university. Two comparative courses are required for these degrees, but other courses are equally divided between English and other language departments. Candidates must be prepared in two languages besides English. This requirement is conceived *in depth* rather than in spread, i.e. graduate students in Comparative Literature are expected to work at the same level of critical understanding in foreign literatures as in English. It is assumed that they will generally be interested in ideas and methods of literary criticism and in problems of literary form and literary history common to two or more literatures.

We believe that *translation* must be one of the areas of concern in any comprehensive program. It is one of the serious modes of criticism and at the same time one of the finest and most neglected of the creative arts, and we consider its cultivation in both these aspects as a special responsibility of comparative literature.

The section in General and Comparative Literature offers courses in The Symbolist Movement, The Art of Translation, Romanticism, and European Literary Criticism since 1900. The various language departments offer a program of at least 30 courses in foreign literatures in English (most of them for undergraduates) in addition to regular courses given in the principal languages: Classical, Far Eastern and Russian, Germanic, Romance, and Scandinavian.

OTHER ACTIVITIES IN THE FIELD OF COMPARATIVE LITERATURE

The University of North Carolina
Studies in Comparative Literature

In order to simplify the commercial problems of the *UNC Studies in Comparative Literature* it was decided to associate the Series with the University of North Carolina Press. The full editorial responsibility is still vested in the Editorial Board consisting of Messrs. W. P. Friederich, Alfred Engstrom, Lyman Cotten and two newly appointed members, Messrs. Howard R. Huse and Walter Allen—but the advertising, selling and book-keeping will henceforth be taken over by the UNC Press. Contracts will be signed between the author, the editor, and the local printer; the author will be responsible for the entire printer's bill, but will receive sixty-six percent of the money obtained from the sales. The increase in our deductions as compared with the deduction of 15% prevailing until now is due to the fact that the Press is obliged to give a 20% discount to libraries, book-dealers and professors—something which we have not often been doing in the past. For further information write to the Editor, Box 775, Chapel Hill, N. C.

International Federation of Modern Languages and Literatures

The third post-war Congress of the *Fédération Internationale des Langues et Littératures Modernes* (Paris, 1948; Florence, 1951) will take place at Oxford, from September 9-16, 1954. The central theme of discussion will be "Modern Languages and Literatures and Science." The number of papers presented will be restricted to 45 and allocated to one of the three sections of the Congress: Middle Ages and Renaissance, Seventeenth and Eighteenth Centuries, From Pre-Romanticism to the Present.

As constituted at present, the following are the officers of the International Federation of Modern Languages and Literatures: Carlo Pellegrini, Florence, President; Charles Dédéyan, Paris, Secretary General—and of the Comparative Literature Section affiliated with it: Jean-Marie Carré, Paris, Chairman; Werner P. Friederich, North Carolina, Secretary.

International Association of Comparative Literature

The April-June issue of the RLC (1953, p. 241) reports as follows about an international meeting at Edinburgh which, it is my understanding, will take place in connection with the above-mentioned meeting at Oxford: "Un certain nombre de comparatistes français et étrangers, . . . sous la présidence de M. Jean-Marie Carré, ont envisagé les moyens de grouper dans une Association Internationale tous ceux qui, de par le monde, s'intéressent à nos études. Un bureau provisoire a été désigné qui convoquera à Edimbourg, en septembre 1954, un Congrès constitutif de cette Association. Outre l'élaboration et l'adoption de Statuts, ce premier Congrès officiel de littérature comparée depuis la fin de la guerre, devra dresser un bilan des recherches poursuivies dans les différents pays."

PART FOUR

REVIEWS OF PROFESSIONAL WORKS

A.

We should be grateful that the editors of the "Que sais-je?" series have gotten around to adding to their remarkable catalogue of titles *La Littérature comparée* by Marius-François Guyard (Presses Universitaires de France, Paris, 1951. 128 p.). And we should probably not demand too much of a little book which is intended as an elementary introduction to comparative literature. But we should hope that such a book would include some re-assessment of the objectives and methods of comparative literature and that this re-assessment would be made from the point of view of the present and the future rather than from that of the past. Indeed, we should hope that such a book—especially one intended as an introduction—would demonstrate that the discipline of comparative literature is truly an evolving one, that its objectives and methods are being constantly modified to contribute to the solving of the very problems which it helps to discover. One can only regret that M. Guyard's little book fails to satisfy these hopes.

M. Guyard has written an admirably clear, precise, and copiously documented introduction to comparative literature. If his book contains virtually nothing that was not expressed just as clearly and precisely in Paul Van Tieghem's *La Littérature comparée*, it is at least considerably shorter than Van Tieghem's little volume, and brevity is a virtue in an elementary introduction. He has taken over Van Tieghem's outline of the problems and methods of comparative literature with only an occasional change in terminology ("agents du cosmopolitisme littéraire" for Van Tieghem's "intermédiaires") and a discussion in a single chapter of "Genres, Thèmes, Mythes" to which Van Tieghem devoted two chapters: "Genres et styles" and "Thèmes, types et légendes." In fact, M. Guyard has in several places even taken over whole sentences from Van Tieghem with only an occasional change in word order.

In one sense it is beside the point that M. Guyard has merely adapted Van Tieghem's *La Littérature comparée* for a more general and more impatient group of readers and that he has made his adaptation without any acknowledgement or mention of Van Tieghem's book, except in a few indirect allusions and undocumented quotations. (Van Tieghem's *La Littérature comparée* is not even listed in M. Guyard's "Bibliographie Sommaire" although it is referred to in a footnote by M. Jean-Marie Carré in his "Avant-Propos" to the Guyard book.) What is to the point is that this oversimplified outline of comparative literature seems curiously sterile of genuinely literary interests. Van Tieghem divided the study of comparative literature into various quasi-scientific problems and methods with the implication that each specific problem could be attacked with a method which would produce "exact" results. But the old master was much too humane and liberal a scholar and critic ever to lose sight of the fact that literature is not and cannot be an exact science. Whatever problem or method he discussed, his eye remained on the real purpose of the method: the study of the individual work of literature. To be sure, M. Guyard professes to be aware that comparative studies may lose sight of their ultimate purpose, and he not infrequently interpolates some such comment as, "Loin d'être arides, de tels travaux peuvent et doivent être finalement oeuvre de moraliste. La littérature comparée s'y épanouit, comme souvent, en psychologie comparée." And, of course, he shows all the more evidently how far away from the individual work of literature his interests really lie. The path leading out of the waste land of "arid" studies leads to comparative psychology, not to the text of a play or a poem or a novel.

In the face of M. Guyard's very great dependence upon Van Tieghem, there seems more than accidental significance in the difference between the definitions of comparative literature which the two propose. M. Guyard defines comparative literature "more exactly" as "l'histoire des relations littéraires internationales." Van Tieghem says, "L'objet de la littérature comparée . . . est essentiellement d'étudier les oeuvres des diverses littératures dans leurs rapports les unes avec les autres." M. Guyard's book, even in its details, implies that the comparatist is interested in the many fields of study which can be reached *through* literature, rather than in literature itself. Van Tieghem, to be sure, often gets into areas that are at best only indirectly related to literature itself, but one is always confident that he knows, no matter how far away he may wander, how to get back to the basic individual work of literature.

In his concluding chapter M. Guyard makes several statements that one wishes he had made in his Introduction. He concedes, despite his precise anatomization of the *science*, that comparatists are far from agreeing on the limits of comparative literature "and even on its orientation." In discussing the causes for the evolving changes in comparative literature he says, "Un changement radical des perspectives de l'histoire littéraire en est la première cause." And then he makes a statement which his whole book contradicts: "L'historien littéraire de 1950 cherche davantage à comprendre la beauté de l'écrivain qu'il étudie; il est moins soucieux de l'expliquer à tout prix par ses antécédents et par son entourage." We cannot but applaud such sentiments. But immediately he enumerates problems which have yet to be solved: problems defined entirely in terms of the quasi-scientific partition of comparative literature into "exact" problems and methods, all of which lead rapidly away from "la beauté de l'écrivain." One does not deny that much more can and should be done in the scholarly studies of influences, sources, genres, etc. But one does wish that M. Guyard had said a little more about the future of comparative literature in the context of the radical changes in literary perspectives and of the modern interest in "la beauté de l'écrivain."

Realizing the purpose of M. Guyard's book, one could accept his making it an adaptation of Van Tieghem. Realizing too that M. Guyard has had to condense much of Van Tieghem's discussion, one could make allowances for the impression of sterility which his account of comparative literature conveys. But one cannot accept the implications of his concluding chapter. After reading M. Guyard's *La Littérature comparée* the American student, at least, must insist that an Introduction to Comparative Literature has yet to be written. Indeed, after reading this book, one feels that an Introduction to Comparative Literature *must* be written. Unless comparative literature in this country is to become the lopsided study of cultural history on the one hand or literary, dilettantism on the other, such a book must, in its ultimate purpose, justify comparative literature as the best means of arriving at an understanding, appreciation, and evaluation of the individual work of literature. It is a truism to note that, with the possible exception of Aristotle, the best critics and the best scholars have always been comparatists in the sense that they were never limited to national or linguistic boundaries. If comparative literature as a field of study and scholarship and criticism in this country is to do more than train teachers for superficial world literature and humanities courses, it needs urgently to get away from the implied scientism found in M. Guyard's book and to declare itself as *the* means of preparing the teacher and the critic for their respective jobs.

DAVID H. MALONE

Alabama Polytechnic Institute
Auburn, Alabama

B.

It has been exactly ten years since the first edition of the useful and well planned critical *Dictionary of World Literature, Criticism—Forms—Technique* (Philosophical Library, New York, 1953. 453 p.) made its appearance. The editor, Joseph T. Shipley, is a drama, and musical, critic, who joins with his sensitivity and aesthetic appreciation a genuine ability as organizer and a faculty for pulling things together into an harmonious whole. In making these remarks I am not seeking for fine language and fulsome praise. I am one of the two hundred and sixty contributors who are listed in the front of the book and, during the compiling of the first edition, I was associated somewhat actively with Dr. Shipley. I know from my own experience as a general editor that it is very hard indeed to give unity to a work which is made up from articles, paragraphs and even short sentences, which have been contributed by many individuals of different backgrounds. My own disposition has been to sacrifice unity to the literal quotation of what the contributor has written. Dr. Shipley has, on the contrary, done more editing. In the case of my own few contributions this has meant improvement and I have not suffered. But it is possible that some who sign with initials may feel aggrieved when they notice sentences here and there that they have not actually written.

I have counted two hundred and twenty-eight articles or definitions under the letter A in the older edition. In this revised volume the same letter has only a hundred and thirty-seven. (Cross references are, of course, not counted). The omissions follow definite trends. There is, for instance, a desire to leave aside what might more properly be found in a companion work, the two-volume *Encyclopedia of Literature*. Here are some of the articles which have been omitted under A: *Abenteuerroman*, Academy, Accadian literature, actor, adaptation, *ad lib.*, agony column, alarums and excursions, Alexandrian school, allegorical interpretation, almanac, Ancients and the moderns, anthropology and literature, apocope, argot, Aristotle, *arlecchino*, *ars moriendi*, art and literature, Arthurian legend, artist and society, astronomy, audience, *avant-garde*. There are a few new articles: action symbolism, affective fallacy, arsis, association of ideas. A few items have been rewritten: analects, Apollonian-Dionysian, aphorism. It is impossible to analyze the additions and subtractions throughout the entire book, but these details for the first letter are indicative.

For the student of Comparative Literature the most informative articles will probably be those on Aesthetics, the national criticisms (American, English, French, German, Greek, Italian, Mediaeval, Russian, Scandinavian, Soviet, Spanish), those on baroque, tragedy, comedy, folktale, Nature, literature and society and Symbolism. There are highly technical subjects such as Gaelic poetry, Welsh versification, prosody, rhyme, and form, which are well handled by experts. Scholars will be disposed to disagree with statements here and there, as we must expect, particularly in a dictionary or encyclopedia where many generalities must be clarified dogmatically. In the article philology I should like to see added the current definition of a philologist: one who uses linguistic knowledge for the better interpretation of literary texts, as opposed to the linguist who is more of a social scientist. Editors of linguistic journals will sometimes reject an article because it is too "philologic".

This new edition is more attractively printed than the previous one. It should serve a very useful purpose for students and mature scholars. There is no subjective slant to any of the material.

URBAN T. HOLMES

The University of North Carolina

C.

In his *Literature through Art: A New Approach to French Literature.* (Oxford University Press, New York, 1952. 247 p.) Professor Helmut A. Hatzfeld sets himself an ambitious task. He wishes "to elucidate French literature with the help of pictorial art," to "put side by side concrete examples of French literature and art as represented by texts and pictures or sculptures from 1100 to 1940 and [to draw] such parallels between them as seemed reasonable," "to shed light on six epochs of French literature and art in the course of six chapters." Moreover, he thinks it possible to interpret "the results of this historical research in terms of their contribution to a critical theory of literary aesthetics."

The results of this investigation are disappointing in the extreme. It soon becomes apparent that, for the most part, such parallels as are offered resolve themselves into treatment of the same subject matter in literature and in painting. Paul Cézanne's *La Montagne Sainte Victoire* is compared to Théophile Gautier's *Dans la Sierra, España* because both treat of mountains; both demonstrate a "majestic approach to nature" and hence belong in a sub-section entitled "Line as Opposed to Color. Ornament rather than Topic." Several paintings of the *Très Riches Heures du Duc de Berry* are compared to literary works: the "Janvier" to the *Petit Jehan de Saintré* because both contain banquet scenes, the "Avril" to the famous *Rondeau* of Charles d'Orléans because both are about spring. These are illustrations of the "Spirit of Minuteness and Its Expression in Genre Scenes and Interiors." The burial scene in *Madame Bovary* is like Courbet's *Funeral at Ornans*. At times, the likeness between two works is so tenuous as to depend upon the possibility of applying the same word to both; thus Brancusi's *Bird in Space* "evidently tries to give an idea of flight," and it thus suggests Mallarmé's sonnet, "Le vierge, le vivace et le bel aujourd'hui," with its "dream of the flights that have not been flown by this swan." When such comparisons are clear and obvious, they merely demonstrate the commonplace remark that at a given time artists in the various arts are ..pt to treat similar subject matters. When they are more farfetched, they merely display a determination to discover parallels at any cost.

The author, however, would not admit that his main concern is with subject matter. At various places, he shows parallelism of "form" as well. Thus the *Chanson de Roland* may be divided into five sections which would correspond to the five sections of the tympanum of the Abbey Church at Moissac. Both works thus demonstrate the principle that "Modern experiments have found that five subunits are the maximum a single glance can catch." One may doubt, first, that the division into five has anything to do with the poetic "form" of the *Roland*, and second that the psychological principle stated is "the acknowledged, unsymbolic, and formal explanation of the five units on the usual Romanesque tympanum." At other places, Mr. Hatzfeld goes beyond subject matter by relating the various works to generalizations of his own about given periods or given literary movements. He begins his section on "Nature Seen through Civilization" with the statement: "Nature, appealing in its primeval immediateness to Germanic and Anglo-Saxon pantheism, is acceptable to the Latin sensibility of the French only in a form refined by art and cultivatea by man" (p. 48.). His introductory section on Baroque Classicism contains the remark that "The reason and *esprit géométrique* of Descartes, the *raison du coeur* and *esprit de finesse* of Pascal in their classical-baroque fusion will also be found in the geometrical *châteaux* and in the immense vistas of their gardens, as well as in the paradoxical logic of the Racinian plots" (p. 63). His conclusion to the chapter on the Rococo declares that "Further investigations may follow the line of interpretation of the rococo forms by such parallels as that between pastel and short sentences, and that between perspective in painting and narrative suspense" (p. 118). He condemns Romanticism, in the introductory chapter on that movement, because—among other things—"The great gift of the seventeenth century, consisting in a psychological anthropology, is temporarily lost" (p. 120). In the section on symbolism in the same chapter, he hazards the generalization: "In the competition between painter and poet during the romantic period, as far as symbolic presentation is concerned, the poet, being symbolic by definition, should in theory be superior to the painter, who is supposed to be a realistic imitator of nature" (p. 148).

There are innumerable statements of this kind throughout the work. I have quoted only a few, and at some length, in order to show on what grounds the reader soon comes to his predominant impression about the book: that it is a book in which there are no definitions, no care in the use of terms, nothing that might be called a consistent and defensible method. Instead, one feels that all of these generalizations spring from a kind of mysticism about art and literature in which all things—grammar, syntax, psychology, religion, history, and the rest—are present and simultaneous, but never distinguished and never clear. This impression is in a sense corroborated by the final chapter, "Consequences for Literary Criticism," in which by passing from a chronological to a categorical arrangement the author believes that he has passed from history to criticism. This rearrangement is meant to "corroborate the indissoluble unit of the historical and the aesthetic method." But no criticism results; the rearrangement merely points up what Mr. Hatzfeld has been doing all along. His sub-headings indicate this: "Details of a Literary Text Elucidated by a Picture"; "Details of a Picture Clarified by a Literary Text"; "Literary-Linguistic Forms Made Comprehensible by Art Forms"; "Art Forms Explained by Literary-Stylistic Expressions"; and "The Constant, Sharp, and Unmistakable Borderlines between Literature and Art." With respect to these divisions, I must take issue with the terms "elucidated, clarified, explained." None of these processes takes place in the course of the work. The parallels strike one as constantly doubtful and forced, the claims of influence of one work on another without any substantial demonstration, the interpretations unsure and readily challenged.

It seems to me that the work represents a transfer to the field of literature of the worst features of the iconographic approach to the history of art. By the "worst" features I mean: the concentration upon isolated details of a work, which are frequently minute and inconsiderable, with the resultant exclusion of any consideration of the work of art as a totality; the satisfaction with partial parallels and imperfect analogies; the complete disregard of the quality of the works involved; the metaphorizing tendency by which far-fetched meanings are ascribed to works without any basis in the works themselves. I fail to see how the method as so applied can bring any new light to literary history or to literary criticism. It would seem, rather, that this type of approach merely adds another kind of confusion to the manifold confusions already existing in the realm of literary studies.

BERNARD WEINBERG

Northwestern University

D.

Although the *Essentials of European Literature* by Vincent F. Hopper and Bernard Grebanier (2 vols. Barron's Educational Series, Brooklyn, N. Y., 1953, 625 p.) is not a perfect answer to the student's need for a convenient and usable manual of European literature, it should be welcomed by those, teachers and students alike, who have long felt handicapped by the lack of a short comprehensive guide to the best literature of Europe. Compact, yet unusually detailed for the area covered, this "Guide to Great Books" is divided into two volumes: I. Early Middle Ages to the Romantic Movement; II. Romantic Movement to the Present (1900). The plan of the material is well designed to achieve one of the objectives of the authors: to relate the outstanding European authors "to the cultural patterns of their respective milieux." Approaching the literature of Europe as a whole, the authors have treated it in terms of phases, eras, or styles, e.g., Height of the Middle Ages, The Renaissance, Neoclassicism, the Rise of Realism, etc. Within each division writers are discussed according to individual countries. A general essay describing the general literary current and often the philosophical, religious, scientific, and political background of the age prefaces each section.

It is always easy to quarrel with a work of this kind — the wide scope of its material and the immense range of the time covered make it a Herculean task to render an accurate, well-proportioned, and readable account of the outstanding literature of Europe during the past seventeen centuries. The actual fact of accomplishment is in itself an achievement, yet the achievement alone should not blind us to certain weaknesses, which if remedied will add to the value of the volumes. Although it is not expected that all share the same opinions on the relative merit or talent of a particular writer, this reviewer finds, for example, the twenty-eight pages allotted to Ibsen out of proportion to the bare fifteen allowed for Dostoievski. One of the causes for this discrepancy brings up a question on the advisability of such long, uninterpretative plot summaries in a guide intended to "heighten the reader's understanding and enjoyment of the books themselves." To use these same authors as further example, we find two and a half pages to retell Dostoievski's *Crime and Punishment,* four pages for *The Brothers Karamazov,* but four and half for Ibsen's *Ghosts* and four and a half for *The Wild Duck.* One questions, too, the necessity for the detail in the summary of a work such as Dante's *The Divine Comedy.* Recounted almost canto by canto, the description of this classic runs to twenty-one pages. There is such a thing as a happy medium which seems to be in order here — an accurate account of a work which will indicate the content, theme, and treatment, but not so detailed that the student might be tempted to let the summary suffice him. Such long summaries do little to heighten enjoyment and understanding and certainly convey nothing of the author's style or literary quality.

In the actual handling of the material it is not quite clear why the authors have seen fit to devote a whole section to romanticism in Germany (The Golden Age of German Literature) and another to the development of realism in Russia (The Rise of Russian Literature) instead of considering German romanticism with that of France and Italy, and Russian realism with that of France and Germany. The result of devoting an entire division to German romanticism has been to burden the description with many minor figures that are scarcely known outside Germany. Since the literature of Russia after Pushkin has been mainly realistic, a better sense of the relation of Russian realism to that of the rest of Europe might have been attained by considering them together. If the bulk of material on romanticism and realism was responsible for these sections, perhaps the divisions could better have been made on the basis of time rather than geography.

One may justifiably ask for more accuracy in some details. Hauptmann's dates are 1862-1946, not 1858-1921. Bérénice is the heroine of Racine's *Bérénice*, not a character in his *Bajazet*. In the statement, "Bérénice has him killed, and then kills herself," Roxanne should be substituted for Bérénice, and "herself" should refer to Atalide. Also for such significant writers as Goldoni and Rilke it seems that it would be well to list the titles of some of their works.

As indicated at the beginning, these volumes serve a useful purpose and personal differences in the handling of the material should not minimize this fact. The third volume, now in preparation, which is to provide an extensive bibliography aimed at the student who depends on English translations, will enhance the worth of the entire project, and indeed, as the authors themselves suggest, justify these first two volumes.

MARY GAITHER

Indiana University

E.

Those teachers who are familiar with the late Philo M. Buck's *An Anthology of World Literature* will be glad to know that a guide for study, *Study Aids for World Literature* (University of Wisconsin, 1952), to be used in connection with the anthology, has been prepared by Professor Hazel S. Alberson of the Department of Comparative Literature at the University of Wisconsin. Although addressed specifically to the student, this outline of the contents of the book and the main literary epochs of the world should be of practical value to the teacher, especially as he may utilize the appendices, Recent Editions of Books and Subjects for Comparative Study. The "Aids for Materials in Text" following each chapter will serve to direct the student's attention to the chief importance of the particular works and help to develop his own selective faculty.

MARY GAITHER

Indiana University

F.

When the late Arthur E. Christy planned *The World Through Literature* (edited by Charlton Laird. Appleton-Century-Crofts, New York 1951, 392 p.), a collection of fifteen essays by various scholars, he had in mind two aims. First, that such a symposium would help people to transcend political and cultural barriers and forward that understanding and sympathy on which the future of mankind seems to depend. Second, that "if thoughtful essays dealing with the great literatures were laid side by side, the implied comparison might reveal a good bit about the way men write, and incidentally about the way men live and what they are." Of the two aims, the second is of most interest to students in our field. Can an essay — or even a course — in a foreign literature be an exercise in comparative literature? A sympathetic reading of this volume will result in an unqualified "yes" as an answer to this question.

F. Scott-Fitzgerald once remarked that a man needs only one window from which to look out at the world. In the home of world literature most of the readers of this collection will have a limited number of windows from which to survey the scene. This limitation can, however, be made the very reverse of a handicap as many essays here prove. From the British-American window are written the excellent essays on "Spanish and Portuguese Literature" by Rudolph Schevill and on "German Literature" by Bayard Quincy Morgan. Each is a brilliant evaluation of a literature like, and yet not identical with, that produced by our culture. The same might be said of J. A. Posin's essay on "Slavic Literature" in spite of the circumstance that the comparison is less obvious. Perhaps the great Russians of the nineteenth century have become so much a part of us that differences have seemed to disappear. Successful in this manner is H. R. Huse's essay on "French Literature", even if it does not completely avoid the tone of an encyclopedia article. More succinct is "Italian Literature" by Giuseppe Prezzolini which concentrates on those aspects of Italian culture which might mislead the American or British student. Such a paragraph as the following is a model of implied comparison:

> The Catholic religious life has left a profound imprint in the literary structure that is sustained by the two columns of Dante and Manzoni — a visible influence even when it manifests itself in negative forms of reaction, whether naturalistic, as in Boccaccio, or anticlerical as in Carducci. Save for Ariosto, whose fantasy seems to elude even Catholicism, it looms for all as an engrossing problem—of conscience for Petrarch, of competition for Mazzini, of philosophy for Leopardi; it torments Tasso, limits Vico, agonizes Michelangelo, irritates Machiavelli, and provides virtually all authors with familiar images, expressions, artistic tricks, starting-off points for thought. It is impossible to understand nine-tenths of Italian literature without the knowledge, not only of the doctrine but of the life of Catholicism.

The authors of the contributions on Scandinavia, Latin America and Hebrew literature adequately evaluate their subjects, though the last might well have been broadened to survey other fields of Jewish literature. Surely the fascinating writings in Yiddish are a part of the patrimony of world literature. Harder to fit in the pattern of the volume is the contribution, "Greek and Latin: The Philosophic Tradition in Literature." This is a good essay on the literary criticism of the ancients but does not deal with literature *per se*.

The hardest task was given the scholars who were asked to write about the Far Eastern, Indian, and Near Eastern literatures. Here the point of view to be taken must have presented a major problem. The implied comparison of the other essays would no longer be effective for the common reader. .Each of the contributors decided — independently apparently —

that the solution to the problem was to quote and cite generously enough so that the reader could judge roughly what was under discussion. All of the essays are good and should inspire linguists to add to the too meager list of translations into English from these languages.

Even though it might theoretically seem the essay the most difficult to write in terms of this collection, "Primitive Literature," by Paul Radin is the best, being both original and thought provoking. The author has succeeded not only in exploding certain prevailing misconceptions about primitive literature, but has done it so brilliantly that the reader learns more about literature in general here than from any other place in the volume. Every modern critic who pretends to a knowledge of "myth" should be required to read Radin's discussion.

Granting the inevitable inequality of the essays, the book as a whole is a good one. Not the least of its virtues is that it sends the readers to the library to read some of the great works that still remain on his list of "works to be read someday". Finally, Charlton Laird is to be congratulated on his editing, and on the introduction in which he neatly suggests what might have been the content of essays on British and American literature if it had been desirable to have included them.

VERNON HALL, JR.

Dartmouth College

... AND OF RECENT TRANSLATIONS AND EDITIONS

I

Every translation is a reminder that the "problem of translation" is inseparable from the "problem" of writing. For a translator aims consciously or unconsciously to produce a successful piece of literature, he aims to be read by some audience with some degree of satisfaction. Like other writers, he is dependent — singularly so, since he is rarely an innovator— on the literary situation in which he writes. But dependence implies an obligation, and if a translator's work is to satisfy his contemporaries, to say nothing of later generations, he must be in contact with the most vigorous literary culture of his time. Only so can he fulfill aims such as those set forth by Mr. Kinchin Smith in the preface to his recent version of the *Antigone* (*The Antigone of Sophocles*, A dramatic translation by F. Kinchin Smith, Oxford University Press, New York, 1951, $.60). Mr. Smith quotes the editors of *The Oxford Book of Greek Verse* as saying that "successful translations have 'two distinguishing marks—the use of a living language, and a proper regard for the claims of the reader, as well as the claims of the author translated'." The "use of a living language" is rightly put first; without success in achieving this aim the other claims will hardly be met. But the goal is perhaps a higher one than many critics realize. Among English translators of the past, it has been surely reached only by a handful of writers, by men like North and Chapman or Dryden and Pope. And these writers stand among the best of their time, their translations rank high when compared with their own original works or with those of their contemporaries. The translations that have aged best have been produced by writers who were responsive to the liveliest literature of their age.

It would be ungracious to measure Mr. Kinchin Smith's *Antigone* by the masterpieces of the translator's art. His intention—to make an acting version for students at the University of London—was modest, and he has undoubtedly succeeded in producing an actable version. The dialogue is speakable and usually easy to follow, and, if subtleties are sacrificed, an audience will at least be clear about the main events and the main relations between the characters. On the whole there are few signs of translators' English and second-hand poetic diction. (Unfortunately there is one lapse in the opening lines of the play: "...do you think there is a single curse that the gods *will not work out upon us* before we die?" The italicized words are individually pure Anglo-Saxon, but combined they are not quite English.) The choral parts have similar and more positive merits. They are neatly phrased and composed in rhythms easy for chanting or singing; and, what is more, they may be comprehensible when heard by a modern audience, a rare experience for listeners accustomed to endure soulful mumblings that they are assured are sublime poetry "in the original Greek."

But "clear" and "neat" are tame words to apply to the dramatist who created a tragic character as passionate and relentlessly heroic as Antigone. The violence of her action and temper, and of Haemon's and Creon's, the continuous and mounting sense of horror as we see them doing what is both right and unwise,— all that is mildly felt in this rather decorous version. If we ask what is wrong in a translation that has so few glaring faults, we must fall back on the hardest of all defects to demonstrate, a failure in rhythm. It is here that we come back to the relation between the translator and the literary life of his time. Mr. Kinchin Smith's "case"—not a bad one, though representative—is instructive to readers interested in the difficulties of twentieth-century translators. His *Antigone* is an example of the now standard "plain-English" version, of which W.H.D. Rouse's *Odyssey* is a good specimen. The great teacher of the new translators, as of the new poets, was Ezra Pound. (His recently published correspondence shows that he found in Rouse an eager and at times exasperating pupil.) But of course Pound gave lessons to few individual translators. His influence on the style of translation is inseparable from his influence as a poet and from the effect of the whole poetic movement of which he and Eliot and Yeats were the leaders. The establishment of the plain new style was salutary in much the same way that the cruder manifestations of functionalism in architecture were salutary; but the revolution in poetry as in architecture did not end with cutting out Victorian gimcrackery. In their mature work Eliot and Yeats made positive contributions to twentieth-century poetic style by the invention of new rhythms and by exploiting new resources of symbol and literary allusion. In poetic drama, as the experiments of both writers show, the revolution has continued up to the present time. And though neither has been certainly successful as a dramatist, they have both proved excellent practical critics of poetry in the theatre. By their plays and their criticism they have helped us to see what poetic drama can and should be.

Mr. Kinchin Smith, as a representative "plain" translator, exhibits the dangers of a demi-revolution. His use of prose and the principles on which he bases his use suggest that he has not gone beyond the first and the negative stage of the Great Reform. "Greek plays," he explains, "were written in verse. Poetry, however, when translated into prose is apt to evaporate. On the other hand, the imposition of a verse pattern in a dramatic translation often fetters the loose rhythm of dramatic speech. Prose can substitute for the regular form of verse the natural cadence of emotional speech, as well as give greater faithfulness to the original." The author of these remarks seems hardly to have passed beyond Wordsworth's confusions about the "language of real life," which Coleridge criticized so effectively in the *Biographia Literaria*. The question inevitably arises as to why Sophocles himself wrote in verse? If by "dramatic speech" is meant speech that brings to our ear a distinct voice, its rhythm can hardly be "loose," whether the medium is prose or verse. Indeed, the prose dialogue of Jonson or Shakespeare, or of Shaw at his best, is very precisely shaped and often beautifully tailored to the character. Yeats's reflections on verse and on "emotion" in tragic drama (see especially "The Tragic Theatre" from *The Cutting of an Age*, in *Essays* [New York, 1924], pp. 294-303) are sound reminders of the fact that verse serves other ends besides rendering the "natural" or actual cadence of speech. Eliot's reading (*Poetry and Drama* [Cambridge, Mass., 1951], pp. 15-20) of the lines from the opening of *Hamlet* testifies to the value of verse for achieving indirectly these other and often more important ends. For creating the large rhythm of rising terror in a play such as the *Antigone*, verse, or prose that is highly stylized, is an all but indispensable tool in translation.

But the prose in this version, and in others of its type, for example the translations of Mr. David Grene, lacks the vibrancy that completes the illusion of a suffering person behind the words, and the urgency that carries us through successive "waves" of the tragic hero's career. We are fortunate in having an excellent version of the *Antigone*, by Dudley Fitts and Robert Fitzgerald, which shows the advantage of good verse over merely honest prose. If we compare almost any speech in this translation with a speech in Kinchin Smith's (or in Grene's *Oedipus*), we feel at once that a drama is really "going on." Fitts and Fitzgerald use prose to similarly good effect, for example, in the opening speeches of Creon, which are cast in a fairly grand oratorical style that may be modelled on the style of Yeats's *Oedipus*. (It is definitely better.) In the choruses they, like Yeats, have taken full advantage of the new freedom: they introduce images and metaphors not in the Greek, though often of a kind that we feel is Sophoclean. By compensation they frequently bring out the large metaphor or the total emotional impact of a strophe, where Kinchin Smith's lyrics come all too close to well-bred bathos. But Fitts and Fitzerald have experienced the complete revolution, and they are poets, Fitzgerald a considerable one. Their versions of Greek drama have been clearly and fully composed as works of literature; they are good for the same reason that other pieces of literature are good — because of the art that has gone into their making.

REUBEN A. BROWER

Amherst College

II

Eugene Mason's translation of *"Aucassin and Nicolette* and other Mediaeval Romances and Legends" in this American edition (Everyman's Library, 1951, $1.25) reproduces fully the British edition. The format is larger, and the type is reset so that the improved printing does not strain the reader's eyes.

Mason appears as a sensitive interpreter in this anthology of mediaeval tales. This new edition bears witness to their lasting vitality, and can assist in further efforts to study their impact upon foreign literatures. Usually, by a felicitous choice of expression, Mason succeeds in imparting the flavor of the Old French language. He is not meticulously faithful to it, but he distorts the text less than others who have attempted to perform the same feat. Most of the slips in this translation can be ascribed to the fact that Mason had to use old, inferior editions. The introduction is deft in presentation and adequate in explanation of the historical, social, religious, and political setting; yet it does not compensate for the omission of bibliographical references. These data are due the reader who intends to trace the prototypes and the imitations of these heterogeneous legends as well as him whose appetite to consult the original is whetted.

Certainly Mason does "bring together a little garland for the pleasure of amateurs of beautiful tales." *Le Lai de l'Oiselet*, edited by Weeks in 1927, was translated into modern French by Oulmont and Pauphilet, into German by Lommatzsch, and into English by Butler. English readers are already familiar with it, because it has been paraphrased delightfully by Shelley just as *La Housse Partie* has been rewritten charmingly by Browning. This tale and *Le Chevalier qui ooit la messe* were both edited in the chrestomathy of Bartsch-Wiese and translated into English by Butler. It seems strange that the Blessed Virgin, deeply venerated as the Mother of Jesus, should be depicted as a warrior fighting in a tournament so that the knight may attend mass. *Sir Hugh of Tabarie* (sc. *L'Ordene de Chevalerie*), edited by Kjellman in 1920, was translated into English by Butler and Morris. The ceremony of dubbing impresses the young knight with the mystical symbolism of chivalry and inculcates in him the ideal of devotion to his God, to his king, and to his beloved. The realization of that ideal can be questioned in *Le Lai de Graelent*. Grimes edited it in 1928, and Mason reprinted his translation of it in "French Mediaeval Romances." The knight, whose conduct is perfect otherwise, is cavalier rather than chivalrous when he spies the lovely fairy bathing in a fountain; she delights in tantalizing him before yielding with reluctance.

Both *The Three Thieves* (sc. *Barat et Haimet*) and *Le Provoire qui mengea les meures* were edited in the collection of Montaiglon-Raynaud and were translated into German by Lommatzsch. The first tale reveals the interior of a peasant's hovel made of mud and containing a filthy pallet, a pitiful byre, crude tools, and fagots under a cauldron. In the *fabliau*, the priest reached the mulberries by standing upon the mare, but he should not have cried aloud: "Gee up!" *Le Vair Palefroi*, edited by Långfors in 1921, was translated into English by Butler and into French by Oulmont and Brandin. Thanks to the palfrey, the heroine escapes from the old suitor and weds her young sweetheart. Lommatzsch edited *Le Tumbeor Notre Dame* in 1920, and translated it into German in 1949. This story of the juggler, who retires to a monastery, has also been translated into French by Brun, Mortier, and Tharaud, and into English by Butler, Wicksteed, Kemp-Welch, and Nesbitt. Its popularity was greatly enhanced when it was revised by Anatole France in his *Etui de Nacre* and when it was set to music, first by Hutter and then by Massenet.

The "chantefable" of *Aucassin et Nicolette* has been edited more often than any other text in Old French. It should be read in the 1946 edition of Suchier by those who have the temerity to face the original, but for the faint of heart versions galore are available in modern French, German, Italian, and English. A theatrical adaptation by René Clermont was performed in Paris only five years ago. True love, thwarted at first by the parents' fear lest the marriage be morganatic, is consummated finally when the heroine reappears as a princess. The literary inspiration, if one is needed, may be found in Ovid, but the unknown author shows originality in setting off passion and idealism against satire and humor. The form of this dramatic recitation marks an affinity with Boethius, but artistry is evident in the author's alternating rhymed sections with heptasyllabic lines to be sung by a minstrel and prose sections to be recited by another jongleur. The writer pokes fun at the stock themes of coëval epics and romances. In the episode of Torelore, he introduces the burlesque interludes of the *couvade*, known to anthropologists universally, and of the battle of women whose ammunition comprises eggs, cheese, and apples. He knows how to blend narration and conversation, monologue and dialogue, unsophisticated realism and pictorial delight. Does he convince you that Nicolette was the most beautiful girl who ever lived? If not, just recall that when the pilgrim was near death, she

> Raised the smock, and bared to him
> Daintily each lovely limb.
> Then a wondrous thing befell,
> Straight he rose up sound and well.

RAPHAEL LEVY

University of Texas

III

When a new translation of an old epic appears (*The Parzival of Wolfram von Eschenbach*, translated into English verse with introduction, notes, and connecting summaries by Edwin H. Zeydel in collaboration with

Bayard Quincy Morgan, Chapel Hill, 1951, $6.50), we professional educators usually want to know whether the author of the original and his work can be defined as genuinely significant literary phenomena. Moreover, if we are inclined to use the new translation in one of our courses, we have every right to know whether the greatness of both original author and his work, as well as the quality of the translation, are all sufficiently high to merit its academic use.

Let us answer immediately that Wolfram, the medieval Bavarian, and his masterpiece, the *Parzival*, are quite unusually appropriate for the great task of stimulating the highest American educational ideals and, furthermore, that this magnificent translation has finally made the great medieval German epic fully accessible to Western academic and lay culture for the first time in literary history.

To begin with, the autobiographical elements in the *Parzival* give the epic such an intimate, realistic flavor that it immediately attracts the average reader, who is almost always fascinated by reading what a great man has to say about himself. This very human character of the narrative is demonstrated repeatedly, such as when the hero, upon winning the Holy Grail at the end, is happy not only because he has won it, but equally so because his devoted wife Condwiramur and the two sons whom he had never seen are approaching the castle to rejoice with him. Wolfram probably had to live apart from wife and children frequently while serving various distant courts and he would naturally feel the joy which Parzival manifests at the family reunion.

Of supreme attractiveness, moreover, to us moderns is the profound interest of Wolfram in the education of youth, particularly masculine youth. Not only does the chivalric code demand that young Parzival be rigorously trained in body (physical strength, skill, bravery, endurance) but he must also approach perfection in artistic accomplishments (music, singing) and, above all, in those spiritual qualities which produce the full-rounded perfect young knight (cleanness of heart, deep fidelity to man and God, genuine tolerance and sympathy, a refined moderation in all things, a profound sense of moral responsibility.) What finer program could we moderns envisage for the development of firmness of character in our own youth than the one which the great Wolfram outlined for his young hero's successful progress to the Kingship of the Holy Grail? The translators in their Introduction summarize it thus (p. 2): "It is the story of the gradual maturing of a naive young lad who becomes a doughty knight but . . . acts blasphemously . . . . and, after doubt and pangs of conscience, is led to a true understanding of and love for God." We moderns can certainly find no nobler description of the gradual inner development of the young manhood of any age than in Wolfram. Other versions of the Parzival story (e.g. Wagner) play down the vital inner struggles of the young knight to become worthy of the Holy Grail, but Wolfram makes these struggles the very heart and center of his great masterpiece.

Another essential feature of the *Parzival* that elicits our admiration and respect is the unusually high status which Wolfram assigns to women.

We contemporary citizens of Western Civilization take this high status for granted, but to find it in a medieval epic is indeed startling. "Not celibacy and 'holiness', but full-blooded living in the forms of decency, loyalty" (Introd., p. 2) are stressed by the translators as major factors in the relationship of the sexes. "Conjugal fidelity" is taken by Wolfram for granted. In fact the poet, deeply devoted to the new chivalric respect for women, demonstrates in his epic that the highest ideals of knighthood and manhood can only take root and flourish in those youths who manifest complete respect and devotion to the refined women of their environment.

What in the final analysis appeals most of all to the modern reader of Wolfram's *Parzival* is that this amazing author treats the deepest problems of human life with the same clear realistic approach and solution, as if he were a cultivated contemporary philosopher. The gnawing doubt, the abandonment of high ideals, the deep inner concern with what constitutes "good" and "evil", the tantalizing problem of Christian asceticism, in fact the vast mental confusion regarding man's efforts to save his difficult, complex civilization—all these and many more spiritual perplexities of contemporary thinkers find liberal humanistic (not ascetic or monastic) answers in this literary masterpiece of Wolfram, answers which are closely analogous to the liberal and humanistic answers we are giving to these questions today (cf. Introd., p. 2). The achievement of ideals, goals, "salvation" to Wolfram is, as to most moderns, almost wholly the problem of improving human character and human environments *on this earth* and not a problem to be left to the uncertainties of immortality. Hence Richard Wagner chose wisely when he made Wolfram's *Parzival* the basis of his profoundest opera, even though no modern version of the story, including Wagner's, has ever attained the almost perfect classical apotheosis of Wolfram's epic.

Having given his major reasons for his faith in Wolfram as an educator and inspirer of youth, this reviewer cannot speak too highly of the magnificent scholarly Introduction (pp. 1-33) furnished us by the translators of Wolfram's great work. After deploring the lack of competent English versions of the epic, the authors lose no time in establishing beyond a doubt that the *Parzival* stands unequivocally first among the great medieval epics of all lands, not only because of its rich pictures of chivalry and its human drama, but essentially because of its incomparable philosophical depth and its lofty idealism. Particularly brilliant are those pages of the Introduction (5-8) which clarify, far more neatly than this reviewer has seen elsewhere, the confusingly interwoven relationship of the old Perceval, King Arthur and Holy Grail legends in medieval and modern literature. The unavoidable conclusion that the Grail is originally non-Christian in origin is faced bravely and with scholarly skill. The possibility of a Kyot source is placed in its proper perspective and is explored in such a way that the non-specialist can really understand this scholarly dilemma, yet all of Wolfram's liberties with his sources and with history do not betray the translators into the fallacy of dubbing the *Parzival* a patch-work of many sources. To them and to most of us it remains a great unified work of art, bound together by the personality of the author. Nothing short of masterful is the highly original explanation by the translators of how the completed *Parzival* probably came into being. Their theory of the combining by Wolfram of the original Crestien material with some second unnamed source, enriching it later by using motifs from the *Lucidarius*, sounds not only plausible but completely convincing. Every modern lover of music and literature will benefit from the translators' fine sketch of the precise relationship between Wolfram's *Parzival* and Wagner's *Parsifal* (Introd. pp. 23-24), which emphasizes once more the essential and central importance of the long period of trial and testing, through which Wolfram's Parzival had to pass, but which Wagner permits his Parsifal to avoid. It is unequivocally affirmed that this great spiritual test alone places Wolfram's work on a loftier humanistic plane than that of Wagner.

As to the actual translation itself, there is very little that one need say to anyone who will take the trouble to read two or three pages of it. Dip in anywhere, especially if you know the story, and you will find it superb reading. The short rhymed couplets are far superior to Jessie L. Weston's (1894) long lines, not only because they are more accurate, but because they truly recover the "spirit and metrical flavor" of Wolfram. The archaic atmosphere is agreeably retained in both the colorful style of the translation and in the occasional use of older English phrases and words. However, the real miracle of the translation is the full preservation of the richness of Wolfram's descriptions of medieval life. Moreover, these translators do not change the original story as others (e.g. Will Vesper's German prose version, 1911) occasionally have done. The outstanding features of this translation are its high degree of accuracy, its simple rhythmic phraseology, its plausible realism and its amazing clarity. Students who read one first-class translation of a medieval epic like this one, will soon ask for others, and it is to be hoped that the future will supply them.

CLEMENT VOLLMER

Duke University

IV

Two recent translations of the first part of Dante's *Divine Comedy*, *The Inferno* by Thomas G. Bergin (Crofts Classics, 1948, $.35) and *The Divine Comedy, I. Hell* by Dorothy L. Sayers (Penguin Classics, 1949, $1.25), are intended for readers of English who know nothing about Dante, and who know no Italian and do not intend to learn any. Their purpose is thus quite different from that of the Temple Classics edition, in which the English, a fairly literal prose version published beside the original, serves to assist the reader to grasp Dante's own words. Both Miss Sayers and Mr. Bergin offer their translations as independent approximations, in English, of Dante's poem. They are thus attempting a very difficult feat, and it is hard to estimate their success. To do so one would have to remember Dante's effects, and at the same time imagine the effect of the translations on a reader who was totally new to the whole subject.

Mr. Bergin has not tried to get very close either to Dante's poetry or to the literal meanings of his words. He has translated most of the *Inferno* into blank verse, a form which is very unlike *terza rima*. English readers, moreover, are sure to have many misleading associations with blank verse, which will take them still farther from Dante. Mr. Bergin has put a few passages into rhymed verse, notably Francesca's speeches in Canto V and Ulysses' narrative in Canto XXVI. Neither is in strict *terza rima*, but both seem to me closer to the original than the blank verse, perhaps because Mr. Bergin likes them especially well. He puts Canto XI into prose, which I think is a mistake; for surely one of the most characteristic virtues of Dante's style is its ability to give philosophic exposition the resonance of poetry, just as it gives the most lyrical passages the clarity we usually associate with prose. Thus Mr. Bergin does not attempt to emulate Dante's style; but neither does he try for literal accuracy. As he explains, he has taken many liberties, especially in the detail, slightly altering many phrases and many images. He tells us that his "aim throughout has been readability," and that perhaps explains his attack on the problem. He seems to have had in mind a reader who would not try to get much more than the main outlines of the story, and endeavored to make a poem which such a reader would find readable. It is a moot question how desirable that is: would the inexperienced reader be tempted by Mr. Bergin's version to investigate further, or would he think there was no more to the *Inferno* than this English reveals?

Miss Sayers has translated the entire poem into *terza rima*. She has evidently worked much harder than Mr. Bergin, has tried for a much closer approximation to the original, and has, on the whole succeeded better. But it is extremely difficult to put a poem of this length into English, especially in *terza rima*, and I fear that anyone who remembers Dante's music will be troubled by many inadequacies, and even misrepresentations of the original. I cannot in this short note attempt to substantiate this impression, but one might compare Miss Sayers' and Mr. Bergin's versions of the illustrious opening tercet:

Bergin: Midway along the journey of our life
I strayed, abandoning the rightful path,
And found myself within a gloomy wood.

Sayers: Midway this way of life we're bound upon,
I woke to find myself in a dark wood,
Where the right road was wholly lost and gone.

Mr. Bergin has used active verbs where Dante used reflexives or passives, substituted adjectives of emotional or moral connotation for Dante's simple sensuous ones, and changed the order, thereby losing most of the helpless terror (and the force) of the original. Miss Sayers has also interpreted Dante's images to some extent, but she has respected his order, and her rhyme scheme helps. The worst feature of her version is its rather jolly, headlong rhythm. Compare the prose of the Temple Classics edition:

> In the middle of the journey of our life
> I came to myself in a dark wood
> where the straight way was lost.

I do not know how readable that prose would be for a reader who did not glance at the Italian, but I think it gives a truer impression of what Dante was up to.

Miss Sayers has not relied solely on her translation to give the reader some idea of the *Inferno*. The best thing about her book is the sixty-page introduction and the explanatory material she includes. I do not know of any better introduction to the reading of Dante than the one she here provides. It shows great understanding and love of the *Divine Comedy*, and I feel sure that it will serve for many years to make that poem accessible to new readers.

FRANCIS FERGUSSON

Indiana University

V

Readers of this generation unschooled in Middle English are fortunate in having available to them a new verse translation of the *Canterbury Tales* by a distinguished Chaucerian (Nevill Coghill, *Chaucer's Canterbury Tales: a New Translation*. The Penguin Classics, 1952, $1.25). This version of the *Tales* has the outstanding virtue of speaking to the reader in his own colloquial English, and in so doing it produces the triumphant impression that this is the kind of English Chaucer himself wrote. In translations of the last generation Alice of Bath seems sometimes to be talking in bad Tennysonian, as if Guinevere had somehow got herself enclosed within her sturdier sister. It is, of course, only natural that a modernizer of poetry, reinterpreting archaically expressed universals to his own age, should employ current poetic idiom. But this procedure is not the happiest one for Chaucer who, at least in the *Canterbury Tales*, largely eschewed all contemporary poetic idiom (except to make fun of it), and who anticipated Wordsworth by reducing—and exalting—poetry to the level of common speech. The result is that Chaucer, speaking as he has generally been made to do, in a consciously "poetic" language, does not sound like Chaucer. Mr. Coghill, recognizing that a modern Chaucer must speak modern colloquial English—and assisted, perhaps, by the resolutely unpoetic nature of modern poetic language—has succeeded in giving his translation an authentic voice that possesses much of the ease, the directness, and the conversational quality of the original.

The voice is, of course, Mr. Coghill's, not Chaucer's. But Mr. Coghill, who is steeped both in Chaucer and in English poetry and who is highly sensitive to the wittiness, the urbanity, and the poetic subtlety of the original, proves himself admirably qualified to imitate Chaucer's voice. No one, least of all the translator, would assert that the translation is an adequate substitute for the Middle English. But while it is fashionable to repeat the half-truth that the original is easy to master, the fact is that a very large number of potential readers will always be cut off from

Chaucer by the difficulty of his language: reading is, after all, a pursuit of pleasure which hard words will inhibit. Mr. Coghill's spirited modernization may be trusted to impart to many otherwise alienated readers some of the pleasure of Chaucer, and will probably even induce a few to make the intellectual effort the original text requires, and thus to reap that pleasure that no translation can transmit.

It is not the least remarkable aspect of Mr. Coghill's work that one may compare it with the original without feeling embarrassment for the translator—although at times one must sympathize with him. He is particularly apt at rendering the subtleties of verbal wit: a random inspection of his handling of certain passages reveals his extraordinary aptitude in this respect and his ingenuity in producing, in cases where the exact effect of Chaucer's lines is untranslatable, at least a similar effect. For instance, there is the delightful list of spicy foods brought to Sir Thopas in his arming:

> . . . gyngebreed that was ful fyn,
> And lycorys, and eek comyn,
> With sugre that is trye.

This satire on chivalric foods—the knight is being offered the child's ideal, a whole candy-counter—concludes with the most commonplace of sweetmeats, sugar, which in Chaucer is described by the self-consciously "poetic" word *trye* ("excellent"), a trite adjective Chaucer elsewhere avoids. This is placed in the most emphatically stressed position that the martial meter affords, and produces a fine anticlimax. Mr. Coghill's modernization,

> And gingerbread, exceeding fine,
> And licorice and eglantyne
> And sugar, very nice,

may not represent the exact pattern of Chaucer's satire, but it will produce in most readers the same shock of pleased surprise. Again, the Wife of Bath comments as follows on the friars' replacement of "faerye":

> Wommen may go now saufly up and doun
> In every bussh or under every tree;
> Ther is noon oother incubus but he,
> And he ne wol doon hem but dishonour.

In translating, it is possible to keep the first three lines almost intact (but not to punctuate them, since Middle English syntax permits the second line to go equally closely with the first and with the third); but the fourth line, with its unusual grammar—a kind of adaptation of the French *ne. . .que* construction, resulting in an anticlimax of dreadful implications for the friars, presents a challenge. Mr. Coghill meets it thus:

> So there is really no one else to hurt you
> And he will do no more than take your virtue.

Here the comic rhyme achieves almost the same result as Chaucer's unusual syntax, although the translation has had to prepare for the anticlimax by adding a line—thus unavoidably forfeiting Chaucerian compactness and the rapidity of the surprise.

One must admire also, I think, the rendering, much discussed by

critics, of one of the concluding lines in the Miller's portrait of Alison,
She was a prymerole, a piggesnye
(literally, a cowslip and a pig's eye). Probably to his audience Chaucer's
humor lay mostly in the perversion of the flower-comparisons convention-
ally applied to heroines: a cowslip, yes, but a pig's eye—even if it was a
flower—no. The convention has passed, and the joke with it. Mr. Coghill
revises,
She was a daisy, O a lollypop,
changing the sense, but certainly providing a properly savorous conclusion for a lip-smacking portrait. To criticize the lollipop as indecorous is
wrong, for much of the humor of the original portrait comes from such
startling departures from normal decorum.

With some of the great passages Mr. Coghill is, understandably,
less successful, but even his comparative failures are valuable in directing
attention to the real nature of Chaucer's art. For to explain why a
translation so intelligent fails now and then to recreate the original, one
is forced to reëxamine Chaucer's text from a fresh point of view. Indeed,
I should recommend comparing this translation with the original to
serious students of Chaucer and of poetry. Observe, for example, the
reply of the mysterious old man in the *Pardoner's Tale* to the rioter's
question, Why do you live so long in so great age?

> This olde man gan looke in his visage,
> And seyde thus, "For I ne kan nat fynde
> A man, though that I walked into Ynde,
> Neither in citee ne in no village,
> That wolde chaunge his youthe for myn age."

The modernization reads thus:

> The old, old fellow looked him in the eye
> And said, "Because I never yet have found,
> Though I have walked to India, searching round
> Village and city on my pilgrimage,
> One who would change his youth to have my age."

The intelligent translation illuminates, in its very failure to render, the
spine-chilling effect of the original. Much of the terror seems to come from
the awful simplicity—a kind of irony of the obvious—and from the
deliberately slow movement, which are products of non-semantic sound
that enhances the poetic sense by emphasizing it without further defining
it: there are five final syllables (*oldë, walkëd,* etc.) pronounced in Chaucer
but not in modern English—ten, if one counts the rhyme words; three
doublets (*ne . . . nat, though that, ne . . . no*) that must be reduced; and
one unrenderable expletive (*gan*). When these are eliminated, nine syllables—virtually one full line out of five—must be compensated for. One
must either omit a line or provide filler; but every line is skeletal—and so
one must provide filler. The result is the "old, old fellow," emphatically old,
but without the slow dignity of "this olde man." The search, which in
Chaucer is a vague and perhaps even metaphorical one, becomes explicit
and literal as words are added to make up for lost syllables: "searching
round" and "I have walked." Did Chaucer's old man actually say he had
walked to India? He may have, but the Middle English verb can be read

ither as a subjunctive, "though I should walk," or as an indicative, as in
he translation. Modern English, on the other hand, tends to be syntacti-
ally less fluid. Thus the rich suggestiveness of the original is lost when
yllables of sense replace syllables of sound, and the old man steps—too
riskly—from the shadows that so enhance his mystery. Mr. Coghill has
made a noble effort; but even if he has failed, because of his attempt those
shadows will, for one reader, always seem the more profound.

Such comparison as this must, of course, appear invidious, and I do
not wish to conclude on an invidious note. Therefore I hope the invidiousness
s more apparent than real, since it merely amounts to saying that Mr.
Coghill is not Chaucer, and that is an imputation we all bear. But Mr.
Coghill's translation, both in its positive and in its negative aspects,
performs a great service to Chaucer, and for this Mr. Coghill deserves the
gratitude of every Chaucerian, as well as of the lay reader.

E. T. DONALDSON

Yale University

VI

The present version of Balzac's *Old Goriot*, translated by M. A.
Crawford (The Penguin Classics, 1951, $.50) appears at a time when
Balzac's reputation, at least in English-speaking countries, is by no
means uncontested. The most recent work on the French novel in English,
Martin Turnell's *The Novel in France*, found Balzac's books "immature,"
unfit to communicate any important experience to discriminating adults.
Mr. Turnell compares Balzac unfavorably with such subtle analysts of
the human heart as Mme. de Lafayette, Stendhal, and Benjamin Constant,
and concludes that a taste for Balzac is an amiable weakness of the French
national character. Nor has Balzac's reputation, even in France, been
free from serious question, once the vogue of realism gave way to other
literary exigencies—though a critic like Albert Béguin, taking a hint from
Baudelaire, has recently evoked the image of a Balzac *visionnaire* to replace
the accepted and somewhat tarnished image of Balzac *réaliste*.

How does *Old Goriot*, taken as a separate work, stand up to these
criticisms of its author? Not very well, it must be admitted, if, like Mr.
Turnell, we seek for some penetrating insight into the finer shades of
human emotions, and are led astray by the usual comparison of *Old Goriot*
and *King Lear*. Balzac's talent lay in a completely different direction; his
was a vision not of Man but of Society; and it is this vision, projected with
obsessive intensity, that gave a new direction to the modern novel. From
this point of view, *Old Goriot* is still a remarkably exciting book, and it is
perhaps unfortunate that Balzac, by naming it after one of the characters,
allowed a misunderstanding to arise. The center of the book is not the
portrait of Goriot—though he is the center of the intrigue; it is the
octopus-like society whose effects are depicted through the momentary
meeting of two lives each in the clutch of the same forces. Eugene Rastignac
is slowly being absorbed into the deadly social machine, struggling
against it in his conscience but unable to resist the allurements of wealth,

beauty and power. Rastignac's rise to social position, for which he has to sacrifice all his moral scruples, is intersected by the decline of Goriot, once a rich and prosperous merchant but now a pitiful derelict whose wealth has been entirely eaten up by the social ambitions of his daughters. Rastignac has before his very eyes, at the Pension Vanquer, an exemplar of the moral tragedies to which consuming social ambitions can lead; and the book's center of interest is not located in the monotonously inevitable decline of Goriot but in the oscillations of Rastignac's conscience.

The irony of the encounter between Rastignac and Goriot is completely understood by only one person—the arch-criminal Vautrin, Balzac's fallen Angel, whose melodramatic origins are undeniable but who is no less fascinating for having sprung from the folk-psyche. "Paris, you see,"— he tells Rastignac, and the speech reminds us that Balzac was an avid reader of Fenimore Cooper—"is like a forest of the New World where a score of savage tribes, the Illinois, the Hurons, struggle for existence; each different social class lives on what it can get by hunting. You are a hunter of millions; to capture them you employ snares, limed twigs, decoys. There are many ways of hunting. Some hunt heiresses, others catch their prey by shady financial transactions; some fish for souls, others sell their clients bound hand and foot. The man who comes back with his game-bag well-lined is welcomed, feted, received into good society. . .If the proud aristocracies of all the capitals of Europe refuse to give a blackguard millionaire admittance to their ranks, Paris holds out her arms to him, runs to his parties, eats his dinners and clinks glasses with his infamy."

This is the Parisian society of Balzac's imagination—and who will deny that it had, and still has, its share of poetic truth, perhaps more now than ever? And it is to this society that Rastignac finally succumbs in the famous last scene of the novel. After attending Goriot's meagre funeral, to which his daughters send only their empty carriages, Rastignac gestures defiance to the lights of Paris glimmering in the distance—and then goes off to dine with his mistress, Mme. de Nucingen, née Goriot. Rastignac has learned his lesson; devotion and self-sacrifice, as in the case of Old Goriot, lead only to a pauper's grave; it is war to the death in the Parisian wilderness, and Rastignac is now fully armed.

Balzac's true greatness, then, cannot be denigrated by comparing him unfavorably with the subtle graces of the *roman intime;* one might as well criticize Adolphe for lacking any graphic portrayal of the social environment in which its drama of the heart is enacted. It must be freely admitted that Balzac, as Henry James once wrote, "has against him that he lacks that slight but needful thing—charm." And this lack will no doubt continue to be re-discovered, as it has recently by Martin Turnell, as long as critics continue to write on Balzac's work. But James, who certainly did not lack charm himself, had enough catholicity of taste to add immediately: "our last word about him [Balzac] is that he had incomparable power"; and this is likely to remain, not only James's last word, but *the* last word.

The translation runs quite well and has been done with great care to make the text read as an English book; whether the translator should

llow himself (or herself, as in this case) unlimited freedom with the
yntax of the original is a debatable point. In comparing the Penguin
ranslation with the older one in the Everyman edition, I found that the
arlier version made greater efforts to preserve the word order and
hrasing of the original wherever this could be done without awkwardness.
3oth translations, however, are marked by an occasional tendency to
owdlerize. The sign on the Pension Vauquer, for example, reads: "Pen-
ion bourgeoise des deux sexes et autres," which is translated as "Lodgings
or Ladies and Gentlemen, etc." The "etc." hardly gets the joke, which
3alzac no doubt intended as a reference to Vautrins proclivity for young
nen. And in the description of the Pension Vauquer garden, which
ontains a statue of Love, Balzac writes: "A voir le vernis écaillé qui la
ouvre, les amateurs de symboles y découvriraient peut-être un mythe de
'amour parisien qu'on guérit à quelques pas de là." This is prudishly
endered: "A statue representing the God of Love is placed in this imitation
hrine and its chipped scaling surface makes it look like a patient for one
f the nearby hospitals and provides an allegory for those who are fond of
ymbols." The French contains a far more unmistakable reference to the
ohysical hazards of Parisian love.

JOSEPH FRANK

Chicago, Illinois

VII

Flaubert's *Madame Bovary* is too good a book to be read in an indif-
ferent translation. The version of Eleanor Marx-Aveling dates from the
closing years of the Victorian era. For its time and place, I have no
doubt that it was a creditable piece of work. Karl Marx's daughter was an
educated woman; she knew French well and for the most part her
translation is accurate enough. But that is no reason why American
publishers, particularly those addressing themselves to college students,
should go on reprinting it year after year, even with slight modifications.
New translations have long been in order and it is good to see that in
recent months three new versions of *Madame Bovary* have appeared here
or abroad; all are available for distribution in this country.

These new translations, by Gerard Hopkins (World's Classics Galaxy
Edition, Oxford University Press, 1949, $2.40), Alan Russell (Penguin
Classics, 1950, $.75), and by Joan Charles (John C. Winston Co., 1949,
$3.50), all testify to an open dissatisfaction with the sentence structure
and diction of translators of the last century. Each in its own way is
intended for the contemporary reader, and this should be enough to
command our interest and attention.

It is too bad, however, that the only version prepared by an American
should be an abridgement. Miss Charles' translation was under the
general editorship of Mr. W. Somerset Maugham, whose convictions find
all too apparent expression in the text. Mr. Maugham, his publishers tell
us, "firmly believes the greatest novels of the world would be more widely
read if they were not too long or too slow in tempo." As a result, perhaps

four-fifths of Flaubert's novel is here; but that is not enough. To be sure, the editor has not removed any whole sections; rather, he has reduced mainly descriptive passages within most of the chapters. This is unfortunate, not only because some of Flaubert's best writing is descriptive, especially in Part Two, but also because relatively little additional space or effort would have given us the complete text. Miss Charles' translation is not great art, but it is uniformly close to the French and has the added advantage, for our readers, of present-day American idiom. I should add at once, however, that the price at $3.50 makes the volume all the more difficult to consider for use as a college text.

One cannot so readily dismiss the translations of Mr. Hopkins or Mr. Russell, nor is it easy to choose between them. Mr. Hopkins is by far the more professional worker. He does not hesitate to modify Flaubert's paragraphing, sentence structure or diction in his evident attempt to communicate the spirit of the novel as well as the lexical meaning. Mr. Russell is less daring and more modest. The risks he takes are few; the rewards correspondingly slender. Yet in attempting to do less, at times he achieves a good deal more. Perhaps a comparison of passages will serve to bring out the principal differences.

Flaubert's memorable description of Dr. Larivière concludes as follows:

> Son regard, plus tranchant que ses bistouris, vous descendait droit dans l'âme et désarticulait tout mensonge à travers les allégations et les pudeurs. Et il allait ainsi, plein de cette majesté débonnaire que donnent la conscience d'un grand talent, de la fortune, et quarante ans d'une existence laborieuse et irréprochable.

Mr. Hopkins translates: :

> His glance, sharper than his scalpel, drove straight to the soul, cutting through every excuse, every defence of modesty, and showing no mercy to lies. He lived among his fellows forever radiating that quiet majesty which comes of the consciousness of great talents, of the security bred of great wealth, and was the result of forty years marked by hard work and an irreproachable private life.

Here is Mr. Russell's version:

> Sharper than a lancet, his eyes looked straight into your soul, piercing through all pretence and reticence to dissect the lie beneath. So he went his way, in all the easy majesty that comes of the consciousness of great talent, wealth and forty years of hard work and irreproachable living.

Now it will be observed at once that Mr. Hopkins' passage is the longer of the two: he employs 67 words to Russell's 50. His ampler version is more colorful and his balanced parallel constructions read more smoothly. Mr. Russell's language is simpler and more direct but it is also closer to Flaubert. Consider Mr. Hopkins' elaboration of "la fortune" in the final sentence, surely a most questionable speculation.

This is not always the case, however, and particularly in rendering Flaubert's expansive panoramas of the country-side, Mr. Hopkins' loose style is more appropriate than Mr. Russell's severely literal manner. The florid speeches at the *Comices* provide a similar illustration. All the same,

Mr. Hopkins is much too uneven, and at times he falsifies the meaning altogether.

Perhaps the most disquieting feature of Mr. Hopkins' version is his abundant use of British idiom. Thus he writes of "pot-houses" and 'town-bred chits," of "plenty of cheek" or "an overplus of feeling." We are told that Charles "had been put in charge of a wholesale ironmonger"; we would say that Charles had been confined to his care. Similar examples may be found on almost every page. Less excusable is Mr. Hopkins' use of Cockney or rustic dialects for "low" characters. Thus Flaubert makes poor Hippolyte exclaim: "Quand est-ce que je serai guéri? . . Ah! sauvez-moi! Que je suis malheureux! que je suis malheureux!" Hopkins renders the passage: "When be Oi going to get well? . . Oh save Oi, zur. . . Oi be terrible low. . ." Russell poses no difficulty here: "When am I going to get better?" he sobbed. "Make me well! It's awful! It's awful!" This feature alone, the persistent use of local idiom and dialect in Mr. Hopkins' text, renders it unsuitable for the American student. Perhaps this weakness could be surmounted in a new edition; at present, the diction creates altogether too many special difficulties.

Mr. Russell too employs British idioms now and then, but so seldom in comparison with Mr. Hopkins that one would almost think that a deliberate effort was made to make the text readable for Americans. Mr. Russell's translation is not an exciting one; it is much too safe and at times seems almost impoverished in its bareness of phrase. An even graver weakness is his badly organized introduction, in which *Les Liaisons dangereuses* (1782) is pushed back to the 17th century and the Romantic Movement made to decline in favor of Realism "by the 1820's and 1830's." All the same, Mr. Russell's translation is in language close to our own and it should find wide acceptance. At present the Penguin Classics edition seems to me clearly the best translation now available of Flaubert's first novel. Let us hope that new versions of his other works will follow soon.

HASKELL M. BLOCK
University of Wisconsin

VIII

Anthologies may well be subjected to periodic re-examination and revision, especially those covering the past century and a half. For even though the literary merit of the selections will not change, our perspective will to a certain extent and with it our concept of what constitutes a truly representative and most effective picture. Nor are, if the anthology is one of foreign literature, the prospects for improvement limited to the matter of substance. They quite naturally extend into the matter of demonstrated skill in the respective translations. — On both of these counts appreciable gains are manifest in the revised edition of *Great German Short Novels and Stories* (Modern Library, 1952, $1.25), thanks to the capable editorship of Victor Lange. And of equal importance, the new version is enriched by a valuable fifteen-page introduction that should delight the more than casually inquisitive reader. Presented in Lange's characteristically vigorous style, this sketch of the history, the nature, and the significance of the short story (*Novelle*) in German literature, and, following it, the incisive characterizations of the individual features as well as the common theme of the selections, make profitable reading. Though the literary selections have to speak for themselves, an informative and enlightening frame of orientation will immeasurably enhance the grasp of the reader who has but a limited knowledge of German literature. Lange's perceptive eye, appreciated particularly in his discerning use of the elusive term "realistic," seems to have been dimmed somewhat only once, namely when he evaluates the German *Novelle's* role in relation to the German novel. This "exceptionally popular and effective form" (the short story), he states, "retarded, certainly, the devolopment of a truly significant and cosmopolitan kind of German novel." This pronouncement smacks suspiciously of passing positive judgment on the old and doubtful question of what came first, the chicken or the egg.

In contrast to the old edition, which in its own way served its purpose satisfactorily for twenty years, the new one is designed to bring into sharper focus the fact that "from the end of the eighteenth century to our own day the intellectual and physical resources of the human being have become vastly extended, and with the larger perspectives and increasing awareness of the potentialities of man, there has emerged an ever sharper perception of the elements of risk and ambiguity that provide the challenging climate of our life." And it provides, in its richer substance, a solid and uniform basis for the editor's final introductory statement, namely that "the balance between thought and action, good and evil, hope and despair is now perhaps more precariously suspended than ever before, and it is this disturbing but revealing modern sensibility that characterizes the stories offered in this volume by an impressive company of German writers."

Whatever the individual reactions to some of the replacements in this anthology may be (Hoffmann's *The Cremona Violin* for *The History of Krakatuk*, Schnitzler's *A Farewell* for his *The Fate of the Baron;* Rilke's *How Old Timofei Died Singing*, Wedekind's *The Burning of Egliswyl*, H. Mann's *Three Minute Novel* and Kafka's *A Country Doctor* for Wassermann's *Lukardis*, St. Zweig's *Amok*, and A. Zweig's *The Parcel*), there should be full agreement on the gain resulting from the inclusion of Kleist's *The Earthquake in Chile*, Brentano's *The Story of the Just Casper and Fair Annie*, Droste-Hülshoff's *The Jew's Beech Tree*, and Meyer's *Plautus in the Convent* at the expense of *Hansel and Gretel, Cinderella*, and Sudermann's *The New Year's Eve Confession*. Nor could one feel anything but warm approval for the substitution of the former rendition of *Werther* by that of William Rose. The latter is more readable and palatable. As against the predecessor's tendency to be a little flowery, it tends to be matter-of-fact without sacrificing, I feel, the flavor of the original. And at the same time, it shows generally greater accuracy and precision.

A similarly commendable degree of competence is observed in most selections, old and new (the unnamed old ones are: Schiller's *The Sport of Destiny*, Heine's *Gods in Exile*, Storm's *Immensee*, Keller's *The Naughty Saint Vitalis*, Hauptmann's *Flagman Thiel*, and Th. Mann's *Death in Venice*), including, to be sure, the editor's own translations of Kleist and Kafka, presented for the first time in a popular edition. In the rendition of Schnitzler's *A Farewell* some of the subtleties of meaning got lost in the process of translation and, by the same token, awkward touches appear occasionally. But these weaknesses are minor compared to the arbitrary omissions and gross inaccuracies encountered in Wedekind's *The Burning of Egliswyl*. Inasmuch as there is no indication that this is not meant to be a true translation, its inclusion in an otherwise praiseworthy array of renditions is somewhat baffling.

JOHN R. FREY

University of Illinois

IX

The recent publication of five of Pirandello's plays edited by Eric Bentley (*Naked Masks*, Everyman's Library, 1952, $1.45) is truly a happy event for those who are interested in dramatic art in general and in Pirandello's drama in particular.

In this book, the best of Pirandello's works are made available to the average reader in England and America, while the introduction and three appendices, with their carefully checked biographical and bibliographical data, are of particular interest to scholars. The first appendix contains an accurate and lucid translation by Eric Bentley of Pirandello's preface to *Six Characters in Search of an Author*, which is a major declaration of the dramatic principles that apply to Pirandello's late plays, just as *Umorismo*, written in 1908, casts a revealing light on the earlier works that show the author's contact with, and departure from, the Naturalism of Verga and Capuana.

There are two statements in Appendix II (p. 379) that are open to question. One refers to the *New Colony*, a play that, according to Mr. Bentley, shows a "definite fascist mentality," just as *Lazarus* is "miracle mongering." Since both Fascism and Christianity are positive and dogmatic systems, they could not be accepted by Pirandello who believed that the essence of Life is unfettered and fluid, and, therefore, every "form" that encloses it gives to it a fixity that dooms it to disintegration and death. This is the basic and unchanging principle of Pirandello's system of ideas. Accordingly, he presents in the *New Colony* the thesis of the impossibility of realizing a perfect government and society on this earth. Likewise, in *Lazarus*, since all religions are "constructions" of the universal concept of God, Pirandello rejected the Christian belief in the personal survival of the soul. For Pirandello, the soul longs to re-enter cosmic Life, whence a strange God detached it to make it live on the bleak desert of this life. Personal form is for him the chief factor in the tragedy of being human.

The second statement of Mr. Bentley to which I take exception refers to Pirandello's *grande passion* for Marta Abba. My exception is based on

Pirandello's own words when he expressed to me, in 1935, during an interview with him in New York, his great resentment against the misconception of his relationship with Marta Abba. I had mentioned to him that the ex-ambassador to Italy, Washburn Child, had cynically referred to that relationship. Whereupon, Pirandello exclaimed, "She is younger than my own children. She has always been like a daughter to me."

The major contribution of Mr. Bentley in this book is his translation of *Liolà*. It is an entirely new translation and it has been beautifully and accurately done by one who knows both Italian and English perfectly. Moreover, Mr. Bentley has a truly lyrical temperament, and he is in love with Sicily. Only a poet can describe the Sicilian landscape as beautifully as this: "Sicily is like that: the African sun shines, the hard rock takes on the soft color of honey, the trees are laden with almonds and oranges, and vagabonds sing." (ix). However, again, I must be allowed to courteously disagree with Mr. Bentley as to the central interpretation of this play. He states that *Liolà* is "Pirandello on holiday. . . . . a truancy on Pirandello's part, an exception to the rules of the maestro's art" (ix-x). To us, *Liolà* presents the positive aspect of Pirandello's central intuition of life. Liolà, the main character, is primitive, spontaneous, fluid, and, is close to primeval life, and capable of living with joy. He is not so tortuous and "cerebral" as many, although not all, of Pirandello's characters. According to Pirandello, by applying the "infernal machine of logic," man forsakes sentiment and offends life in its very essence. Thinking is not a "gift" for man. Since it implies objectivity and consciousness, it leads to our "constructing ourselves," and, hence, is a negative force. Pirandello, while of necessity indulging himself in thought, punishes his characters by showing their tortuous thinking through which they "immobilize the continuous flux of life through concepts" (*Umorismo*, p. 214). By denying to his characters the gift of logical thinking, Pirandello reaches the absolute in his system of tragedy, the essence of which lies in incomprehension of others as well as of ourselves. In his plays, it is primarily the incomprehension of the characters of the plight in which they find themselves that creates tragedy.

In *Liolà*, the main character is the opposite of being "constructed." The characters that are "constructed," although they are too elementary to be aware of it, are Zia Croce and Zio Simone. Zia Croce conceives the scheme of attributing to Zio Simone, her wealthy cousin, the fatherhood of the baby that her unwed daughter Tuzza is going to have by Liolà. She not only wants to save appearances but also hopes to get her cousin's money. The latter, since he has not been able to have a son from his young wife Mita, agrees to the base pact in order to save his masculine pride. Liolà realizing that this offends and ruins Mita, a former sweetheart of his, intervenes and spoils the scheme. Unsuspectingly, Zia Croce and Zio Simone have thrown Liolà and Mita into each other's arms. Mita, too, is soon expecting a baby by Liolà. Zio Simone will now appear to be the father of two children who are in reality of Liolà. The only person who is left defenseless and exposed is Tuzza who in the very end tries to stab Liolà, but in vain. All this is very far from being an idyll, "the last

Sicilian pastoral" (x). Indeed, *Liolà* bears a marked resemblance to the traditional Italian comedy and particularly to Machiavelli's *Mandragola*. In both works, the plot is basically the same and the two dishonest husbands, Ser Nicia and Zio Simone, are punished through the triumph of the romantic lovers Callimaco and Liolà.

An objective and critical reading of the text makes it questionable whether this play can be included among those that deal with the contrast of truth and appearance. It is difficult to agree with Mr. Bentley that in *Liolà* Pirandello wanted to prove that "reality is not more real than appearance" (xii), (Tuzza would not grant this) and that Zio Simone "only appears to appear to be the father" (xii). Basically, Zio Simone wants to appear to be a father, but Pirandello unmasks him and holds him up to ridicule. This is all. More simply, *Liolà* belongs to that section of Pirandello's drama that is closely related to his early contacts with Naturalism. Even in technique, like many plays of this group, *Liolà* has been given a solid background, and its characters possess traits quite different from those so effectively described in the above-mentioned preface to *Six Characters*. The theoretical roots of *Liolà* are in *Umorismo*, just as those of the later play are in the preface of *Six Characters*.

In discussing *It Is So (If You Think So)*, the term "reality" is rather misleading. In Pirandello, what exists in the observable and tangible world is an *actuality* that the artist uses in order to transform it, first into a psychological, and then into an artistic reality. The epilogues of many of Pirandello's plays contain in a very living and human manner the result of this transformation. The playwright is not at all interested in the actuality of the situation presented. It does not matter to him whether Ponza's wife is Lina or another person. Indeed, if this be ascertained, the play would lose its *raison d'être*. What counts is the nobility of the veiled wife who proclaims that she is, to Ponza and to Signora Frola, what each wants her to be, and she is nobody to herself. With infinite compassion she has obliterated her own identity and consciously has lent herself to be whatever the two want her to be. This is a new type of "construction" in Pirandello. It possesses positive connotations and it is distinguishable from that of the comedies conceived under the guidance of the artistic principles contained in *Umorismo*. Tragedy shuns laughter and this is the ancient principle that Pirandello followed only in the later period of his artistic career. In this context, the statement that *It Is So (If You Think So)* is "outside the boundary of realism" (xviii) clashes with the deep significance of the play. Pirandello's system of ideas, far from being abstract, is full of human understanding. Life being what it is, only simplicity, humility, kindness, and, especially, illusion, help us to bear its burden.

One of the merits of Mr. Bentley is to have championed the reality of Pirandello's ideas. This is precisely what Adriano Tilgher had failed to do in his essays written in the twenties. Pirandello was fully aware of this when he came to the United States in 1935, at which time he, in accepting my own analysis of his dramaturgy, repudiated Tilgher's theory to which he had previously given official sanction.

The greatest praise that can be rightly and gladly given to both Mr. Bentley and Everyman's Library rests on the fact that this new volume serves the average man as well as the scholar. This combination is befitting democratic society that constantly aims at raising the intellectual level of its citizens.

DOMENICO VITTORINI

University of Pennsylvania

PART FIVE

BIBLIOGRAPHY OF COMPARATIVE LITERATURE

PREFACE

This second annual supplement to the Baldensperger-Friederich *Bibliography of Comparative Literature* (Chapel Hill, N. C. 1950) can happily point to two great corrections and to one very promising innovation.

Professor P. M. Mitchell of the University of Kansas has kindly agreed to rewrite the entire Scandinavian chapter (pp. 682-88 in the BFB), eliminating erroneous items, correcting occasional mistakes, and supplementing individual data, so that his chapter henceforth should be used in lieu of the one in BFB.

Professors Gleb Struve of the University of California at Berkeley and Thomas G. Winner of Duke University undertook the important task of filling the exceedingly many gaps with regard to Slavic scholarship. In their division of labor Professor Struve supplied the vast majority of cards dealing with the Slavs as receivers or intermediaries, while Professor Winner is almost solely responsible for the last chapter of this Supplement dealing with the Slavs as emitters. My debt of gratitude to these three scholars is great and lasting, and I sincerely do hope that this Bibliography may enjoy the benefit of their collaboration also in future years. I am further indebted to Professor Winner for having consented to supervise the proof-reading of the galleys containing Slavic entries.

The decision of Professor H. Blair Rouse of Emory University and of his fellow-bibliographers in the annual Prose-Bibliography compiled by the Comparative Literature Group I of the MLA to incorporate their findings in the present Bibliography opens up the promising possibility that also other Comparative Literature Groups in the MLA may see fit to join forces with us. To include their items in the framework of the BFB, to be sure, means that these must have a distinctly comparative value and that their titles and comments, instead of being presented in compact form, will be scattered according to the pattern originally worked out by Professor Baldensperger; on the other hand, however, the advantages of uniting all comparative titles in one all-encompassing annual supplement may seem big enough for these gentlemen to wish to continue this arrangement and may also induce others (e.g. those in the Anglo-German or Franco-American field) to join us. At least I hope so and I do not mind the somewhat mixed aspect of the present bibliography (comments to some titles, no comments to most of them) if by this gradual transition we can attract other groups of bibliographers to support a thoroughly worthwhile annual bibliography which in its world-embracing scope is altogether too big for one single man anyhow. The scholars to whom I am deeply indebted for their contributions to prose literature are the following:

American literature: H. B. Rouse, Emory University (and Chairman and Editor).

English literature: R. C. Boys, University of Michigan.
　　　　　　　　　　R. M. Kain, University of Louisville, Ky.
　　　　　　　　　　J. P. Kirby, Randolph-Macon Woman's College.
French literature: I. Putter, University of California at Berkeley.
German literature: L. Bergel, Queens College, N. Y.
Hungarian literature: J. Remenyi, Western Reserve University.
Italian literature: D. Vittorini, University of Pennsylvania.
Polish literature: M. Kridl, Columbia University.
Russian literature: G. Struve, University of California at Berkeley.
South-American literature: J. E. Englekirk, Tulane University.
Spanish literature: J. López-Morillas, Brown University.

The choice of chapters presented in this supplement differs from that contained in last year's listings, and in the *Yarbook* 1954 other chapters will be brought in or deleted, as the necessity of restricting ourselves to less than 3000 items per year will require. The many reviewers of the BFB—all of them generous, encouraging and helpful (with the sole exception of the disappointing attitude displayed by S. Skard in JEGP, 1953)— have urged various improvements in the big Bibliography which I shall be glad to make in these successive supplements, though I still do not have the courage to tackle the depressing problem of an Index.

The following pages are doubly numbered, with the larger number (761 ff) continuing where the BFB and *Yearbook* No. 1 had left off. Many new cross-references endeavor to facilitate the search for certain items, with pages 1-701 referring to the BFB and 702-60 to the first, and 761-822 to this second supplement. Items marked with an asterisk indicate that they were faulty, incomplete or wrongly classified in the BFB and that they are now corrected. For abbreviations of journals inadvertently omitted from the following list, please consult the listings in the BFB.

To Mrs. Kenneth M. McIntyre in the Reference Department of our University Library I am warmly indebted for her constant and gracious helpfulness in tracing incomplete or ambiguous bibliographical items.

W.P.F.

List of Abbreviations

A	Apollon. St. Petersburg.
AB	Bulletin of the American Association of Teachers of Slavic and East European Languages. Philadelphia.
AC	L'Antiquité classique. Wetteren.
ACUM	Annales du centre universitaire méditerranéen de Nice.
AFR	Anglo-French Review. London & Paris.
AGR	American-German Review. Philadelphia.
AHR	American Historical Review. New York.
AJPh	American Journal of Philology. Baltimore.
AL	American Literature. Durham, North Carolina.
AM	Atlantic Monthly. Boston.
AQ	American Quarterly. Philadelphia.
A & R	Atene e Roma. Bullettino della Società italiana per la diffusione degli studi classici. Firenze.
Archiv	Archiv für das Studium der neueren Sprachen & Litteraturen. Braunschweig.
ASEER	American Slavonic and East European Review. New York.
ASR	American-Scandinavian Review. New York.
AUA	Annals of the Ukrainian Academy of Arts and Sciences in the United States, New York.
B	Brazda, Sarajevo.
BA	Books Abroad. Norman, Oklahoma.
BAGB	Bulletin de l'Association Guillaume Budé. Paris.
BDB	Börsenblatt für den deutschen Buchhandel. Leipzig.
BH	Bulletin Hispanique. Bordeaux.
BHR	Bibliothèque d'Humanisme et Renaissance. Paris.
Bí	Bulletin Italien. Bordeaux.
BNYPL	Bulletin of the New York Public Library. New York.
BRL	Bulletin of the John Rylands Library. Manchester.
BSS (or BHS)	Bulletin of Spanish (or: Hispanic) Studies. Liverpool.
BSSL	Bulletin de la Societé des sciences et des lettres de Łodz.
C	Critique. Paris.
CB	Classical Bulletin. Chicago.
CE	College English. Chicago.
CJ	Classical Journal. Chicago.
CL	Comparative Literature. Eugene, Oregon.
C & M	Classica et Medievalia. København.
CMF	Časopis pro moderni filologii. Praha.
Conv.	Convivium, Rivista di lettere, filosofia e storia, Università Catt. del Sacro Cuore. Milano-Torino.
CP	Classical Philology. Chicago.
CQ	Classical Quarterly. London.
CS	Cahiers du Sud. Marseilles.
CW	Classical Weekly. Lancaster, Pennsylvania.
DAN	Doklady Akademii Nauk SSSR. Moscow.
DJ	Dźiś i Jutro. Warsaw.
DN	Družba Narodov. Moscow.
DVLG	Deutsche Vierteljahrsschrift für Literaturwissenschaft und Geistesgeschichte. Halle.
EC	Etudes Classiques. Namur.
EG	Etudes Germaniques. Paris.
EL	Ezik i literatura. Sofia.
ELH	English Literary History. Baltimore.

E & S	Essays & Studies by Members of the English Association. Oxford.
ESn	Englische Studien. Leipzig.
ESs	English Studies. Groningen.
FAR	French-American Review. Washington.
FM	Filosofska Mis'l. Sofia.
FR	French Review. New York.
FS	French Studies. New Haven, Connecticut.
Gxvi	God šestnadcatyj. Almanach. Moscow.
GD	Giornale dantesco. Firenze.
GLAIU	Gledališki list Akademije za igralsko umetnost. Ljublana.
GLL	German Life and Letters. Oxford.
GLSNG-L	Gledališki list Slovenskega narodnega gledališča v Ljubljane. Ljubljana.
GLSNG-M	Gledališki list Slovenskega narodnega gledališča v Mariboru. Maribor.
GQ	German Quarterly. Lancaster, Pennsylvania.
G & R	Greece and Rome. Oxford.
GR	Germanic Review. New York.
GRM	Germanisch-romanische Monatsschrift. Heidelberg.
GSLI	Giornale Storico della letteratura italiana. Torino.
Hi	Hid. Novi Sad
Hisp.	Hispania. Stanford (1918 ff.); also Paris, 1918-22.
HK	Hrvatsko Kolo. Zagreb.
HLQ	Huntington Library Quarterly. San Marino, California.
Ho	Hochland. Monatsschrift für alle Gebiete des Wissens. München.
H & R	Humanisme et Renaissance. Paris.
HR	Hispanic Review. Philadelphia.
HSPhL	Harvard Studies and Notes in Philology and Literature. Cambridge, Mass.
IAN	Izvestija Akademii Nauk. Moscow.
IAN, OLJA	Izvestija Akademii Nauk SSSR, Otdelenie literury i jazyka. Moscow.
IAN, OON	Izvestija Akademii Nauk SSSR, Ordelenie obščestvennyx nauk. Moscow.
IAN, ORJaSL	Izvestija Otdelenija russkogo jazyka i slovesnosti Akademii Nauk. Moscow.
IANUz	Izvestija Akademii Nauk Uzbekistanskoj SSR. Taškent.
ICS	L'Italia che scrive. Roma.
ILGU	Izvestija Leningradskogo Gosudarstvennogo Universiteta. Leningrad.
IRJaSl	Institut Russkogo Jazyka i Slovesnosti Pri Akademii Nauk SSSR.
IS	Italian Studies. London.
Ital.	Italica. Chicago.
IVGPI	Izvestija Voronežskogo gosudarstennogo pedagogičeskogo instituta. Voronež.
Iz	Izvor. Zagreb.
JAAC	Journal of Aesthetics and Art Criticism. Cleveland, Ohio.
JAF	Journal of American Folklore. Lancaster, Pennsylvania.
JaiL	Jazyk i Literatura. Leningrad.
JbDG	Jahrbuch der Dante Gesellschaft. Leipzig.
JbShG	Jahrbuch der Shakespeare Gesellschaft. Weimar.
JEGP	Journal of English and Germanic Philology. Urbana, Illinois.
JHI	Journal of the History of Ideas. New York.
JIFM	Journal of the International Folk Music Council. Cambridge, England.

JWI	Journal of the Warburg and Courtauld Institute. London.
K	Književnost. Belgrade.
KB	Komunist. Belgrade.
KiR	Kniga i Revoljucija. Leningrad.
KN	Krasnaja Nov'. Moscow.
KnN	Književne novine. Belgrade.
KP	Kulturní Politika. Prague.
KR	Kenyon Review. Gambier, Ohio
Kž	Kulturni Život. Belgrade.
LDL	Letopis Doma Literatorov. Petrograd.
LG	Literaturnaja Gazeta. Moscow.
LiM	Literatura i Marksizm. Moscow.
LitM	Literaturnaja Mysl. Petrograd.
LM	Les Langues Modernes. Paris.
LMS	Ljetopis matice srpske. Novi Sad.
LN	Literaturnoe Nasledstvo. Moscow.
LT	Levende Talen. Bruxelles.
LZ	Literaturnye Zapiski. St. Petersburg.
MA	Medium Aevum. Oxford.
MDU	Monatshefte für deutschen Unterricht. Madison, Wisconsin.
Me	Meander. Warsaw.
MF	Mercure de France. Paris.
MG	Molodaja Gvardija. Mosrow.
Ml	Mladost. Belgrade.
MlR	Mladinska Revija. Ljubljana.
MLF	Modern Language Forum. Los Angeles.
MLJ	Modern Language Journal. Menasha, Wisconsin.
MLN	Modern Language Notes. Baltimore.
MLQ	Modern Language Quarterly. Seattle.
MLR	Modern Language Review. London.
MP	Modern Philology. Chicago.
NAnt	Nuova Antologia di Scienze, Lettere ed Arti. Roma.
NaR	Naša Reč. Paris.
NBLU	Naučnyj Bjulleten' Leningradskogo Universiteta. Leningrad.
NCF	Nineteenth Century Fiction. Los Angeles.
NEQ	New England Quarterly. Baltimore.
NG	Neue Gesellschaft. Berlin.
NISGU	Naučnye Izvestija Smolenskogo Gosudarstvennogo Universiteta. Smolensk.
NJK	Nastava Jezika i Književnosti u srednoj školi. Belgrade.
NL	Nouvelles Littéraires. Paris.
NO	Nova Obzorja. Maribor.
NoM	Novyj Mir. Moscow.
Nož	Nový Život. Svaz čsl. spisovatelů. Praha.
NP	Neophilologus. Groningen.
N & Q	Notes and Queries. London.
NR	Neue Rundschau. Berlin.
NRF	Nouvelle Revue Française. Paris.
NRFH	Nueva Rivista de Filología Hispánica. México.
NS	Novi Svet. Ljubljana.
NSR	Neue Schweizer Rundschau. Zürich.
NTBB	Nordisk Tidskrift för Bok- och Biblioteksväsen. Stockholm.
NTIPI	Naučnye Trudy Industrial'no-Pedagogičeskogo Instituta. Moscow.
NW	Neue Welt. Berlin.
Nž	Naša žena. Ljubljana.
Nžu	Novyj Žurnal. New York.
O	Oktjabr'. Moscow.

Os	Osvit. Belgrade.
P	Polonystyka. Warsaw.
PAPS	Proceedings of the American Philosophical Society. Philadelphia.
PAU-AN	Polska Amademia Umiejętnosci. Archivum Neophilologicum. Warsaw.
PBA	Proceedings of the British Academy. London.
PBSA	Papers of the Bibliographical Society of America. New York.
PCA	Proceedings of the Classical Association. Cambridge, England.
PiR	Pečat' i Revoljucija. Moscow.
PiS	Puškin i ego sovremenniki. Leningrad.
PL	Poet Lore. Philadelphia.
PMLA	Publications of the Modern Language Association. New York.
Po	Polet. Belgrade.
PPL	Prace Polonysticzne. Lódz.
PPW	Prace Polonystyczne. Wrócław.
PQ	Philological Quarterly. Iowa.
PS	Pamiętnik Słowianski. Cracow.
PWTN-A	Prace Wrócławskiego towarzystwa naukowego. Seria A. Wrócław.
PZ	Przegląd Zachodni. Poznań.
PZM	Pod Znamenem Marksizma. Moscow.
QQ	Queen's Quarterly. Kingston, Ontario.
R	Republika. Zagreb.
RA	Revue Archéologique. Paris.
RBPh	Revue Belge de Philologie et d'Histoire. Bruxelles.
RCC	Revue des Cours et Conférences. Paris.
RCLI	Rassegna critica della letteratura italiana. Roma.
RDM	Revue des Deux Mondes. Paris.
REA	Revue des Etudes Anciennes. Paris.
REH	Revue des Etudes hongroises. Paris.
REL	Revue des Etudes Latines. Paris.
RES	Review of English Studies. London.
RF	Romanische Forschungen. Erlangen.
RFC	Rivista di Filologia Classica. Torino.
RFE	Revìsta de Filología Española. Madrid.
RFH	Revista de Filología Hispánica. Buenos Aires.
RH	Revue Hispanique. Paris.
RHLF	Revue d'Histoire littéraire de la France. Paris.
RI	Rivista d'Italia. Roma.
RIA	Revista Iberoamericana. México.
RIL	Rendiconti dell'Instituto lombardo. Milano.
RiSL	Rossija i Slavjanstvo. Paris.
RLC	Revue de Littérature comparée. Paris.
RLM	Rivista di Letterature moderne. Firenze.
RLV	Revue des Langues vivantes. Paris.
RM	Russkaja Mysl'. Before 1918: Moscow-Petrograd; after 1918: Sofia, Prague, Berlin, Paris.
RMM	Revue de Métaphysique et de Morale. Paris.
RP	Revue de Paris.
RPh	Romance Philology. Berkeley, California.
RR	Romanic Review. New York.
RS	Ricerche Slavistiche. Napoli.
RuB	Russkoe Bogatstvo. St. Petersburg.
RyF	Razon y Fe. Madrid.
SAB	Shakespeare Association Bulletin. New York.
SAQ	South Atlantic Quarterly. Durham, North Carolina.

SAU	Sprawodzania Akademii Umiejętnosci. Cracow.
SBAW	Sitzungsberichte der Bayrischen Akademie der Wissenschaften. München.
SEER	Slavonic and East European Review. London.
SF	Socialistički Front. Zagreb.
SIFC	Studi italiani di filologia classica. Firenze.
SL	Soviet Literature. Moscow.
Sla	Slavia. Praha.
SlP	Slovenski poročevalec. Ljubljana.
SloP	Slovanský přehled. Praha.
SlPo	Slovenské pohl'ady. Turčiansky Svätý Martin.
SlR	Slavistična Revija. Ljubljana.
SN	Sovetskaja Nauka. Moscow.
SoZ	Sovremennye Zapiski. Paris.
SP	Studies in Philology. Chapel Hill.
Spec	Speculum. Cambridge, Mass.
SQ	Shakespeare Quarterly. Washington.
SRL	Saturday Review of Literature. New York.
SS	Scandinavian Studies. Lawrence, Kansas.
SV	Slovesná Věda. Praha.
SZ47	Šekspirovskij Sbornik, 1947. Moscow.
T	Teatr. Moscow.
TB	Tvorba. Bratislava.
TBGU	Trudy Belorusskogo Gosudarstvennogo Universiteta. Minsk.
TLS	Times Literary Supplement. London.
TNT-FF	Towarzystwo Naukowe w Toruniu. Prace Wydziału Filologiczno-Filosoficznego. Toruń.
TODRL	Trudy Otdela drevnerusskoj literatury, Akademija Nauk SSSR. Moscow-Leningrad.
Tov	Tovariš. Ljubljana.
TTPI	Trudy Tbiliskogo Gosudarstvennogo Pedagogičeskogo Instituta im. Puškina. Tiflis.
TVIIJ	Trudy Voennogo Instituta Innostrannykh Jazykov. Leningrad.
Tw	Twórczość. Cracow.
UCPP	University of California Publications in Modern Philology. Los Angeles.
UKCR	University of Kansas City Review.
UQ	Ukrainian Quarterly. New York.
UTQ	University of Toronto Quarterly.
UZII	Učenye Zapiski Instituta Istorii. Moscow.
UZLU	Učenye Zapiski Leningradskogo Universiteta. Leningrad-Saratov.
UZLU-FN	Učenye Zapiski Leningradskogo Universiteta, Serija Filologičeskix Nauk. Leningrad-Saratov.
UZMPI	Učenye Zapiski Moskovskogo Gosudarstvennogo Pedagogičeskogo Institua im. Potemkina. Moscow.
UZSGU	Učenye Zapiski Saratovskogo Gosudarstvennogo Universiteta. Saratov.
UZTI	Učenye Zapiski Tixookeanskogo Instituta. Vladivostok.
UZUPI	Učenye Zapiski Ural'skogo Pedagogičeskogo i Učitel'skogo Instituta im. Puškina. Sverdlovsk.
VE	Vestnik Evropy. St. Petersburg.
Ver	Versty. Paris.
VJ	Voprosy Jazykoznanija. Moscow.
VLU	Vestnik Leningradskogo Universiteta. Leningrad.
VND	Vprašanja naših dni. Ljubljana.
VNFH	Vjesnik Narodnog Fronta Hrvatske. Zagreb.

Vozr	Vozroždenie. Paris (Before 1936, daily; 1936-40, weekly. Since 1948, bimonthly).
VPD	Vremennik Puškinskogo Doma. Moscow-Leningrad.
VR	Volja Rossii. Praha.
VZ	Vostočnye Zapiski. Moscow.
WSJ	Wiener Slavistisches Jahrbuch. Vienna.
XF	Xudožestvennyj Fol'klor. Moscow.
Yb	Yearbook of Comparative and General Literature. Chapel Hill.
Z	Zora. Sarajevo.
ZDMG	Zeitschrift der deutschen morgenländischen Gesellschaft. Leipzig.
ZDP	Zeitschrift für deutsche Philologie. Halle.
ŽMNP	Žurnal Ministerstva Narodnogo Prosveščenija. St. Petersburg.
ZRNI	Zapiski Russkogo Naučnogo Instituta. Belgrade.
ZSP	Zeitschrift für slavische Philologie. Leipzig.
Zv	Zvezda. Leningrad.
ZvV	Zvezda Vostoka. Taškent.

Other Abbreviations: C.R.: Compte rendu; Jb: Jahrbuch; n.d.: no date; Zs: Zeitschrift; Zt: Zeitung.

Bibliography

A. GENERALITIES, INTERMEDIARIES, THEMATOLOGY, LITERARY GENRES

I. COMPARATIVE LITERATURE, WORLD LITERATURE, EUROPEAN LITERATURE

Comparative Literature

Carré, J.-M. L'Institut de Littérature comparée de l'Université de Paris. Yb, 1, 1952.

Gillies, A. Some Thoughts on Comparative Literature. Ibid.

Laird, C. G. A Guide for Comparative Literature. Ibid.

Levin, H. The Department of Comparative Literature. Ibid.

Peyre, H. A Glance at Comparative Literature in America. Ibid.

Pypin, A. O sravnitel'no-istoričeskom izučenii russkoj literatury. VE, 10, 1875, 641-77.

Rosenberg, R. American Bibliographies Pertaining to Comparative Literature. CL, 2, 1950.

Teesing, H. P. Die Bedeutung der vergleichenden Literaturgeschichte für die literarhistorische Periodisierung. Forschungsprobleme der vergl. Lit. gesch. Tübingen, 1951.

Texte, J. L'histoire comparée des littératures. In: Etudes de littérature européenne. Paris, 1898.

Varia. Comparative Literature Departments in American Universities. Yb, 1, 1952.

Veselovsij, A. Istoričeskaja poétika. Ed. with Introduction by V. Žirmunskij. Leningrad, 1940. [Reprints of some of V.'s major studies in comparative literature, world literature, folklore.]

Wais, K. Vergleichende Literaturbetrachtung. In: Forschungsprobleme der Vergleichenden Literaturgeschichte. Tübingen, 1951.

Wilkinson, E. Neure Strömungen der angelsächsischen Aesthetic in ihrer Beziehung zur vergleichenden Literaturwissenschaft. Ibid.

Willoughby, L. A. Stand und Aufgaben der vergleichenden Literaturgeschichte in England. Ibid.

Wollman, F. Les comparatistes de Prague et leur école. SV, 1951.

World Literature, European Literature.

Auerbach, E. Philologie der Weltliteratur. Festschrift Strich. Bern, 1952.

Carlsson, Anni. Die Entfaltung der Weltliteratur als Prozess. Ibid.

Curtius, E. R. Kritische Essays zur europäischen Literatur. Bern, 1950.

Eppelsheimer, H. W. Weltliteratur. Ein Versuch. Imprimatur, 10 (Hamburg), 1951.

Fuchs, A. Grundriss der Geschichte des Schriftenthums der Griechen und Römer und der romanischen und germanischen Völker. Halle, 1846.

Haantjes, J. & Smit, W. A. P. Meesterwerken der literatuur. Inleidende beschouwingen over tien der voornaamste werken uit de wereldliteratuur. Amsterdam, 1948.

Korsch, V. (ed.). Všeobščaja istorija literatury. St. Petersburg, 1880.

Millett, F. B. Teaching the Humanities. Yb, 1, 1952.

Mitov, D. Istorija na zapadno-evropejskata literatura. 4 vols. Sofia, 1951-52.

Schneider, H. Weltliteratur und Nationalliteratur im Mittelalter. Euphorion, 45, 1950.

Strich, F. Weltliteratur und vergleichende Literaturgeschichte. In: Philosophie der Literaturwissenschaft. Berlin, 1930.

Varia. France and World Literature. FS, 6, 1950. Cf. CL, 4, 1952.

Weatherley, E. H. et al (eds.). The Heritage of European Literature. 2 vols. Boston, 1948-49.

Wells, H. W. World Literature Today. Yb, 1, 1952.

Žirmunskij, V. M. (ed.). Istorija zapadnoj literatury. Moscow, 1947.

Individual Authors and Scholars.

Orcibal, J. Le cosmopolitisme d'ANGELUS SILESIUS. RLC, 26, 1952.

Friederich, W. P. Fernand BALDENSPERGER. Yb, 1, 1952.

Ernst, F. Louis BETZ. Ibid.

Silvestri-Giorgì, A. Un geniale comparatista: W. P. FRIEDERICH. Idea, 22, VI, 1952.

Jaime, E. Stefan GEORGE und die Weltliteratur. Ulm, 1949.

Mann, K. André **GIDE**. Die Geschichte eines Europäers. Zürich, 1948.

Muret, W. **GOETHE** européen. RDM, Aug., 1949.

Strich, F. Gœthes europäische Sendung. Der kl. Bund (Bern), 21, VII, 1929.

―――― Goethe and World Literature. London, 1949.

Torre, G. de. Goethe y la literatura universal. Realidad, 6, 1949.

Bergstraesser, A. **HOFMANNSTHAL** und der europäische Gedanke. Universitätsreden. Kiel, 1951.

Zappa, F. **KÖSTLER** scrittore internazionale. Studium, 44, 1948.

Schalk, E. **MONTESQUIEU** und die europäischen Traditionen. In: Forschungsprobleme der vergleichenden Literaturgeschichte. Tübingen, 1951.

Anon. **PUSCHKIN** und die Weltliteratur. Roland von Berlin, 23, 1949.

Tomlinson, M. D. Albert **THIBAUDET**, European. MLQ, 12, 1951.

Macrì, O. Paul **VALÉRY**, uomo europeo. Rassegna d'Italia, 4, 1949.

Bray, R. Paul **VAN TIEGHEM**. Yb, 1, 1952.

Doyle, J. George E. **WOODBERRY**. Ibid.

II. LITERATURE AND POLITICS

Sociology, Bourgeoisie, Capitalism, Democracy, Marxism, Communism, Nationalism, Imperialism, Cosmopolitanism, Pacifism, Utopias.

Alonso, D. La injusticia social en la literatura española. In: Hora de España. Valencia, 1937.

Altheim, F. Literatur und Gesellschaft im ausgehenden Altertum. Halle, 1948-50.

Anisimov, I. et al. Krizis kapitalizma i sojusniki proletariata v literature Zapada. Moscow, 1933, 123 p.

Arsen'ev, K. Staryj vopros o tendencioznosti v iskusstve. VE, 1, 1889, 340-55.

Averbach, L. Klassovaja bor'ba v sovremennoj literature. Zv, 1, 1929, 139-59.

Balet, L. Die Verbürgerlichung der deutschen Kunst, Literatur und Musik im 18. Jahrhundert. Strassburg, 1936.

Bel'čikov, N. Narodničestvo v literature i kritike. Moscow, 1934.

Brinton, C. English Political Thought in the Nineteenth Century. Harvard U. P., 1950.

Canavan, P. J. A Study of English Drama as a Reflection of Stuart Politics from 1603 to 1660. U. of Southern Calif. Diss., 1950.

Diaz-Plaja, G. La literatura española como documento social. Revista Internacional de Sociologia, 4, 1944.

Doyle, P. A History of Political Thought. London, 1949.

Drenovec, B. Nekaj misli o vlogi marksistično-leninistične ideologije v literarnem ustvarjanju. MlR, 5, 1949-50.

Evnina, E. Literatura francuzskogo soprotivlenija, 1940-1944. Moscow, Akademija Nauk SSSR, 170 p., 1951. [A general survey of French Resistance literature written from the Communist standpoint.]

Fišman, O. Novejšaja kitajskaja literatura kak otraženie bor'by demokratičeskix i reakcionnyx sil (China). VLU, 8, 1948.

Frey, V. Die Stellung der attischen Tragödie und Komödie zur Demokratie. Diss., Zürich. Aarau, 1946.

Fritsche, V. Poezija imperializma i poezija demokratii. Moscow, 1918.

Gal'perina, E. Pervye šagi marksistskogo literaturovedenija vo Francii. LiM, 3, 1929, 177-82.

Golovin, K. Russkij roman i russkoe obščestvo. St. Petersburg, 1897.

Grinberg, I. K probleme socialističeskoj liriki. In: Bor'ba za stil'. Sbornik statej. Leningrad, 1934.

Juzovskij, J. Voprosy socialističeskoj dramaturgii. Moscow, 1934, 197 p.

Kamegulov, O. Ob osnovnyx voprosax marksistskogo literaturovedenija. Zv, 2, 1929, 183-200.

Kluckhohn, P. Dichterberuf und bürgerliche Existenz. Tübingen, 1949.

Leites, A. Literatura dvux mirov. Moscow, 1935, 182 p.

Lelevič, G. Principy marksistskoj kritiki. Zv, 2, 1925, 235-42.

―――― Marksistskoe literaturovedenie i biografija xudožnika. Zv, 3, 1926, 181-88.

Ležnev, A. Prolekul't i proletarskoe iskusstvo. KN, 2-3, 1924.

―――― Iz istorii marksistskoj kritiki. Voprosy o proletarskom iskusstve i kul'turnom nasledstve v germanskoj social-demokratii. Naši Dni, Moscow, 5, 1925, 315-50.

Lifšic, M. K voprosu o vzgljadax Marksa na iskusstvo. Moscow, 1933, 131 p.

Lixačev, D. Nekotorye voprosy klassovogo xaraktera russkoj literatury XI-XVII vekov. IAN,OLJA, 5, 1951, 461-73.

Lukács, G. Fortschritt und Reaktion in der deutschen Dichtung. Berlin, 1947.

L'vov-Rogačevskij, V. & Mandelštam, R. Raboče-krestjanskie pisateli. Bibliografičeskij ukazatel'. Moscow, 1926.

Maffre de Beaugé. Du sens international chez les provincialistes. Montpellier, 1896.

Mandel'štam, R. Xudožestvennaja literatura v ocenke russkoj marksistskoj kritiki. 4th ed. Moscow, 1928.

Manning, C. A. Socialistic Realism and the American Success Novel. SAQ, 1949.

Markiewicz, H. O marksistowskiej teorii literatury. Wrócław, 1952, 126 p.

Mead, R. G. Dictatorship and Literature in the Spanish World. BA, 25, 1951.

Noether, Emiliana. Seeds of Italian Nationalism, 1700-1815. Columbia U. P., 1951.

Novicov, M. La littérature de la République Populaire Roumaine sur la voie du réalisme socialiste. Revue Roumaine (Bucarest), 7, 1950.

Nusinov, I. Social'nyj zakaz. LiM, 2, 1928, 3-33.

Polet, A. Le communisme dans la pensée grecque. Le Caire, 1947.

Ratner, M. Problemy idealizma v russkoj literature. RuB, 8-10, 1903.

Sakulin, P. Russkaja literatura i socializm. Moscow, 1924.

Sapir, J. Frejdizm i marksizm. PZM, 11, 1926, 59-87.

Schenk von Stauffenberg, A. Dichtung und Staat in der antiken Welt. München, 1950.

Šiller, F. Marksizm, psixoanaliz i iskusstvo. Vestnik Kommunisticeskoj Akademii, Moscow, 18, 1926, 244-57.

———— Marksizm v nemeckom literaturovedenii. LiM, 2, 1928, 130-44.

Slonimskij, L. Gosudarstvennvj socializm v politike i literature. VE, 7, 1884, 287-315.

———— Učenie Marksa v žizni i literature. VE, 2, 1897, 768-90.

Spektorskij, E. Russkij anarxizm. RM, 1-2, 1922, 232-53.

Stepanov, N. Obraz bol'ševika v sovetskoj poezii. In: Grinberg, I. et al. Obraz bol'ševika. Leningrad, 1938, 94-176.

Strich, F. Der Dichter und der Staat. In: Dichtung und Zivilisation. München, 1928.

———— Der Dichter und die Zeit. Bern, 1947.

Trifonova, T. Obraz bol'ševika v detskoj literature. In: Grinberg, I. et al. Obraz bol'ševika. Leningrad, 1938, 213-45.

Verhaaren, T. E. The Idea of the State in the Creative Writings of German Romanticism. Diss., Stanford U., 1946.

Vinogradov, I. Voprosy marksistskoj poètiki. Leningrad, 1936, 428 p.

Waters, B. Politics and Literature. Prairie Schooner, 25, 1951.

Webster, T. B. L. Political Interpretations in Greek Literature. Manchester U. P., 1948.

Zalkind, A. Frejdizm i marksizm. KN, 4, 1924, 163-86.

Zlotorzycka, M. Les Polonais et la Commune de Paris. Wiedza i Życie, 3 (Warszawa), 1951. (In Polish.)

Individual Authors and Works.

Greenleaf, R. History, Marxism, and Henry **ADAMS**. Science & Society, 15, 1951.

Squitieri, G. Il preteso communismo di S. **AMBROGIO**. Sarno, 1946.

Paronzini, V. L'ideale politica d'**ARISTOFANE**. Dioniso, 1948.

Schwarz, F. Der beste Staat des **ARISTOTELES** und das politische Antlitz der Zeit. Diss., Wien, 1940.

Kohn, H. **ARNDT** and the Character of German Nationalism. AHR, 54, 1949.

Zwick, M. I. Berthold **AUERBACHS** sozialpolitischer und ethischer Liberalismus. Stuttgart, 1933.

Dupuy, A. **BALZAC** colonial. RHL, 50, 1950.

Duveau, G. Balzac et le prolétariat. Esprit, 18, 1949.

Ferran, A. **BAUDELAIRE** et la révolution de 1848. Ecrits de Paris, March, 1948.

Natoli, G. Baudelaire e il '48 in Francia. Rassegna d'Italia, 3, 1948.

Jampolskij, I. Valerij **BRJUSOV** i pervaja russkaja revoljucija. LN, 15, 1934, 201-20.

Dowden, W. S. The Consistency in **BYRON'S** Social Doctrine. Rice Institute Pamphlet, 37, 1950.

Hackelsberger, F. J. Die Staatslehre des Marcus Tullius **CICERO**. Diss., Köln, 1948.

Rudčenko, O. Benžamen Konstan i ego učenie o ličnyx pravax. (**CONSTANT**). RM, 12, 1905, 42-72.

Couton, G. **CORNEILLE** et la Fronde. Clermont-Ferrand, 1951.

Lesevič, V. Daniel Defo kak čelovek, pisatel' i obščestvennyj dejatel'. (**DEFOE**). RuB, 5-8, 1893.

Johnson, E. Bleak House: The Anatomy of Society. (**DICKENS**). NCF, 7, 1952, 73-89. [A revolutionary indictment of legal injustice and of the whole cor-

rupt structure of Victorian society.]
Kulišer, E. Dikkens kak kriminalist. RM,
5, 1912, 94-102.
Naumov, N. Čarlz Dikens i njegovo doba.
Po, 10-11, 1950.
Anon. Theodor **DREISER**—glasnik na-
predne miselnosti i borec proti im-
perializmu. NO, 3, 1950, 230-33.
Higgins, D. Pierre **DUPONT**, a Chanson-
nier of the 1848 Revolution. FS, 3,
1949.
Polet, A. Deux utopies hellénistiques. La
Panchaïe d'**EVHÉMÈRE** et la Cité du
Soleil de Jambule. Bull. of the Fac. of
Arts, Cairo, 1947.
Lukács, G. Gestalten und Probleme des
Bürgerkriegs. Aufbau, 7-8, 1951. [A
study of **FADEYEV'S** Civil War novel
(The Rout) from point of view of correspondence between form and ideological content.]
Gaffiot, M. Les théories d'Anatole
FRANCE sur l'organisation sociale de
son temps. Paris, 1928.
Mommsen, W. Die politischen Anschauungen **GOETHES**. Stuttgart, 1948.
Sauvage, P. P. L'économie et l'homme
dans les Années de Voyage de Wilhelm
Meister. EG, 7, 1952, 88-104. [Author
examines the degree of affiliation between Wilhelm Meister and the utopian novel. Instead of establishing an
ideal framework into which the individual has to fit himself, Goethe starts
from the existing economic and social
realities of his time and has man
change them.]
Klejnbort, L. Maksim **GOR'KIJ** i čitatel'
nizov. VE, 12, 1913, 171-93.
Prozhogin, V. Labor in Maxim **GORKY'S**
Works. Soviet Literature (Moscow),
June, 1950.
Lenz, H. Franz **GRILLPARZER'S** Po-
litical Ideas and Die Jüdin von Toledo.
New York, 1938.
Barnstorff, H. Die soziale, politische und
wirtschaftliche Zeitkritik im Werke
Gerhart **HAUPTMANNS**. Jena, 1938.
Dosenheimer, E. **HEBBELS** Auffassung
vom Staat und sein Trauerspiel Agnes
Bernauer. Leipzig, 1912.
Dresch, J. **HEINE** et la révolution de
1848. EG, 4, 1949.
Knipovič, E. Gejne kak političeskij lirik.
Moscow, 1932, 140 p.
Stern, I. Heinrich Heine: der Dichter der
Revolution. Berlin, 1948.
Barradas de Carvalho, J. As ideias politi-
cas e sociais de Alexandre **HERCU-
LANO**. Lisboa, 1949.

Schierenberg, R. Der politische **HERDER**.
Graz, 1932.
Stolte, H. **HÖLDERLIN** und die soziale
Welt. Gotha, 1949.
Salmon, E. T. The Political Views of
HORACE. Phoenix, 1-2, 1946.
Solari, A. Il tradizionalismo antiimperiale
de Orazio. Rendiconti dell'Accad. dei
Lincei, Roma, 8, 1950.
Ekstrom, W. F. The Equalitarian Prin-
ciple in the Fiction of W. D. **HOW-
ELLS**. AL, 24, 1952, 40-50. [The so-
cialistic ideas in his novels were not
the expression of wild-eyed Utopianism
but appeals to mankind to eliminate
rudeness, unkindness, and snobbish-
ness—all that sears in man's relation-
ship to man.]
Arsen'ev, K. Viktor Gjugo kak političeskij
dejatel'. (**HUGO**). VE, 4, 1876, 601-
47.
Kott, J. Wiktor Hugo—pisarz walczący.
Warsaw, 1952.
Messières, R. de. Victor Hugo et les Etats-
Unis d'Europe. FR, May, 1952.
Nekora, L. Social'nyj roman Viktora
Gjugo. Moscow, 1932, 481 p.
Roos, J. Victor Hugo und sein Gedanken
der vereinigten Staaten Europas. In:
Forschungsprobleme der vergleichen-
den Literaturgeschichte. Tübingen,
1951.
Vinogradov, A. Social'naja tematika
Otveržennyx V. Gjugo. NoM, 11, 1929,
206-21.
Zatloukal, A. Les problèmes sociaux dans
les romans de Victor Hugo. CMF, 1951.
(In Czech.)
Bagolini, L. Esperienza giuridica e poli-
tica nel pensiero di David **HUME**.
Siena, 1947.
Lana, I. L'utopia di **IPPODAMO** di Mileto.
Riv. di Filosofia, 40, 1949.
Klatt, F. **JEAN PAUL** als Verkünder von
Frieden und Freiheit. Hamburg, 1947.
Pogodin, M. Idei **KARAMZINA** kak pub-
licista. VE, 1866, 11-22.
Kriesi, M. Gottfried **KELLER** als Politi-
ker. Frauenfeld, 1918.
Iwanowa, G. Der nationale Gedanke bei
Heinrich von **KLEIST**. Sofia, 1942.
Reisner, M. **KORAN** i ego socialnaja
ideologija. KN, 8-9, 1926.
Montagne, R. H. de la. Histoire de la
démocratie chrétienne de **LAMEN-
NAIS** à Georges Bidault. Paris, 1949.
Rémond, R. Lamennais et la démocratie.
Paris, 1948.
Anon. Sinclair **LEWIS**—kritičar američke
srednje klase. R, 7, 1951.

Bixalji-Merin, O. **LOPE DE VEGA** i njegovo doba. Os, 1, 1951.

Alekseev, A. **MAKKIAVELLI** kak političeskij myslitel'. Moscow, 1880.

Gewirth, A. **MARSILIUS** of Padua, The Defender of Peace, I: Marsilius of Padua and Medieval Political Philosophy. New York, 1951.

Karl **MARX**: See also Marxism above.

Lukács, G. Karl Marks i Fr. T. Eiser. Ekscerpty Marksa iz "Estetiki" Fišera (Vischer). LN, 15, 1934, 1-56.

Slonimskij, L. Karl Marks v russkoj literature. VE, 8-10, 1897.

Struve, P. Marks o Gete. (Goethe). K xarakteristike dvux umov. In: Na raznye temy. St. Petersburg, 1902.

Wolfson, S. Marks i Lassal' v perepiske s Gejne. (Heine). TBGU, 2-3, 1922, 292-303.

Zaleski, Z. L. Adam **MICKIEWICZ** et le mouvement de 1848. Revue des travaux de l'Acad. des Sciences Morales et Politiques, 24, V, 1948.

Kovalevskij, M. **MIL'TON** kak pobornik narodnogo samoderžavija i avtonomii ličnosti. VE, 11-12, 1909.

Hexter, J. H. **MORE'S** Utopia: The Biography of an Idea. Princeton U. P., 1952.

Rooy, N. de. Utopia gewonnen en verloren. De tragedie van Thomas More en Erasmus. 's Gravenhage, 1950.

Tarle, E. Obščestvennye vozzrenija Tomasa Mora v svjazi s ekonomičeskim sostojaniem Anglii ego vremeni. St. Petersburg, 1901.

Bell, J. A Study of Arthur **MORRISON**. In: Essays and Studies. London, 1952. 76-89. [Evaluation of his short stories and novels about slum life in London as contributory to Realism in England.]

Rey, W. H. The Destiny of Man in the Modern Utopian Novel. (**ORWELL** and Jünger). Symposium, 6, 1952, 140-56.

Perpiñá, R. Los tres pensadores griegos sobre el fenómeno colonial. (**PINDAR**, Plato, Aristotle.) Helmantica, 1, 1950.

Koz'min, B. D. I. **PISAREV** i socializm: O vlijanii na Pisareva zapadnoevropejskogo socializma. LiM, 6, 1929, 27-59.

Croiset, M. La République de **PLATON**. Paris, 1946.

Field, G. C. Plato's Political Thought and its Value Today. Philosophy, 16, 1941.

Marcuse, L. Der Philosoph und der Diktator: Plato und Dionys. Berlin, 1950.

Percev, V. Social'no-političeskoe mirovozzrenie Platona. TBGU, 1-2, 1922.

Ziegler, L. Von Platons Staatsheit zum christlichen Staat. Olten, 1948.

Viereck, P. Pure Poetry, Impure Politics and Ezra **POUND**. Commentary, 12, 1951.

Budde, E. A. S. **PUSKIN** v bor'be za prava russkogo graždanina. RM, 10, 1900, 130-46.

Lednicki, W. Pushkin, Tyutchev, Mickiewicz and the Decembrists: Legend and Facts. SEER, 29, 1951.

Derathé, R. J. J. **ROUSSEAU** et la science politique de son temps. Paris, 1950.

Gurvic, G. Russo i deklaracija prav. Petrograd, 1918.

Hubert, R. Rousseau et l'Encyclopédie. Essai sur la formation des idées politiques de Rousseau (1742-56). Paris, n.d.

Rozanov, M. Z. Z. Russo i demokratičeskij ideal žizni. RuB, 10, 1912, 47-55.

Gilbert, F. Bernardo **RUCELLAI** and the Orti Oricellari; a Study on the Origins of Modern Political Thought. JWI, 12, 1949.

Butler, Eliza M. The **SAINT-SIMON**ian Religion in Germany; a Study of the Young German Movement. Cambridge U. P., 1926.

Ivanov, I. Sen-Simon i sen-simonizm. Moscow, 1901.

Rouget, Marie T. George **SAND** socialiste. Lyon, 1931.

Kogan, P. Političeskie idealy Šillera. (**SCHILLER**). RM, 6, 1905, 57-72.

Flaker, A. Taras **ŠEVČENKO**—borac i revolucionar. Iz, 3, 1950, 421-32.

Ehrmann, Ruth. George Bernard **SHAW** und der viktorianische Sozialismus. Antwerpen, 1937.

Fatur, B. Bernard Shaw—satirik kapitalistične civilizacije. VND, 31, XII, 1950.

Humo, Olga. Džordž Bernard Šo (Shaw). B, 11-12, 1950.

Cameron, K. N. The Young **SHELLEY**: Genesis of a Radical. New York, 1950.

Spasowicz, W. Vl. S. **SOLOV'EV** kak publicist. VE, 1, 1901, 211-38.

Mohl, Ruth. Studies in **SPENSER**, Milton, and the Theory of Monarchy. New York, 1949.

Dédéyan, C. **STENDHAL** et le Risorgimento dans La Chartreuse de Parme. RLC, 26, 1952.

Fechner, E. Recht und Politik in Adalbert **STIFTERS** Witiko. Tübingen, 1952, 87 p. Cf. Wort und Wahrheit, 7, 1952.

Collinson, R. I. R. S. **SURTEES**: Satirist and Sociologist. NCF, 1952, 202-07.

[A satirical commentator upon the early Victorian social scene.]

Rhodes, B. R. **SWIFT** and Mandeville as Critics of Society. Bull. of Vanderbilt U., 51, 1951.

Grene, D. Man in his Pride. A Study in the Political Philosophy of **THUCYDIDES** and Plato. Chicago U. P., 1950.

Méautis, G. Thucydide et l'impérialisme athénien. Neuchâtel, 1950.

Romilly, J. de. Thucydide et l'impérialisme athénien. Paris, 1947.

Maklakov, V. Lev **TOLSTOJ** kak obščestvennyj dejatel'. RM, 2, 1912, 54-82.

—— Tolstoj i sud. RM, 3, 1914, 35-72.

Schifman, A. Lev Tolstoj o kolnial'nom razboe. IAN,OLJa, 11, 1952, 509-26. [As a fighter against imperialism Tolstoy influenced Anatole France, Rolland, Shaw, and others.]

Struve, P. Tolstoj i social'naja revoljucija. RM, 1, 1911 and in: Patriotica. St. Petersburg, 1911.

Polonskij, L. Očerki anglijskogo obščestva v romanax A. **TROLLOP**a. VE, 8-10, 1870.

Annenkov, P. Russkaja sovremennaja istorija v romane I. S. **TURGENEV**a "Dym." VE, June, 1867, 100-20.

Veksler, I. I. S. Turgenev i političeskaja bor'ba šestidesjatyx godov. Leningrad, 1935, 96 p.

Flottes, P. La pensée politique et sociale d'Alfred de **VIGNY**. Paris, 1927.

Grace, W. J. Evelyn **WAUGH** as a Social Critic. Renascence, 1, 1949, 28-41.

Čukovskij, K. Uot Uitmen. Poezija grjaduščej demokratii. (**WHITMAN**). Petrograd, 1919.

Szewczyk, W. Fryderyk **WOLF** w pracy i walce. Wizerunek niemieckiego pisarza antyfaszystowskiego. Zeszyty Wrócławskie, 3-4, 1950.

Luccioni, J. Les idées politiques et sociales de **XÉNOPHON**, Paris, 1947.

V. COMPARISONS, SOURCES, IMITATIONS, SIMILARITIES AND CONTRASTS

Among Nations.

Buescu, V. Analogias temáticas nos românticos **BRASILEIROS** e romenos. Brasilia, 4. (Coimbra), 1947.

Gilman, M. Revival and Revolution in **ENGLISH** and French Romantic Poetry. FS, 6, 1950.

Leroy, A. La pensée britannique et la pensée française devant les problèmes philosophiques. Rev. de psych. des Peuples (Le Havre), 1949.

Goodman, H. P. Original Elements in the **FRENCH** and German Passion Plays. Diss., Bryn Mawr, 1951.

Malblanc, A. Pour une stylistique comparée du français et de l'allemand. Paris, 1944.

Marchand, R. Parallèles littéraires franco-russes. Mexico, 1949.

Hocket, C. F. & Moulton, G. **GERMANIC** and Algonquian: A Modern Myth. ASR, 39, 1951.

Heimann, Betty. The Philosophy of Flux, an Analogous Study in Heraclitean and Indian Thought. (**GREEK**). Annals of Bhandarkar Oriental Research Inst., 23, 1942, 177-86.

Ruben, W. Die Philosophen der Upanischaden. Bern, 1947.

Saksena, S. K. **INDIAN** and Western Idealism. Rev. of Philosophy & Religion, 11, 1942, 46-50.

Figueiredo, F. de. Pirene. Ponto de vista para uma introdução á história comparada das literaturas **PORTUGUESA** e espanhola. Lisboa, 1935.

Bertini, G. M. Drammatica comparata ispano-italiana (**SPAIN**). Letterature Mod., July, 1951.

Castro, A. Ensayo de historiologia. Analogias y diferencias entre hispanos y musulmanes. New York, 1950.

Poyatos y Atance, V. Historia de la literatura española comparada con las extranjeras. 9. ed. Valencia, 1930.

Puisbusque, A. de. Histoire comparée des littératures espagnole et française. Paris, 1843.

Schanzer, O. Parallels between Spanish American and Russian Novelistic Themes. Hisp., 35, 1952, 42-48. [A discussion of three thematic parallels representing common social and moral problems.]

Schuchardt, H. Analogia entre los Cantares Alpinos y los Andaluces. El Folklore Andaluz, Sevilla, 1882-83.

Yela Utrilla, J. F. Literatura española comparada con la extranjera. Lerida, 1928.

Among Authors and Types.

Abel, D. Strangers in Nature—**ARNOLD** and Emerson. UKCR, 15, 1949.

Cossio, J. M. **BECQUER** y Grün. Bol. Biblioteca de Menéndez Pelayo, 2-4, 1950.

Vincent, E. R. **BYRON**, Hobhouse, and Foscolo: New Documents in the History of a Collaboration. Cambridge U. P., 1949.

Vitaletti, G. Vite parallele: **CAMOENS** e Cervantes. Colombo, 2, 1927.

Grubbs, H. A. Albert **CAMUS** and Graham Greene. MLQ, 10, 1949.

Di Sarra, D. D. Materiali per uno studio sulla tecnica del romanzo novecentesco: Povĕtroň di K. **CAPEK**. RS, 1, 1952, 38-66. (Gide and Huxley). [One of the major renovators of European novelistic technique, with special reference to Meteor and the trilogy of which it forms part.]

Meister, C. W. Comparative Drama: **CHEKHOV**, Shaw, Odets. PL, 55, 1950.

Red'ko, A. Zadači žizni u Ibsena. RuB, 1, 1905, 22-56.

Dreyer, K. **COMMYNES** and Machiavelli: A Study in Parallelism. Symposium, 5, 1951.

Bowen, R. P. A Comparison of the Methods of Composition of **COOPER** and Balzac. FAR, 3, 1951.

Grubb, G. E. The Personal and Literary Relationships of **DICKENS** and Poe. NCF, 5, 1950.

Rouse, H. B. Charles Dickens and Henry James: Two Approaches to the Art of Fiction. Ibid.

Key, Ellen. Seelen und Werke (**DIDEROT**, Goethe, Maeterlinck). Berlin, 1911.

Gornfeld, A. Don-Kixot i Gamlet (**DON QUIXOTE** and Hamlet). In: Boevye otkliki na mirnye temy. Leningrad, 1924, 18-28.

Cejtlin, A. Prestuplenie i nakazanie i Les Misérables, sociologičeskie paralleli. (**DOSTOEVSKY**). LiM, 5, 1928, 20-58.

Pujals, E. Paralelismo e independencia de **ESPRONCEDA** y Lord Byron. Arbor, 11, 1948.

Quinlan, M. J. Dr. **FRANKLIN** meets Dr. Johnson. Pa. Mag. of Hist. & Biog., 73, 1949.

Anon. **GALSWORTHY**, Kuprin in Stevenson. SlP, 6, VII, 1951.

Muchnic, Helen. Circe's Swine: Plays by **GORKY** and O'Neill. CL, 3, 1951.

Tynjanov, J. Sjužet Gorja ot Uma. (**GRIBOEDOV** & Baumarchais). LN, 47-48, 1946, 147-88.

HAMLET: See also 63, 566.

Jones, E. Hamlet and Oedipus. London, 1949.

West, R. B. Three Methods of Modern Fiction: Ernest **HEMINGWAY**, Thomas Mann, Eudora Welty. CE, 12, 1951.

Winstedt, R. O. A Literary Device Common to **HOMER** and the East. Journal Royal Asiatic Society, 3, 1941.

Weil, F. Victor **HUGO** et Richard Wagner, leurs conceptions dramatiques. Zofingen, 1926.

Salvan, J. L. Le scandale de la multiplicité des consciences chez **HUXLEY**, Sartre, et Simone de Beauvoir. Symposium, 5, 1951.

Knapp, F. A. Two Contemporary Historians: José María **IGLESIAS** and Hubert Howe Bancroft. Pacific Hist. Rev., 20, 1951.

McFarlane, I. D. A Literary Friendship. Henry **JAMES** and Paul Bourget. Cambridge Journal, 1950-51.

Smith, Jane A. (ed.). Henry James and Robert Louis Stevenson: A Record of Friendship and Criticism. New York, 1949.

Burns, W. **KAFKA** and Alex Comfort: The Penal Colony Revisited. Arizona Quart. 8, 1952, 101-20. [Comfort's On This Side Nothing contrasts with Kafka's expressionistic abstraction, but his vision is Kafka's nightmare become reality.]

Feise, E. **KELLERS** Romeo und Julia und Stifter's Brigitta: Aufbau und Gehalt. In: Xenion. Baltimore, 1950.

McClain, W. H. **KLEIST** and Molière as Comic Writers. GR, 24, 1949.

Maritain, J. Trois réformateurs: **LUTHER**, Descartes, Rousseau. Paris, 1947, New York, 1948.

Rhodes, S. A. The Friendship between Gérard de **NERVAL** and Heinrich Heine. FR, 23, 1949.

Gilson, E. L'école des muses. (**PETRARCA**, Baudelaire, Wagner). Paris, 1951.

Tate, A. Three Commentaries: **POE**, James, and Joyce. Sewanee Rev., 58, 1950.

Felsen, J. O Pruste i Džojse. (**PROUST**, Joyce). čisla, Paris, 6, 1932, 215-18.

Batjuškov, F. **PUŠKIN** i Rasin. (Racine). Pamjati Puškina, St. Petersburg, 1900, 1-34.

Lang, Renée. **RILKE** and Gide: Their Reciprocal Translations. FS, 7, 1951.

Castex, P. G. Walter **SCOTT** contre Hoffmann. Les épisodes d'une rivalité littéraire. Mélanges Mornet. Paris, 1951.

Ure, P. On some Differences between **SENECAN** and Elizabethan Tragedy. Durham U. Journal, 10, 1948.

Fergusson, F. The Theater of **SHAW** and Pirandello. Partisan Rev., 16, 1949.

Faddegon, B. (**SUDRAKA'S**) Mrcchakatoka and King Lear. In: India Antiqua,

Festschrift Vogel, Leiden, 1947, 113-23.

Lang, C. Y. A Further Note on **SWIN-BURNE** and Whitman. MLN, 64, 1949.

Chaudhury, P. **TAGORE** and Croce. Visva-Bharati Quart., 12, 1947, 277-85.

Red'ko, A. **TOLSTOJ** i Ibsen. RuB, 1, 1907, 89-104 & 12, 1910, 124-33.

Havelock, E. A. **VIRGIL'S** Road to Xanadu. (Coleridge). Phoenix, 1, 1946.

Roditi, E. Oscar **WILDE** and Henry James. UKCR, 15, 1949.

Church, Margaret. Thomas **WOLFE**: Dark Time (and Proust). PMLA, 64, 1949.

VI. LITERARY THEMES: CHARACTERS, FABLES, FAIRY TALES, FOLKLORE, LEGENDS, MYTHS, MYTHOLOGY, SAGAS AND TYPES.

General Works

Allen, R. E. B. The Nature and Dissemination of the Märchen with Special Reference to the Cabinet des Fées. Diss. U. of Illinois, 1941.

Bassi, D. La mitologia nei cantici delle tragedie greche. RIL, 77, 1943-44.

Benz, R. Märchen und Aufklärung im 18. Jahrhundert. Gotha, 1907.

Boggs, R. S. Folklore Classification. SFQ, 13, 1949.

Bradbrook, M. C. Themes and Conventions of Elizabethan Tragedy. Cambridge, 1935.

Commelin, P. Mythologie der Griechen und Römer. Luzern, 1948.

Crum, R. H. Additions to the Bibliography of Greek and Roman Folklore. CW, 42, 1948-49.

Dontenville, H. La mythologie française. Paris, 1948.

Dorson, R. M. Five Directions in American Folklore. Midwest Folklore, 1, 1951.

Ebeling, E. Ein neuer Beitrag zur Kenntnis der akkadischen Fabelliteratur. Journal of Cuneiform Studies, 4, 1950, 215-22.

Espinosa, A. M. La clasificación de los cuentos populares. Bol. de la Academia Española, 21, 1934.

Gaer, J. Lore of the Old Testament. Boston, 1951.

Gaster, T. H. Ugaritic Mythology. Journal of Near Eastern Studies, 7, 1948, 184-93.

Gifford, E. W. Fijian Mythology, Legends, and Archaeology. Festschrift Popper. Berkeley, 1951.

Goodwyn, F. A Proposed Terminology for Clarifying the Relationship between Folklore and Literature. SFQ, 14, 1950.

Goossens, R. Notes de mythologie comparée indo-européenne. Nouvelle Clio (Bruxelles), 1, 1949.

Green, O. H. Fingen los poetas—Notes on the Spanish Attitude toward Pagan Mythology. Festschrift Menéndez Pidal. Madrid, 1950.

Guastalla, R. M. Le mythe et le livre: essai sur l'origine de la littérature. Paris, 1940.

Haywood, C. A Bibliography of North American Folklore and Folksong. New York, 1951.

Hightower, J. R. Topics in Chinese Literature. Harvard U. P., 1950.

Hubaux, J. Les grands mythes de Rome. Paris, 1945.

Hudson, A. P. La poesia folklorica. Folklore Americas, 10. (Chapel Hill), 1951.

Kagarov, E. Očerk sovremennogo sostojanija mifologičeskoj nauki. In: Voprosy teorii i psixologii tvorčestva, 5. Kharkov, 1907-16.

Kampman, A. A. Hethietische Mythen en Legenden. Ex Oriente Lux, 10, 1945-48, 407-14.

Klaiber, J. Das Märchen und die kindliche Phantasie. Stuttgart, 1866.

Kleijntjens, J. & Knippenberg, H. H. Van goden en helden. Mythen en sagen van Grieken, Romeinen en Germanen. Groningen, 1950.

Korfmacher, W. C. Character Portrayal in Early Roman Epic. CW, 42, 1948-49.

Leach, Maria & Fried, J. (eds.). Standard Dictionary of Folklore, Mythology, and Legend. New York, 1949 ff.

Malcolm, D. M. Zulu Literature: Unwritten Lore. Africa, 19, 1949, 33-39.

Miller, A. B. Themes and Techniques in Mid-Tudor Lyric Poetry. Diss. Northwestern U., 1950.

Muschg, W. Dichtertypen. Festschrift Strich. Bern, 1952.

Neri, F. Letteratura e Leggende. Torino, 1951.

Nossag, O. Volksmärchen und Volksinteresse im 18. Jahrhundert bis 1770. Diss., Greifswald. Cottbus, 1931.

Obermann, J. J. Ugaritic Mythology. New Haven, 1948.

Otten, H. Vorderasiatische Mythen als Vorläufer griechischer Mythenbildung. F&F, 1949.

Philippson, P. Origini e forme del mito greco. Coll. di Studi religiosi, 10. (Torino), 1949.

Portuondo, J. A. Caribbean Literary Themes in the Last Fifty Years. In: The Caribbean at Mid-Century (ed. by A. C. Wilgus). Gainesville, 1951.

Prescott, F. C. Poetry and Myth. New York, 1927.

Pypin, A. Legendy i apokrify v drevnej russkoj pis'mennosti. VE, 3, 1894, 291-331.

Rahv, P. Image and Idea, Fourteen Essays on Literary Themes. Norfolk (Conn.), 1949.

Roussel, L. Mythologie et folklore. Bull. de Correspondance Hellénique, 70, 1946.

Sangin, M. Nekotorye nabljudenija iz oblasti antičnogo fol'klora. ILGU, 1, 1928, 89-99.

Sauerbrey, R. Zur Typologie der Mythendeutung. Bonn, 1943.

Schott, S. Mythe und Mythenbildung im alten Ägypten. Leipzig, 1945.

Seidenfader, E. Fairy Tales of Common Origin. Journal of Thailand Research Society, 33, 1941, 143-45.

Smethurst, S. E. The Growth of the Roman Legend. Phoenix, 3, 1949.

Taylor, A. Folklore and the Student of Literature. Pacific Spectator, 2, 1949.

Thompson, S. The Future of Folklore Research in the United States. PAPS, 93, 1949.

——— Folklore at Midcentury. Midwest Folklore, 1, 1951.

Vermeil, L. L'origine et le développement de la fable. Lausanne, 1882.

Virolleaud, C. Légendes de Babylone et de Canaan. Paris, 1949.

Whiteford, R. N. Motives in English Fiction. New York, 1918.

Wolf, J. W. Beiträge zur Deutschen Mythologie. 2 vols. Göttingen, 1852.

Xarciev, V. Mifotvorstvo, poezija i nauka. In: Voprosy teorii i psixologii tvorčestva, 5. Kharkov, 1907-16.

Individual Authors and Works.

Schultz de Mantovani, F. ANDERSEN y la fabula. Sur, 186, 1950.

Elisseeff, N. Thèmes et motifs des Mille et une Nuits; Essai de classification. (ARABIAN NIGHTS). Beirut, 1949.

Paton, L. A. Fairy Mythology of ARTHURIAN Romance. Boston, 1903.

Gross, J. J. After FRAZER: the Ritualistic Approach to Myth. Western Humanities Rev., 5, 1951.

Kempter, L. HÖLDERLIN und die Mythologie. Diss. Zürich. Leipzig, 1929.

Bassi, D. La mitologia in Orazio. (HORACE). RIL, 76.

Taine, H. LA FONTAINE et ses fables. Paris, 1914.

Ostrogorskij, V. Motivy LERMONTOVskoj poezii. RM, 1-2, 1891.

Albrecht, L. Der magische Idealismus in NOVALIS' Märchentheorie und Märchendichtung. Hamburg, 1948.

Nordick, Agnes. Der Stil der Märchen PERRAULTS. Diss., Münster, Bochum-Langendreer, 1934.

Bassi, D. La mitologia in PINDARO. RIL, 74, 1940-41.

Rivier, A. Mythe et poésie. Leurs rapports et leur fonction dans trois épinicies de Pindare. Lettres d'humanité, Suppl. à BAGB, 1950.

Bassi, D. La mitologia in PLATONE. RIL, 73, 1939-40.

Edelstein, L. The Function of the Myth in Plato's Philosophy. JHI, 1949.

Guillen, J. PRUDENCIO y la Mitologia. Helmantica, 1, 1950.

Noskov, N. (ed.) SLOVAR literaturnyx tipov. Tipy Puškina. St. Petersburg, 1912.

Moser, H. UHLANDS schwäbische Sagenkunde und die germanistisch-volkskundliche Forschung der Romantik. Schwäb. Beitr. Philol. & Volkskunde, 1. Tübingen, 1950.

Herzofi, Alice. Die Märchen von Oscar WILDE. Mülhausen, 1930.

Individual Motifs.

Dédéyan, C. Stendhal adaptateur dans Vittoria ACCORAMBONI. Symposium, Nov., 1951.

Dewitte, J. Le mythe d'ADRASTE. Etude de tradition littéraire. Diss., Bruxelles. RBPh, 25, 1946-47.

Hritzu, J. N. AENEAS, the Noblest of Romans. CW, 42, 1948-49.

Fletcher, F. Notes to the AGAMEMNON of Aeschylus. Oxford, 1949.

Scholtze, J. Der Charakter des Agamemnon von Homer bis Euripides. Diss., Wien, 1939.

Luzzatto, G. L. L'ALCESTE di Wieland. Dioniso, 1949.

Janouch, V. O poměru ALEXANDREIDY staročeské k Ulrichu von Eschenbach. Praha, 1951.

Struve, V. U istokov romana ob Aleksandre. VZ, 1, 1927, 131-46.

Osella, G. Intorno alla leggenda di S. ALESSIO. Convivium, 1948.

Lecomte, B. **ANDROMAQUE** dans l'oeuvre d'Euripide. Diss., Louvain. RBPh, 1949.

Frayn, J. M. The Cult of **APOLLO** and Early Christianity. LQHR, 1947.

Hausmann, U. Die Apollosonette Rilkes und ihre plastischen Urbilder. Berlin, 1947.

Enk, P. J. The Romance of **APOLLONIUS** of Tyre. Mnemosyne (Leiden), 4.

Nilsson, N. A. Die Apollonius-Erzählung in den slavischen Literaturen. Uppsala, 1949.

Leitich, R. Der Einfluss der **ARGONAUT-IKA** des Apollonios von Rhodes auf Vergil and Ovid. Diss., Wien, 1940.

Kuehnemund, R. **ARMINIUS** or The Rise of a National Symbol. Chapel Hill, 1953.

Maticetov, M. **ATTILA** fra Italiani, Croati e Sloveni. Ce Fastu?, 25-26, 1948-49.

Romano, D. Due storici di Attila, i Greco Prisco e il Goto Jordanes. Antiquitas, 2, 1947.

Levi, E. La leggenda di **BARLAAM** e Josaphat in Ispagna. Leonardo, 7, 1931.

Campion, A. La personalidad eúskara en la Historia, el Derecho y la Literatura. (BASQUES), Bilbao, 1901.

Eguia Ruiz, C. De literatura regional: Euskeria. RyF, 87, 1929.

Farinelli, A. Guillaume de Humboldt y el País Vasco. Bilbao, 1922.

Reicher, G. G. Les Légendes basques dans la tradition humaine. Paris, 1946.

Wright, R. W. M. The City of **BATH** and its Literary Associations. Addresses to English Association. London, 1948.

BORIS GODUNOV: See also Demetrius, 94.

Bernštejn, D. Boris Godunov Puškina i russkaja istoričeskaja dramaturgija v epoxu dekabrizma. In: Puškin—rodonačal'nik novoj russkoj literatury. Moscow, 1941, 217-62.

Nikolaieff, A. M. Boris Godunov and the Ouglich Tragedy. Russian Rev., 1950.

Loehr, R. C. Some More Light on Paul **BUNYAN**. JAF, 64, 1951.

Pérez de Guzman, J. El emperador **CARLOS** V en la poesía lírica italo-castellana. Ilustración Española y Americana, 51, (Madrid), 1907.

Templin, T. H. **CAROLINGIAN** Titles in the Spanish Drama before 1800. RR, 26, 1935.

Meessen, H. J. **KASSANDRA** als Endform in Paul Ernsts religiöser Dramatik. MDU, 43, 1951.

Lukman, N. The **CATALAUNIAN** Battle (451) in Medieval Epics. C & M, 10, 1948.

Blume, B. Die Stadt als seelische Landschaft im Werk Rainer Maria Rilkes. (CITY). MDU, 43, 1951.

Rees, J. Samuel Daniel's **CLEOPATRA** and Two French Plays. MLR, Jan., 1952.

Illjin, K. Die Gestalt der **KLYTAIM-NESTRA** in der klassischen Dichtung der Hellenen. Diss., Wien, 1939.

Guengerich, R. Die Küstenbeschreibung in der griechischen Literatur. (COAST). Orbis Antiquus, 4, (Münster), 1950.

Bédarida, H. Christophe **COLOMB**, héros de quelques drames français de Rousseau à Claudel. Annales de l'U. de Paris, Oct. 1951.

CRIME: See 177 and also Sociology.

Porena, M. **CRISTINA** di Svezia in una commedia di Calderón de la Barca. Colombo, 2, 1927.

Benveniste, E. La légende des **DANAIDES**. Rev. de l'Histoire des Religions, 136, 1949.

Dohet, E. La légende des Danaïdes dans l'oeuvre d'Eschyle. Diss., Louvain. RBPh, 1948.

Gruenther, R. Formen des **DANDYSMUS**. Eine problemgeschichtliche Studie über Ernst Jünger. Euphorion, 46, 1952, 170-201. [The author relates Jünger to the pseudo-aristocratic, antibourgeois tradition of the 19th century (Sénancour, Gautier, Flaubert, Wilde, d'Annunzio). The ultimate ancestor of this attitude is found in German romanticism].

Grossman, L. Puškin i dendizm. In: Etjudy o Puškine. Moscow, 1923.

Balseiro, J. A. Cuatro enamorados de la muerte. (DEATH). Memoria del 4. Congreso del Inst. de Lit. Iberoamericana. (Habana), 1949.

Diego López, V. G. de. Estudio psicológico-lingüistico del temor a la muerte entre los clásicos latinos. Anales de la U. Hispalense (Sevilla), 1945.

Haugh, R. F. Death and Consequences: Joseph Conrad's Attitude toward Fate. UKCR, 18, 1953, 191-97. [Theme of the "Nigger" is the conflict between death, disorder, fear and human solidarity.]

Johnsson, J. W. S. Notes on the Black Death in Danish Folklore and Tradition. Leyden, 1928.

Mewaldt, J. Liebestod bei Platon. Anzeiger der Akad. d. Wissenschaften, Wien, 80, 1943.

Rosales, L. La figuración y la voluntad de morir en la poesía española. Cruz y Raya, 38, (Madrid).

Salinas, P. Lorca and the Poetry of Death. Hopkins Rev., 5, 1951.

Vedia y Mitre, M. de. El Dr. Johnson y la obsesión de la muerte. Nacion (Buenos Aires), 21, I, 1951.

Werner, F. Das Todesproblem in den Werken T. G. von Hippels. Halle, 1938.

Werner, H. Houston S. Chamberlain über den Untergang Rome. Gedanken zum DEKADENZproblem um die Jahrhundertwende. Zs. f. Kirchengeschichte, 1942.

Rabinowitsch, M. Der DELPHIN in Sage und Mythos der Griechen. Basel, 1947.

Wormhaudt, A. The DEMON Lover: a Psychoanalytical Approach to Literature. New York, 1949.

DEVIL: See also Faust 629 & 755.

Robe, S. L. Four Mexican Exempla about the Devil. Western Folklore, 10, 1951.

Shoeck, R. J. More, Erasmus, and the Devil. N&Q, 196, 1951.

Valera Jacome, B. El pacto diabólico en la literatura española. Guía (Midrad), Jan., 1946.

Hollevoet, A. De DIANA-mythus bij de latijnsche scholiasten. Diss., Gand. RBPh, 25, 1946-47.

Essen, C. van. DIDO. Hermeneus, 20, 1949.

Turner, R. E. Didon dans la tragédie de la Renaissance italienne et française. Diss., Paris, 1926.

Ceretelli, G. Novyj gimn v čest' DIONISA, IAN, 9-11, 1918.

Wiesmann, L. Das Dionysische bei Hölderlin und in der deutschen Romantik. Basel, 1948

Zelinskij, F. Dionis v religii i poezii. RM, 7, 1915, 1-21.

Levi, E. La leggenda di DON CARLOS nel teatro spagnuolo del Seicento. RI, 16, 1913.

—— Il principe Don Carlos nella leggenda e nella poesia. Roma, 1925.

Glicksberg, C. I. Modern Literature and the Sense of DOOM. AQ, 6, 1950.

Baumann, Marianne. Der Traum im Werk von Jeremias Gotthelf. (DREAM). Bern, 1945.

Bem, A. Razvertyvanie sna (Večnyj muž Dostoevskogo). Učenye Zapiski Russkoj Učebnoj Kollegii (Praha), 2, 1924, 45-59.

Cordle, T. H. The Role of Dreams in A la recherche du temps perdu. RR, 42, 1951.

Éigis, M. O Lermontove (k metafizike snovidenij). A, 10, 1914, 51-69.

Schueler, H. Hebbel and the Dream. New York, 1941.

Straxov, I. Xudožestvennoe poznanie snovidenij. NBLU, 7, 1946, 44-46.

Leuridant, L. Les rapports entre l'ELECTRE d'Euripide et l'Electre de Sophocle. Diss., Bruxelles. RBPh, 25, 1946-47.

Hutcherson, D. R. Milton's Epithets for EVE. U. of Virginia Studies, 4, 1951.

Saintyves, P. Des fées et de leur littérature en France. (FAIRIES). RDM, 38, 1862.

Wentz, W. Fairy-Faith in Celtic Countries. Oxford, 1911.

Rogers, P. P. A Spanish Version of the Mateo FALCONE Theme. MLN, 45, 1930.

Amand, D. FATALISME et liberté dans l'antiquité. Louvain, 1945.

Greene, W. C. Moira. FATE, Good and Evil in Greek Thought. Harvard U. P., 1944.

Maerkisch, A. Das Problem des Schicksals bei Adalbert Stifter. Berlin, 1941.

Psaar, W. Schicksalsbegriff und Tragik bei Schiller und Kleist. Berlin, 1940.

Saz, A. del. Los Reyes Católicos en el teatro. (FERDINAND & Isabella). Bol. de la U. de Madrid, 1929.

Edsman, C. M. Ignis divinus. Le feu comme moyen de rajeunissement et d'immortalité. Contes, légendes, mythes et rites. (FIRE). Skrifter Vetenskaps. Soc., 34. Lund, 1949.

Kovalevskij, M. Masonstvo vo vremena Ekateriny. K istorii nemeckogo vlijanija v Rossii. (FREEMASON). VE, 9, 1915, 95-115.

Pypin, A. Russkoe masonstvo v XVIII veke. VE, 2-7, 1867-68.

—— Materialy dlja istori masonskix lož. VE, 1-2, 7, 1872.

—— Kto byl avtor Antidota? Iz istorii literaturnoj dejatel'nosti imp. Ekateriny II. VE, 5, 1901, 181-216.

Jacoby, D. FRIEDRICH der Grosse und die deutsche Literatur. Basel, 1875, 43 p.

Dallaire, H. La notion de l'amitié chez Aristote. (FRIENDSHIP). Diss., Ottawa, 1948.

Diederich, M. D. Cicero and Saint Ambrose on Friendship. CJ, 43, 1948.

Purdy, R. R. The Friendship Motif in Middle English Literature. Vanderbilt Studies in Humanities, 1, 1951.

Teixeira de Pascoaes, J. Hieronymus, der Dichter der Freundschaft. Amsterdam, 1941.

Restori, A. GENOVA nel teatro classico di Spagna. Genova, 1912.

—— Ancora Genova nel teatro classico di Spagna. Riv. ligure scienze, lett. ed arti, 40, 1913.

Lee, C. P. Decline and Death of the Southern GENTLEMAN. Southwest Rev., 36, 1951.

McCluney, D. C. The Reception of the Gentleman Concept in Germany. Diss., Stanford U., 1949-50.

Mary Jeremy, Sister. Caxton's Original Additions to the Legenda Aurea. (GOLDEN LEGEND). MLN, 64, 1949.

Friedrich, P. Die Stunde, die anbrach. (GOLEM). Die Besinnung, 7, 1952, 56-65. [A stimulating survey of the theme in contemporary literature, beginning with Meyrink's Golem and Kafka's Trial. Among the authors discussed are Jünger, Orwell, Gheorgiu, Papini, Hemingway, Graham Greene, etc.]

Beer, E. S. de. GOTHIC: Origin and Diffusion of the Term; the Idea of Style in Architecture. JWI, 11, 1948.

Weigand, H. J. Thomas Mann's GREGORIUS. GR, 27, 1952. [The author identifies the medieval French and German sources for the novel: Chrétien, the Adam and Eve play, Hartmann, Wolfram; he examines the importance of Gregorovius' Geschichte der Stadt Rom im Mittelalter and of a host of minor sources; he studies the transformation of this material in the novel.]

Jungandreas, W. Die GUDRUNsage in den Ober- und Niederlanden, eine Vorgeschichte des Epos. Göttingen, 1948. 221 p.

Clavería, C. Estudios sobre los gitanismos del español. (GYPSIES). Suppl. RFE, 53, 1951.

Benoît, P. Les idées de Sénèque sur l'audelà. (HEAVEN). Rev. des sciences philos. & théol., 32, 1948.

Benz, R. HEIDELBERG und die Romantik. Heidelberg, 1948.

Boggs, R. S. The HERO in the Folktales of Spain, Germany and Russia. JAF, 44, 1931.

Grinberg, I. Geroj sovetskogo romana. In: Obraz bol'ševika. Leningrad, 1938, 3-93.

Gifford, H. Hero of His Time: a Theme in Russian Literature. New York, 1950.

Mehnert, K. Der Sowjetautor und sein Held. Osteuropa, Oct., 1951.

Minkov, C. Položitelnijat geroj v B'lgarskata literatura. EL, 6, 1951, 274-83.

Timofeev, L. O položitel'nom geroe sovetskoj literatury. NoM, 1, 1952, 217-31. [Soviet writers are constantly blamed by Soviet critics for their inability to create a positive hero. Here one of the leading Soviet literary scholars discusses this controversial subject.]

Eremin, I. Drama-igra Car' Irod. (HERODES). TODRL, 4, 1940, 223-40.

Wolffheim, H. Wielands Begriff der HUMANITÄT. Hamburg, 1949.

Grande, C. del. HYBRIS. Colpa e castigo nell' espressione poetica e letteraria degli scrittori della Grecia antica da Omero a Cleante. Napoli, 1947.

Hadamowsky, W. Studien zur Entwicklung des Hybrisbegriffs von Homer bis Euripides. Diss., Wien, 1948.

ILIAS: See Troy, 153 & 712.

Ulrich, L. Petrarca, Ariost und die Unsterblichkeit. (IMMORTALITY). RF, 63, 1951.

Alba, V. Les INDIENS et la naissance de la littérature latino-américaine. Preuves, March, 1952.

Aldridge, A. C. Franklin's Deistical Indians. PAPS, 94, 1950.

González, Beatrice E. The Emergence of the Indian in Mexican Imaginative Literature. Bucknell U. Studies, 2, 1951.

Pearce, R. H. Melville's Indian-Hater. A Note on a Meaning of The Confidence-Man. PMLA, 67, 1952, 942-48. [The blackness of the novel is complete; Indian-hating is as false and unreasoning as its opposite, confidence.]

Rehm, W. Nachsommer. Zur Deutung von Stifters Dichtung. München, 1951. 141 p. [The author traces the motif of INDIAN SUMMER from Jean Paul to Burckhardt and Nietzsche, stressing the importance of Claude Lorrain, and linking this theme with the cult of the Mediterranean world.]

Bertini, G. M. L'Orlando Furioso e l'INQUISIZIONE spagnuola. Convivium, 7, 1935.

Castanien, D. G. A Seventeenth Century Mexican Library and the Inquisition. Diss., U. of Michigan, 1951.

Gordon, D. H. & Torrey, N. L. The Censoring of Diderot's Encyclopédie and the Reestablished Text. New York, 1947.

Iouben, H. H. Verbotene Literatur von der klassischen Zeit bis zur Gegenwart. Berlin, 1924.

Iaceina, A. Der Grossinquisitor. Geschichtsphilosophische Deutung der Legende Dostojewskys. Heidelberg, 1952. 340 p. Cf. Welt und Wort, 7, 1952.

Iorozov, A. Zapadnye pisateli v carskoj cenzure. In: Zapadnyj sbornik, 1. Moscow, 1937.

Iiermann, W. T. Romantische IRONIE nach Jean Paul und Solger. Diss., New York U., 1949.

Iudrick, M. Jane Austen: Irony as Defense and Discovery. Princeton U. P., 1952. 267 p. [Jane Austen's ironic perception of the incongruities of her orthodox world was inhibited by her moral commitments to the genteel society of her day. Emma is the most artistic embodiment of her irony, as it is most free from evidences of her need to justify bourgeois morality.]

arcía Villada, Z. San ISIDRO Labrador en la Historia y en la Literatura. RyF, 62, 1922.

Brockmeyer, F. Cicero und ITALIEN. Diss., Münster, 1947.

Kaufmann, W. A. Faust and JACOB. GR, 26, 1951.

Desfourneaux, M. JEANNE D'ARC en Espagne. Hisp., 26, 1943.

Saix, G. de. Jeanne d'Arc dans la littérature espagnole. Hisp., 2 (Paris), 1919.

Echegaray, B. de. La legenda de San JULIAN el Hospitalario en romances castellanos. BH, 1951.

Coster, R. de. JUPITER et Fortuna dans l'oeuvre d'Horace. RBPh, 25, 1946-47.

Schmid, B. Studien zu griechischen KTISISsagen. Diss., Fribourg, 1947.

Lerena, M. Función del paisaje en la novela hispanoamericana. (LANDSCAPE). Hisp., 32, 1949.

Maple Arce, M. El paisaje en la literatura mexicana. Mejico, 1944.

Rosenberg, S. L. M. Paisaje en la lirica mejicana. BH, 36, 1938.

Keller, H. Goethe und das LAOKOON-Problem. Frauenfeld, 1935.

Clavería, C. Los lapones y su literatura. (LAPPS). Insula, 63, 1951.

Giergielewicz, M. Elements of LAW in Słowacki's Life and Writings. (In Polish). In: Słowacki Centenary Volume. London, 1951.

McNair, A. Dr. Johnson and the Law. Cambridge U. P., 1948.

Zavattari, E. Il mito di LEDA. Festschrift P. Capparoni. Torino, 1941.

LEGENDA AUREA: See Golden Legend, 105.

Castro, A. El Libro de Buen Amor del Arcipreste de Hita. (LOVE). CL, 4, 1952.

Green, O. H. Courtly Love in Quevedo. U. of Colorado Stud., 1952.

Holman, C. H. Courtly Love in the Merchant's and Franklin's Tales. ELH, 18, 1951.

Jones, R. O. The Idea of Love in Garcilaso's Second Eglogue. MLR, 1951.

Levin, S. Love and the Hero in the Iliad. TAPhA, 80, 1949.

Müller, L. Der Sinn der Liebe and der Sinn des Lebens (Der ideologische Plan der Anna Karenina). ZSP, 21, 1951, 22-39. [Tolstoy's novel as "a phenomenology of sexual love, shown in all its varieties." His ideas about love and marriage are related to Schopenhauer's philosophy, but he is shown to have had, as an artist, a deeper grasp of the dialectics of love and life.]

Ruiz de Conde, J. El amor y el matrimonio secreto en los libros de caballeria. Aguilar, 1948.

Suxotin, L. Ljubov' v russkoj lirike XIX v. Beograd, 1927.

Vincent, L. George Sand et l'amour. Paris, 1917.

Nikol'skij, N. Sledy magičeskoj literatury v knige Psalmov. (MAGIC). TBGU, 4-5, 12, 1923.

Towne, F. White Magic in Friar Bacon and Friar Bungay. MLN, 1952.

Manresa, R. M. de. La Virgen MARIA en la literatura hispana. Roma, 1904.

Pérez, N. La Inmaculada en la literatura española. RyF, 9, 1904.

Chauvin, Sister Mary John. The Role of MARY MAGDALENE in Medieval Drama. Washington, 1951.

Garth, H. M. Saint Mary Magdalene in Mediaeval Literature. Baltimore, 1950.

Ruggieri, J. Frammenti castigliani delle leggende di SS. MARTA e Maddalena. AR, 17, 1933.

Wonderley, A. W. Some Notes on Hypochondria and MELANCHOLY in German Literature of Early Eighteenth Century. PQ, 30, 1951.

Carrère, J. B. Sénèque et Rousseau: le thème des MINES, Mélanges D. Mornet. Paris, 1951.

Bogdanova, N. Stixi XVIII veka o rudokopnom dele. TODRL, 1, 1932, 231-46.

Littmann. **MOHAMMED** in Volksepos. Kopenhagen, 1950.

Miquel y Planas, R. La leyenda de Fray Juan Garin, ermitaño de **MONTSER-RAT**. Barcelona, 1940.

Achoukine, N. **MOSCOU** dans la vie et dans les oeuvres de Pouchkine. (In Russian). Moscow, 1949

Stefanek, J. Moscou dans la littérature tchèque. (In Czech). Prague, 1949.

Bates, R. H. A Study of the Literature of the **MOUNTAINS** and of Mountain Climbing Written in English. Diss., U. of Pa., 1951.

MULATTO: See Negro, 129 & 710.

Boeniger, Yvonne. Lamartine et le sentiment de la **NATURE**. Paris, 1934.

Crowther, M. Nature in Spanish Poetry. BSS, 22, 1945.

Wimsatt, W. K. The Structure of Romantic Nature Imagery. In: The Age of Johnson: Essays Presented to C. B. Tinker. Yale U. P., 1949.

Augustin, H. Goethes und Stifters **NAU-SIKAA**-Tragödie. Basel, 1941.

Blomberg, H. La **NEGRA** y la mulata en la poesía americana. Atenea, 80 (Concepción), 1945.

Boratav, P. N. The Negro in Turkish Folklore. JAF, 64, 1951.

Glicksberg, C. I. Bias, Fiction, and the Negro. Phylon, 13, 1952, 127-35. [Sees the real American tragedy—that of race relations and the plight of the Negro in America—as waiting to be written; perhaps a Negro author will best do this.]

Howe, I. William Faulkner and the Negroes. Commentary, 12, 1951.

Malkiel, Y. The Amulatado Type in Spanish. RR, 32, 1941.

Ocvirk, V. Književnost črne Amerike. MlR, 6, 1950-51, 271-81.

Pivano, F. Letteratura negra americana. Rassegna d'Italia, 3, 1948.

Snowden, F. M. The Negro in Ancient Greece. American Anthropologist, 50, 1948.

Spratlin, V. B. The Negro in Spanish Literature. Journal of Negro History, 19, 1934.

Heinz, K. Das Bild Kaiser **NEROS** bei Seneca, Tacitus, Sueton und Cassius Dio. Diss., Bern. Biel, 1948.

Kerenyi, K. **NIOBE**. Neue Studien über antike Religion und Humanität. Zürich, 1949.

Oliver, R. P. The **OEDIPUS** of Plautu: CP, 1950.

Arms, E. F. d' & Hulley, K. K. Th **ORESTEIA**-Story in the Odysse; TAPhA, 77, 1946.

Weisert, J. J. Two Recent Variations o the Orestes Theme (Hauptmann (Sartre). MLJ, 35, 1951.

Boutemy, A. Une version médiévale in connue de la légende d'**ORPHÉF** Hommages Bidez-Cumont. Bruxelle: 1949.

Dornseiff, F. Goethe und Orpheus. F&F 26, 1950.

Rehm, W. Orpheus: Der Dichter und di Toten: Selbstdeutung und Totenku] bei Novalis, Hölderlin, Rilke. Düsse] dorf, 1950.

Herbig, R. **PAN**, der griechische Bock: gott. Frankfurt, 1949.

Fucilla, J. G. Pasquale **PAOLI** in Eight eenth-Century Italian Literature. Ital 28, 1951.

Avalle Arce, J. B. Sobre la difusión de ¶ leyenda del Purgatorio de San **PA TRICIO** en España. NRFH, 2, 1948.

PEASANTS: See Professions, 173-77.

Hulst, C. S. **PERSEUS** and the Gorgor La Salle (Ill.), 1946.

Douglas, R. The **PESSIMISM** of Mar Twain. Mark Twain Quart., 9, 1951.

Evlaxov, A. I. S. Turgenev—poét mirovo skorbi. RuB, 6, 1904, 1-45.

Pypin, A. Petr Velikij v narodnom pre danii. (**PETER** the Great). VE, 8 1897, 640-90.

PETERSBURG: See St. Petersburg, 144

Kulczycka-Saloni, J. Geneza literacka Far aona. Pamiętnik Literacki, Lwów, 4(93-128. [Reviewing the history o Egyptian motifs in Polish and foreig literatures, the author states tha **PHARAOH** (by Prus) owes to his pre decessors the political conflict as back ground and sensational motifs; but th originality of his novel consists in hi treatment and interpretation of th characters.]

PHILIP II: See also Don Carlos, 95-96 ‹ 707.

Guerrieri Crocetti, C. Il Filippo dell'A: fieri, studio introduttivo sulle fonti lo sviluppo della leggenda di D. Carlo: Firenze, 1928.

Radermacher, L. Zur **PHILOKTET**sag‹ Annuaire de l'Inst. de Philol. & d'His: orientales, 9 (Bruxelles), 1949.

Thompson, D. B. The **PHOENIX**. Phoeni; 1, 1946.

Dricot, L. La légende de **POLYXENE**. Diss., Liége. RBPh, 25, 1946.

Schirokauer, A. Die Legende vom Armen Heinrich. (**POOR HENRY**). MDU, 43, 1951.

Foerster, D. M. Scottish **PRIMITIVISM** and the Historical Approach. PQ, 29, 1950.

Schmidt, R. Pervobytnoe myšlenie v obrazax Iliady. JaiL, 4, 1929, 93-109.

Frankel, C. The Faith of Reason: the Idea of **PROGRESS** in the French Enlightenment. New York, 1948.

Keller, A. C. The Idea of Progress in Rabelais. PMLA, 66, 1951.

Balthasar, H. U. von. **PROMETHEUS**: Studien zur Geschichte des deutschen Idealismus. Heidelberg, 1947.

Deratani, N. Obraz tirana v tragedii Esxila Prometej prikovannyj. DAN, 4, 1929, 70-74.

Gadamer, H. G. Prometheus und die Tragödie der Kultur. Anales de Filol. Clásica, 4, (Buenos Aires), 1947-49.

Loy, J. R. Prometheus, Theseus, the Uncommon Man and an Eagle. (Gide). FS, 7, 1951.

Riggs, T. Prometheus, 1900. AL, 22, 1951.

Crane, M. **PYGMALION**: Bernard Shaw's Dramatic Theory and Practice. PMLA, 1951.

Guerrieri Crocetti, C. La leggenda di **RODRIGO**. Contributo allo studio dell'epopea spagnuola. In: Nuovi Studi Medievali. Bologna, 1926.

Krappe, A. H. The Legend of Rodrick, Last of the Visigoth Kings, and the Ermanarich Cycle. Heidelberg, 1923.

Menéndez Pidal, R. Leyendas del último rey godo (Notas e investigaciones). Madrid, 1906.

———— El rey Rodrigo en la literatura. Bol. Real Acad. Española, 11, 1924.

Hämel, A. Die **ROLAND**legende des Pseudo Turpin. Festschrift A. M. Huntington. Wellesley (Mass.), 1952.

Peckham, P. G. La Chanson de Roland dans les littératures française et espagnole au Moyen Age. RR, 1952.

Marsili, A. **ROMA** nella poesia di Claudiano. Romanità occidentale contrapposta a quella orientale. Antiquitas, 1, 1946.

SALOMON: See Solomon, 48.

Lo Gatto, E. Il mito di Pietroburgo nella letteratura russa. (**ST. PETERSBURG**). Lett. Moderne, 3, 1952, 38-57. [The theme has played an important part in Russian literature from Pushkin through Gogol and Dostoevsky to Merezhkovsky and Andrey Bely.

Here it is related to the debate about the historical destinies of Russia between the Slavophiles and the Westernizers.]

Rehm, W. Roquairol. Eine Studie zur Geschichte des Bösen. (**SATANISM**). Orbis Litterarum, 8, 1950, 161-258. [The author examines the literary ancestors of Jean Paul's character in Der Titan, broadening his investigation into a study of libertinistic and "satanic" characters in the European novel of the 18th century, as presented by Laclos, de Sade, Restif de la Brétonne, Jacobi, and Tieck.]

SCEPTICISM: See Religion, 327-38, 730-33.

Veselovskij, A. Slavjanskie skazanija o **SOLOMONE** i Kitovrase i zapadnye legendy o Morol'fe i Merline. St. Petersburg, 1872.

Niesten. De **SPORT** bij Homeros. Diss., Louvain. RBPh, 25, 1946-47.

Dumézil, G. Pères et fils dans la légende de **TARQUIN** le Superbe. In: Hommages Bidez-Cumont. Bruxelles, 1949.

Hahn, W. **TEMISTOKLES** w Genezis z Ducha Juliusza Słowackiego. Kornelia, matka Gratchów u Juliusza Słowackiego. Me, 5, 1950.

Lovers of **TERUEL**: See 120.

Häny, A. Hölderlins **TITANEN**mythus. Zürich, 1948.

Maeztu, R. de. La brevedad de la vida en nuestra poesía lírica. (**TRANSITORINESS**). Academia Española, 1935.

Geppener, N. K istorii perevoda povesti o Troe Gvido de Kolumna. (**TROY**). In: Festschrift Orlov. Leningrad, 1934, 351-60.

Jarxo, B. Il'ja, Ilias, Xil'tebrant. IAN, ORJaSl, 22, 1917, 326-37.

Young, A. M. Troy and her Legend. Pittsburgh U. P., 1948.

Val'denberg, V. Ponjatie o tiranne v drevnerusskoj literature v sravnenii s zapadnoj. (**TYRANT**). IRJasl, 2, 1929, 214-36.

Davaux, J. Etude sur le personnage d'**ULYSSE** dans la littérature grecque d'Homère à Sophocle. Diss., Louvain. RBPh, 25, 1946-47.

Stanford, W. B. Studies in the Characterization of Ulysses. Hermathena, 73, 1949.

———— Ulysses from Homer to Joyce. PCA, 46, 1949.

Voevodskij, L. Vvedenie v mifologiju Odissei. Odessa, 1881. 235 p.

Masson, A. **VENISE** retrouvée (Goethe, Chateaubriand, Nietzsche, Barrès,

Byron in Venice) Critique, Nov., 1951.
Bolis, W. Francisco de Quevedo y Villegas e i suoi Sueños. (VISIONS). Napoli, 1935.
VICE & Crime: See 177-78, 714 and also Sociology 12 & 702.
Politzer, H. The Indelible Seal of Elisabeth Langgässer. (WANDERING JEW). GR, 27, 1952, 200-09. [The author relates the novel to the tradition of the Wandering Jew. Ahasveric elements can be discovered in James Joyce's Bloom and even in Marcel Proust's Swann.]
WAR & Peace: See also Politics, 12 ff & 702-03.
Anisimov, I. Problema nemeckogo voennogo romana. MG, 14, 1929, 51-57.
Bledsoe, T. Guerra ideológica y militar. Cuatro novelistas contemporáneos de Norteamérica. Cuadernos americanos, 61, 1952, 237-55. [War and ideological conflict in the novels of Hart Stilwell, Mari Sandoz, Irwin Shaw and Howard Fast. Commends their style, treatment, and profound social and human preoccupation.]
Folejewski, Z. Polish Poetry during the Last War. ASEER, 10, 1951.
Oliver, K. The Study of Literature in a World at War. Pacific Spectator, 5, 1951.
Tamarčenko, D. Tema vojny v literature. Leningrad, 1933, 134 p.
Tanner, L. E. WESTMINSTER Abbey in English Literature. Addresses to the English Assoc. London, 1948.
Christoffel, K. Rebe und Wein in Goethes Weltbild. (WINE). Heidelberg, 1948.
Feyereisen, R. Horace et le vin. Diss., Louvain. RBPh, 1949.
Eitrem, S. Der Kranz. Seine religiösmagische Bedeutung bei den Griechen und Römern. (WREATH). Serta Hoffilleriana. Zagreb, 1940.

VII. LITERARY AND SEMI-LITERARY GENRES AND FORMS.

Novel, Short Story, Prose.
General Works.

Aldridge, J. W. (ed). Critiques and Essays on Modern Fiction, 1920-51. New York, 1952. 610 p. [A fine selection of essays emphasizing technical theory, textual criticism, the problems of experience, naturalism, myth, fantasy. Extensive bibliography of general studies, and works on nineteen British and American novelists.]
Aleksandrova, F. Istoričeskij roman i ego kritiki. NoM, 8, 1948.

Alonso, A. Literatura y literatos regionales en España. In: Estudios. Buenos Aires, 1929.
Aseev, N. Ključ sjužeta. PiR, 7, 1925, 67-88.
Boborykin, P. Evropejskij roman v XIX stoletii. St. Petersburg, 1900. See also: Gornfel'd, A. RuB, 1, 1901; Kogan, P. RM, 9, 1900; Spasowicz, W. VE, 10, 1900; Boborykin, P. RM, 8-9, 1901; Kogan, P. RM, 12, 1901.
Benton, T. H. American Regionalism: A Personal History of the Movement. UKCR, 18, 1951.
Boeschenstein, H. The German Novel, 1939-44. Toronto, 1949.
Bonnet, H. Roman et Poésie. Essai sur l'esthétique des genres. Paris, 1951, 243 p. [Distinguishes the objective world and social considerations of the novelist and the self-contained approach of the poet as stemming from distinct temperaments.]
Brickell, H. What Happened to the Short Story. AM, 188, 1951.
Brunetière, F. Le roman naturaliste. Paris, 1883.
Buslaev, F. O značenii sovremennogo romana i ego zadačax. Moscow, 1877.
Curcio Altamar, A. La novela historicoromántica. Bolívar, 15, 1952, 861-90. [Well-documented review of the romantic-historical novel in Colombia; especially good for sources and influences.]
Dobraczyński, J. Niemiecka powieść katolicka. Tygodnik Powszechny, Cracow, 43, 1952. [Gertrude von Le Fort and others.]
Enk, P. J. Antieke "short stories." Groningen, 1949.
García, G. La novela argentina. Buenos Aires, 1952. [A catalog of names and titles, superficial in approach and irresponsible in tone. Cf. Sur, 215-16, 1952.]
Gardiner, H. C., S. J., (ed.) Fifty Years of the American Novel. New York, 1952. 304 p. [The American novel as seen by a number of Catholic critics.]
Gonçalves Rodrigues, A. A novelística estrangeira em versão portuguesa no período préromantico. Bol. da Biblioteca da U. de Coimbra, 20, 1951.
Greenberg, J. H. Swahili Prosody. Journal American Oriental Soc., 67, 1947, 24-30.
Grifcov, B. Teorija romana. Moscow, 1927. 150 p.
Hadas, M. Cultural Survival and the

Origins of Fiction. SAQ, 51, 1952, 253-60. [Ancient Greek romances were written by authors who sought to preserve the memory of a race's once glorious past in later, less happy days.]

Hicks, G. Fiction and Social Criticism. CE, 13, 1952, 355-61. [There has been a falling off in the novel of social criticism; nevertheless, such novels will probably continue to be written. Mr. Hicks sees little evidence of the true novel of manners in America.]

Hoffman, F. J. The Modern Novel in America: 1900-1950. Chicago, 1951. 216 p. [A useful account, critical and historical, with emphasis on ideological and aesthetic tendencies.]

Hoog, A. The Surrealist Novel. FS, 8, 1950.

Jenny, E. Die Heimatkunstbewegung. Basel, 1934.

Jensen, M. Regionalism in America. Madison, (Wis.), 1951.

Kettle, A. An Introduction to the English Novel. vol. 1. London, 1952. 200 p. [Critically discerning analyses of six 19th century novels from Emma to Middlemarch. The essay on Wuthering Heights is best. Not a primer.]

Kirchner, Anna. Zagadnienie opisu w powieśći. Wieś, 21, 1952. [A polemic with the formal attitude attributing to the description purely artistic function. The author stresses the role of description as a constituent element of the realistic picture of the world.]

Koltonovskaja, E. Vozroždenie romana. RM, 5, 1916, 26-41.

Lalou, R. Le roman français depuis 1900. Paris, 1951.

Lydenberg, J. Mobilizing Our Novelists. AQ, 4, 1952, 35-48. [Attacks on contemporary novelists by those who demand patriotic American virtues and praise of the status quo are in the tradition of conservatism and gentility which has favored the innocuous, sentimental, and unreal; against these stronger voices have been raised, from Emerson and Whitman to the present.]

Margouliès, G. Histoire de la littérature chinoise: Prose. Paris, 1949.

Mish, C. C. English Prose Fiction. vol. 1, 1600-40; vol. 2, 1641-60. Charlottesville, Va. 34 & 21 p. [A most useful mimeographed check-list arranged chronologically.]

—————— English Prose Fiction, 1610-1642: a Survey. U. of Michigan Microfilms, No. 2500.

—————— Comparative Popularity of Early Fiction and Drama. N&Q, 197, 1952, 269-70. [Tudor-Stuart fiction had a popularity surprisingly close to that of the drama as reading matter.]

Motyljova, T. O progressivnoj francuzskoj proze. NoM, 5, 1952, 180-201. [A study of French Communist and proletarian writers (including Louis Aragon and others) who combine the traditions of Balzac with Socialist Realism.]

O'Connor, W. The Novel as a Social Document. AQ, 4, 1952, 169-75. [The novel is not to be read as though it were literally a document. It is written in accordance with its peculiar aesthetic conventions. Hence, it should no more be considered a direct report than is a drama or an epic poem.]

Petrow, S. Der historische Roman in der Sowjetliteratur. SL, 1949.

Polonskij, L. Sovremennyj roman v Anglii. VE, 11, 1875, 245-82.

—————— Sovremennyj pol'skij roman. VE, 6-7, 1906.

Pongs, H. Im Umbruch der Zeit. Das Romanschaffen der Gegenwart. Göttingen, 1952, 291 p. [Classifies fiction according to the simplicity of heart and the degree of nihilism it exhibits. The most prominent black sheep are Joyce, Gide, Kafka, Sartre. There is a grey zone (Melville, Conrad, Hesse, Dreiser, Faulkner) while darkness is completely overcome by neo-Catholic French writers and a host of recent German non-entities. Pongs warns especially against the sinister influence of Kafka.]

Ramanujam, M. S. Modern Tamil Prose. Bull. Rama Varma Research Inst., 10, 1942, 20-25.

Reformatskij, A. Opyt analiza novellistićeskoj kompozicii. Moscow, 1922.

For REGIONAL NOVEL see also Realism, 357 & 786-89.

Roland, A. A Rebirth of Values in Contemporary Fiction. Western Humanity Rev., 6, 1952, 59-69. [Neo Thomism (Greene, Mauriac, Waugh), existentialism (Beauvoir, Camus), social consciousness (Farrell, Caldwell, Dos Passos, Steinbeck, Faulkner), and Oriental mysticism (Huxley, Maugham, Isherwood), in the novel.]

Seymour, A. R. The Mexican Novela de Costumbres. Hisp., 8, 1925.

Sipovskij, V. Iz istorii russkogo romana i povesti. St. Petersburg, 1903.

—— Russkaja povest' XVII-XVIII st. St. Petersburg, 1905.

—— Očerki po istorii russkogo romana. 2 parts. St. Petersburg, 1909, 715 p. & 1910, 951 p.

Spies, O. Die türkische Prosaliteratur der Gegenwart. Leipzig, 1943.

Spriel, S. & Vian, B. Un nouveau genre littéraire: la Science-Fiction. Temps Modernes, Oct., 1951.

Stedmond, J. M. English Prose of the Seventeenth Century. Dalhousie Rev., 30, 1950.

Sylvester, G. The Recent Development of the French-Canadian Novel. UTQ, 21, 1951.

Thorp, M. The Motion Picture and the Novel. AQ, 3, 1951.

Tiemann, H. Zur Geschichte des altfranzösischen Prosaromans. RF, 63, 1951.

Tindall, W. Y. The Symbolic Novel. AQ, 3, 1951.

Torres-Rioseco, A. (ed.). La novela iberoamericana. Albuquerque, N. M., 1952. 212 p. [This memorial volume of the Fifth Internat. Congress on Ibero-American Literature contains thirteen outstanding essays by as many authorities on trends, characteristics, types, and theories of the novel from early 19th century to the present.]

Veselovskij, A. Iz istorii romana i povesti. 2 vols. St. Petersburg, 1886-88. (See also: Novye otkrytija v poetičeskoj starine. VE, 12, 1888, 710-42.)

Vinogradov, V. Problema skaza v stilistike. In Poétika. Sbornik statej, 1, Leningrad, 1926, 24-40.

Vossler, K. La novela de los pueblos románicos. Formas literarias en los pueblos románicos. Madrid, 1944.

Wagenknecht, E. Cavalcade of the American Novel. New York, 1952. 575 p. [An encyclopaedic account which contains much useful material, especially its bibliographies. The book is marred by its peculiar emphases and is scarcely the final critical work on its subject.]

Watkins, Alma T. The Origin and Destiny of the Erotic Spanish Novel. MLJ, 35, 1951.

Weisser, H. Die deutsche Novelle im Mittelalter, auf dem Untergrunde der geistigen Strömungen. Freiburg, 1926.

Winther, S. K. The Limits of Region-

alism. Arizona Quart. 8, 1952, 30-36 [Attacks the idea of prose fiction having a regional significance so far as adequate criticism is concerned.]

Zimmermann, F. Zum Stand der Forschung über den Roman in der Antike Gesichtspunkte und Probleme. F&F 26, 1950.

Individual Authors.

Guillaumie, G. J. L. Guez de **BALZAC** e la prose française. Paris, 1927.

Rejsov, B. G. Problema istoričeskogo romana u Balzaka. UZLU FN, 13, 1948

Gallaher, C. The Predecessors of **BECQUER** in the Fantastic Tale. Bull Southeastern Louisiana Coll., 6, 1949

Di Sarra, D. Materiali per uno studio tec nica del romanzo novecentesco: Po větroň di K. **CAPEK**. RS, 1, 1952, 38 66.

Grossman, L. Kompozicija v romani **DOSTOEVSKOGO**. VE, 9, 1916, 121 55 & In: Tvorčestvo Dostoevskogo Moscow, 1928.

—— Iskusstvo romana u Dostoevskogo Svitok (Moscow), 1922, 73-82.

—— Dostoevskij i teatralizacija ro mana. In: Mastera slova. Moscow 1928, 99-104.

Ivanov, V. Dostoevskij i roman-tragedija RM, 5-6, 1911.

Anon. Francuzskoe obščestvo v novom ro mane Gustava Flobera. (**FLAUBERT**) VE, 1-2, 1870.

Borcherdt, H. Der Roman der **GOETHE** zeit. Stuttgart, 1949.

Eixenbaum, B. O. Genri i teorija novelly (**O.HENRY**). Zv, 6, 1925, 291-300.

Patterson, C. I. Charles **LAMB**'s Insigh into the Nature of the Novel. PMLA 67, 1952, 375-82. [Lamb did not car for the moralizing, didactic, or senti mental novels; he preferred fictior which penetrated psychological depth and which pointed toward later de velopments of the art.]

Trahard, P. Prosper **MÉRIMÉE** et l'art d la nouvelle. Paris, 1952.

Castex, P. G. Le conte fantastique er France de **NODIER** à Maupassant Paris, 1951.

Jakubovič, D. Rabota **PUSKINA** nac xudožestvennoj prozoj. In: Rabotɛ klassikov nad prozoj. Leningrad, 1929 7-29.

Lopatto, M. Opyt vvednija v teoriju prozɣ (povesti Puškina). Petrograd, 1918.

Šklovskij, V. Zametki o proze Puškina Moscow, 1937, 144 p.

rane, M. SHAKESPEARE's Prose. Chicago U. P., 1951.

ooth, W. C. The Self-Conscious Narrator in Comic Fiction before Tristram Shandy. PMLA, 67, 1952, 163-85. [An analysis of the use of the narrator,

touching on Cervantes, Marivaux, Scarron, Congreve, Fielding, and STERNE.]

Šklovskij, V. Tristram Šendi Sterna i teorija romana. Petrograd, 1921.

B. THE ORIENT, GREECE, ROME, JUDAISM

II. CLASSICAL ANTIQUITY

Generalities.

ubin, H. Vom Altertum zum Mittelalter. Absterben, Fortleben und Erneuerung. München, 1949.

aldry, B. H. The Classics in the Modern World. Capetown & Oxford U. P., 1949.

ernardini, A. & Righi, G. Il concetto di filologia e di cultura classica nel pensiero moderno. Bari, 1947.

stelrich, J. L'utilisation des classiques gréco-latins. Actes du Congrès de l'Assoc. G. Budé. Grenoble, 1948.

oerlich, E. Antike Stoffe in der Dichtung des 19. Jahrhunderts. Gymn., 54-55, 1943-44.

ighet, G. A. The Classical Tradition: Greek and Roman Influences on Western Literature. New York, 1949. (Cf. CL, 2, 1950).

Iöeg, C. Les études classiques et l'Unesco. BAGB, N.S.8, 1949.

raiker, W. Die Gegenwart der Antike. Gymn., 57, 1950.

ukenheim, L. Contributions à l'histoire de la grammaire grecque, latine et hébraïque à l'époque de la Renaissance. Leiden, 1951.

ida de Malkiel, Maria R. Perduración de la literatura antigua en Occidente. RPh, Nov. 1951.

öfstedt, E. Klassische Dichterreminiszenzen im Mittelalter. C&M, 9, 1947.

ot, F. La fin du monde antique et le début du moyen âge. Paris, 1927.

Iomigliano, A. Ancient History and the Antiquarian. JWI, 13, 1950.

epe, G. La cultura classica e l'uomo moderno. Belfagor, 1949.

ehm, A. Die Internationalität der klassischen Altertumswissenschaft. Gymn, 56, 1949.

eynold, G. de. La formation de l'Europe, I: Qu-est-ce que l'Europe? II: Le monde grec et sa pensée. III: L'hellénisme et le génie européen. IV: L'empire romain. Paris, 1947.

ostagni, A. Classicità e spirito moderno. Torino, 1939.

Rüegg, W. Ein Führer zum Nachleben antiker Autoren in Mittelalter und Renaissance. Museum Helveticum, 1950.

Salis, A. von. Antike und Renaissance. Ueber Nachleben und Weiterwirken der alten in der neueren Kunst. Zürich, 1946.

Schwander, A. M. Das Fortleben des spätantiken Romans in der mittelalterlichen Epik. Diss., Frankfurt, 1945.

Skutsch, K. L. Das Fortleben der Antike in den Dichtern. Berlin, 1947.

Snell, B. (ed.). Antike und Abendland. Beiträge zum Verständnis der Griechen und Römer und ihres Nachlebens. Hamburg, 1947.

Stellwag, H. W. F. The Psychological Significance of the Conception of Antiquity through the Ages and its Consequences for the Evaluation of Greek Culture in Modern Times. Festschrift C. W. Vollgraff. Amsterdam, 1948.

———— De waarde der klassieke vorming, een cultuur-historische, paedagogisch-psychologische en didactische inleiding. Groningen, 1949.

Thompson, A. H. Classical Echoes in Medieval Authors. History, 33, 1948.

Influences upon Individual Nations.

Houghton, H. P. The Study of the Classics in the United States in the Seventeenth, Eighteenth, Nineteenth and Twentieth Centuries. (AMERICA). Humanitas, 2, 1948-49.

Espinosa Polit, A. Los clásicos y la Literatura Ecuatoriana. Quito, 1938.

Brüggemann, W. L. A View of the ENGLISH Editions. Translations and Illustrations of the Ancient Greek and Latin Authors. Stettin, 1797.

Brunner, K. England und die Antike. Ewiger Humanismus, 17 (Innsbruck), 1947.

Rice, G. P. The Classics and the Bible in English Public Address, 1550-1650. CW, 42, 1948-49.

Schoder, R. V. John Bull on Helicon. The State of the Classics in England. CJ, 44, 1949.

Thomson, J. A. K. Classical Influences on English Poetry. London, 1951.

Hutton, J. The Classics in Sixteenth-Century **FRANCE**. CW, 1950.

Nostrand, H. L. Le théâtre antique et à l'antique en France de 1840 à 1900. Genève, 1934.

Scheel, H. L. Die Urteile Sainte-Beuves über das Verhältnis der französischen Literatur zur Antike (1500-1800). Kiel, 1950.

Taille, J. de la. La manière de faire des vers en françois comme en grec et en latin. Paris, 1572.

Benz, R. Wandel des Bildes der Antike in Deutschland im geistesgeschichtlichen Ueberblick. (**GERMANY**). München, 1948.

Frings, T. Antike und Christentum an der Wiege der deutschen Sprache. Abhandl. der sächs. Akad., Phil. hist. Kl., 97. Berlin, 1949.

Gabrieli, F. L'eredità classica del Medievo **MUSULMANE**. Scientia, 84, 1949.

Hammer, S. Traductions **POLONAISES** des classiques grecs et latins. Bull. du Centre Polon. de Rech. Scient. de Paris, 4, 1949.

Buescu, V. Les études classiques en **ROUMANIE** (des origines à 1943). Mélanges Marouzeau, Paris, 1948.

Bilinski, B. Les voies du monde antique vers les terres **SLAVES** à la lumière des témoignages littéraires de l'antiquité. (In Polish). Archeologia, 1 Wrocław, 1947.

Bataillon, M. Influences antiques en Espagne. (**SPAIN**). BH, 24, 1922.

Galiano, F. Les études classiques en Espagne. Actes du Congrès de l'Assoc. G. Budé, Grenoble, 1948.

Grismer, R. L. Introduction to the Classical Influence in the Literatures of Spain and Spanish America. Bol. del Inst. Caro y Cuervo, 5, 1951.

Lida de Malkiel, Maria R. La tradición clásica en España. NRFH, 5, 1951.

Pellicer y Saforcada, J. A. Ensayo de una Biblioteca de Traductores Españoles donde se da noticia de las traducciones que hay en castellano de la Sagrada Escritura, Santos Padres, Filósofos, Historiadores, Médicos, Oradores, Poetas, asi griegos como latinos, y de otros autores que han florecido ante de la invención de la imprenta. Madrid, 1778.

Heinimann, F. Gli studi di filologia classica in **SVIZZERA**. Belfagor, 1948.

Influences upon Individual Authors and Works.

Latimer, J. F. American Classical Scholarship and Caleb **ALEXANDER** TAPhA, 80, 1949.

*Reichenberger, A. **BOSCÁN** and the Classics. CL, 3, 1951.

Cordasco, F. Notes on **BULWER-LYTTON**'s Classical Scholarship. N&Q 196, 1951.

Salis, A. von. Jakob **BURCKHARDT**s Vorlesungen über die Kunst des Altertums. Basel, 1948.

Bogaerts, T. Louis **COUPERUS** en de grieks-romeinse oudheid. Hermeneus 21, 1950.

Marmorale, E. V. Benedetto **CROCE** e l'antichità greco-latina. Giornale ital. di filologia, 1, 1948.

Casella, M. Le guide di **DANTE** nella Divina Commedia. Firenze, 1944.

Hudson-Williams, T. Dante and the Classics. G&R, 1951.

Pézard, A. Le nom grec et le nom latin chez Dante. ACUM, 3, 1948-50.

Renucci, P. Dante, disciple et juge du monde gréco-latin. Diss., Paris. ACUM, 4, 1950-51.

Silvestre, H. Les citations et réminiscences classiques dans l'oeuvre de Rupert de **DEUTZ**. Rev. d'hist. ecclesiastique, 45, 1950.

Pumpjanskij, L. **DOSTOEVSKIJ** i antičnost'. Petrograd, 1921.

Bainton, R. H. The Querela Pacis of **ERASMUS**, Classical and Christian Sources. Archiv f. Reformationsgeschichte, 42, 1951.

Brown, Ruth W. Classical Echoes in the Poetry of Philip **FRENEAU**. CJ, 45, 1949.

Flemming, W. **GOETHE**s Gestaltung des klassischen Theaters. Köln, 1949.

Grumach, E. Goethe und die Antike, eine Sammlung. 2 vols. Berlin, 1949.

Reinhardt, K. Goethe and Antiquity: The Helen Episode of Goethe's Faust. In: Goethe & the Modern Age ed. by A. Bergstraesser. Chicago, 1950.

Svoboda, K. **HALEK** a Antika. SV, 1950, 100-03.

Jaureguizar, E. San **JERONIMO** y los clásicos. Humanidades, 1, 1949.

Keyl, F. Samuel **JOHNSON** und die Antike. Diss., Erlangen, 1945.

Schelling, F. E. Ben **JONSON** and the Classical School. PMLA, 13, 1898.

Pritchard, J. P. A Glance at **LOWELL**'s Classical Reading. AL, 21, 1950.

Kleiner, G. Die Begegnungen **MICHEL-ANGELO**s mit der Antike. Berlin, 1949.

Pianko, G. **MICKIEWICZ** et le monde antique. Me, 1947.

Morenz, S. Die Zauberflöte im Lichte der Altertumwissenschaft. (**MOZART**). F&F, 21-23, 1947.

Semerano, G. La Lirica Greca e Latina del **POLIZIANO**: Epigrammata. Convivium, 1951.

Jakubovič, D. Antičnost' v tvorčestve **PUŠKINA**. (Unfinished). VPD, 6, 1941, 92-159.

Weinreich, O. Franz **SCHUBERT**s Antikenlieder. Bodenseebuch (Ulm), 1943.

Thompson, W. L. Classical Echoes in **SEWALL**'s Diaries, 1674-1729. NEQ, 24, 1951.

Boas, F. **SHAKESPEARE**'s Handling of Classical Legend and History. In: Queen Elizabeth in Drama and Related Essays. London, 1950.

Leon, H. J. Classical Sources for the Garden Scene in Richard II. PQ, 29, 1950.

Wickert, Maria. Antikes Gedankengut in Shakespeares Julius Caesar. JbShG, 82-83, 1946-47.

Miščenko, F. Antičnye motivy v proizvedenijax Genrika Šenkevica. (**SIENKIEWICZ**). RM, 8, 1897, 62-85.

Manning, C. A. Classical Influence on the **SLOVO**. Mem. Am. Folklore Soc., 42, 1949.

Jahn, W. Echa klasyczne w utworach Juliusza **SLOWACKI**ego. Me, 3-4, 1950, 158-65.

Custis, A. A. Hippolyte **TAINE** and the Classical Genius. U. of Calif. P., 1951.

García Calvo, A. Unas notas sobre la adaptación de los metros clásicos por D. Esteban **VILLEGAS**. Bol. Bibl. Menéndez Pelayo, 26, 1950.

IV. LATIN CONTRIBUTIONS.

General Latin Influences, Medieval and Neo-Latin Literature, Quarrel of the Ancients and the Moderns.

Alfonsi, L. Forme e caratteri della poesia latina moderna. Paideia, 1947.

Buechner, K. & Hofmann, J. B. Lateinische Literatur und Sprache in der Forschung seit 1937. Bern, 1951.

Bouhours, Le Père. Pensées ingénieuses des Anciens et des Modernes. Paris, 1693.

Pain, A. Mediaeval and Renaissance Latin

Translations   a n d   Commentaries. BAGB, 7, 1949.

Faria, E. O latim e a cultura contemporanea. Rio de Janeiro, 1941.

Franceschini, E. Lineamenti di una storia letteraria del medioevo latino. Milano, 1944.

Ghellinck, J. de. L'essor de la littérature latine au XII. siècle. Bruxelles, 1946.

Goossens, R. L'oeuvre de Rome. La contribution du génie romain à la formation et à l'éducation de l'Europe. Paris, 1944.

Groult, P. La formation des langues romanes. Tournai & Paris, 1947.

Hélin, M. A History of Medieval Latin Literature. New York, 1949.

Keller, A. C. Ancients and Moderns in the Early Seventeenth Century. MLQ, 11, 1950.

Klauser, T. Der Uebergang der römischen Kirche von der griechischen zur lateinischen Liturgiesprache. Festschrift G. Mercati. Città del Vaticano, 1946.

Marouzeau, L. Les études latines dans le monde: en Allemagne, en Pologne, aux Etats-Unis, en Colombie. REL, 1949.

Marshall, M. H. Boethius' Definition of persona and Mediaeval Understanding of the Roman Theater. Speculum, 25, 1950.

Mohrmann, Christine. How Latin Became the Language of Early Christendom. Studies, Sept., 1951.

Salvatore, A. Attualità e modernità dei poeti latini. Caserta, 1947.

Schoell, F. L. Une discipline négligée; la littérature latine de la Renaissance. Lettres d'humanité, 7, (Paris), 1948.

Wencélius, L. La Querelle des Anciens et des Modernes et l'Humanisme. Le XVIIe Siècle, 9, 1951.

Winbolt, S. E. **BRITAIN** under the Romans. New York, 1945.

Rivas Sacconi, J. M. El latin en **COLOMBIA**. Bosquejo histórico del humanismo colombiano. Caro y Cuervo, Bogotá, 1949.

Barrière, P. La littérature française de langue latine. (**FRANCE**). Lettres d'humanité, 6 (Paris), 1947.

Müller, O. Das lateinische Einschiebsel in der französischen Literatur des Mittelalters. Zürich, 1919, 258 p.

Pope, M. K. From Latin to Modern French. Manchester, 1952.

Betz, W. Der Einfluss des lateinischen Sprachschatzes auf den althochdeutschen. (**GERMANY**).Heidelberg, 1936.

Accame, S. Il dominio romano in **GRECIA**

dalla Guerra arcaica ad Augusto. Roma, 1946.

Lankes, I. Das Geschichtsbild der römischen Antike und der Begriff der Virtus bei den Florentiner politischen Humanisten des 14.-16. Jahrhunderts. (ITALY). Diss., Freiburg, 1948.

Thorndike, L. Latin and Italian Grammar in the Year 1486. RR, 41, 1950.

Menéndez y Pelayo, M. Bibliografía hispano-latina clásica. Códices, ediciones, comentarios, traducciones, estudios críticos, imitaciones y reminiscencias; influencia de cada uno de los clásicos latinos en la literatura española. (SPAIN). Madrid, 1902 ff. and 1950.

Parducci, A. I drammi spagnuoli che s'inspirano alla Storia di Roma. In: Italia e Spagna. Saggi sui rapporti tra le due civiltà. Firenze, 1941.

Webber, E. J. Origins of the Spanish Theater as Related to the Classical Latin Drama. Diss., U. of California, 1949.

Roman Authors.

Daly, W. L. The Greek Version of CAESAR's Gallic War. TAPhA, 77, 1946.

Martellotti, G. Petrarca e Cesare. Annali Scuola Normale Superiore di Pisa, 16, 1947.

Whiting, B. J. Notes on the Fragmentary Fairfax Version of the Disticha CATOnis. Mediaeval Studies, 10 (Toronto), 1948.

Mabbott, T. O. Walt Whitman and CATULLUS. N&Q, 196, 1951.

Delhaye, P. Deux adaptations du De amicitia de CICÉRON au XII. siècle. Recherches de théologie ancienne et médiévale, 1948.

Ferrara, O. Ciceron y Mirabeau. La moral de dos grandes oradores. Madrid, 1949.

Klingner, F. Cicero als Erwecker Petrarkas. Gymnasium, 57, 1950.

Roessel, S. Des Johannes Sambucus Schrift De imitatione a Cicerone petenda und des Verfassers Stellung im Streite der Ciceronianer und Anticiceronianer. Diss., Graz, 1944.

Baron, H. Aulius GELLIUS in the Renaissance and a Manuscript from the School of Guarino. SP, 48, 1951, 107-25.

—— The Scribe of the Newberry Gellius of 1445: A Supplementary Note. SP, 49, 1952, 248-50.

Diez Canedo, E. HORACIO en México. Rev. de Lit. Méxicana, 1, 1940.

Fischer, W. Alexander Pope und Horaz Diss., Hamburg, 1948.

Henriquez Ureña, P. Horacio en México RFH, 6, 1944.

Mele, E. Una reminiscenza oraziana nell Oráculo Manual del Gracián. Marzocco, 37, 1932.

Menéndez y Pelayo, M. Traductores castellanos de Horacio. Revista Europea 9, 1877.

—— La poesía horaciana en Castilla Ibid., 10, 1877.

—— Adiciones a Horacio en España Solaces bibliograficos. Madrid, 1926.

Riba, C. Horaci en les literatures iberiques Revista, 21 (Barcelona), 1935.

Riber, L. Un poète horatien. (Manuel de Cabanyes y de Ballester). In: La mission de l'Espagne. Paris, 1941, 288-95

Staedler, E. Horaz-Analekten bei Rabelais. Gymnasium, 56, 1949.

Trowbridge, H. Dryden and Horace TAPhA, 77, 1946.

Weinreich, O. Horatius christianus. Universitas (Stuttgart), 2, 1947.

Malein, A. JUVENAL v russkoj literature. Festschrift Orlov, Leningrad 1934, 227-32.

Rusev, R. Johnson i Juvenal. Annuaire de l'U. de Sofia. Fac. Hist. philol., 43 1946-47.

Sanford, E. M. Renaissance Commentarie on Juvenal. TAPhA, 1948.

Engstrom, A. G. LUCRETIUS and Micromégas. (Voltaire). Festschrift W. M Dey. Chapel Hill, 1951.

Nicolosi, I. L'influsso di Lucrezio su Lat tanzio. Raccolta di Stud. di Lett. Crist ant. (Catania), 1946.

Tremoli, P. Mario Rapisardi traduttore d Lucrezio. Ann. Triest., 4, 1949.

Ghisalberti, F. Mediaeval Biographies of OVID. JWI, 9, 1946.

Jakubovič, D. K stixotvoreniju Taitsj peščora. (Pushkin). Gedenkschrif Vengerov. Moscow, 1922, 282-94.

Malein, A. Puškin i Ovidij. PiS, 23-24 1916, 23-66.

Castorina, E. Ancora su PETRONIO e Novelli. Giornale ital. di filologia, 2 1949.

MacKendrick, P. L. The Great Gatsby an Trimalchio. (Fitzgerald). CJ, 45 1951.

Herrmann, L. Autour des fables d PHEDRE. Latomus, 1948.

Agnew, M. E. Lessing's Critical Opinion o the Captivi of PLAUTUS. CW, 39 1945.

Bebenkowna, M. Plautus, Terentius i Molière. Me, 3, 1948.

Mariotti, S. Sul testo e le fonti comiche della Chrysis di E. S. Piccolomini. Annali Scuola normale superiore di Pisa, 15, 1946.

Prete, S. Plautus und Terenz in den Schriften des Francesco Petrarca. Gymnasium, 57, 1950.

Stevens, C. H. Study of the Menaechmi Theme in Spanish Literature. New York, 1939.

Becatti, G. PLINIO e l'Aretino. Arti Figurative, 2 (Roma), 1946.

Huerga, A. Plinio en la ascética de Fray Luis de Granada. Helmantica, 1, 1950.

Alfonsi, L. Biografie umanistiche di PROPERZIO. RIL, 79, 1945-46.

Robathan, D. M. Cristoforo Landino's Use of Propertius. TAPhA, 78, 1947.

Merone, E. Dante, RUTILIO e le città che muiono. Giornale ital. di filologia, 3, 1950.

Bolaffi, E. SALLUSTIO e la sua fortuna nei secoli. Roma, 1949.

Brummer, R. Auf den Spuren des Philosophen SENECA in den romanischen Literaturen des Mittelalters und der Frührenaissance. Festschrift, F. Neubert. Berlin, 1948.

Fontán, A. Algunos códices de Séneca en bibliotecas españolas y su lugar en la tradición de los Diálogos. Emerita, 17, 1949.

Préchac, F. Sénèque lecture royale sous le dernier Valois. Lettres d'humanité, Suppl. à BAGB, 1950.

Reserbat, P. Sénèque et les Pères du IV. siècle. REL, 1948.

Vooys, C. J. Renatus Descartes over Seneca. Hermeneus, 22, 1950.

Williamson, G. The Senecan Amble: A Study in Prose Form from Bacon to Collier. London, 1951.

Pézard, A. Rencontres de Dante et de STACE. Mélanges A. Renaudet. BHR, 14, 1952.

Amusin, I. Puškin i TACIT. VPD, 6, 1941, 160-80.

Castiglione, G. Tacito e Cicerone commentati dal Pinelli. Aevum, 1948.

Franz, L. 450 Jahre Forschung über die Germania des Tacitus. Anzeiger f.d. Altertumswissenschaft (Wien), 3, 1950.

Gippius, V. Aleksandr I v puškinskix zamečanijax na Annaly Tacita. VPD, 6, 1941, 181-82.

Arias, A. VIRGILIO en castellano. Hisp., 18, 1935.

Caro, M. A. Virgilio en España. Repertorio Colombiano, 3 (Bogotá), 1879.

Gerhardt, M. I. Les premières traductions des Bucoliques. NP, 1949.

Gómez Restrepo, A. Virgilio en la América latina. Colombo, 22 (Roma), 1930.

Gutierrez, J. M. Virgilio en América. Revista del Rio de la Plata, 1, II, 1875.

Leo, U. The Unfinished Convivo and Dante's Rereading of the Aeneid. Mediaeval Studies (Toronto), 13, 1951.

Llobera, J. Virgilio y los jesuitas españoles. RyF, 92, 1930.

MacKail, J. W. Virgilio y su influencia en el mundo de hoy. Buenos Aires, 1946.

MacVay, A. P. Dante's Strange Treatment of Vergil. CJ, 43, 1948.

Menéndez y Pelayo, M. Traductores españoles de la Eneida. Apuntes bibliográficos. In: Virgilio, La Eneida. Traducción de Miguel Antonio Caro. vol. 2. Madrid, 1879.

O'Brien, J. Gide's Nourritures Terrestres and Vergil's Bucolics. RR, 43, 1952, 117-25. [A convincing survey of Gide's contact with Vergil's pastoral poetry with reasons for this penchant, the influence of the latter on certain characters, on the general theme, form and stylistic devices.]

Rodríguez Moñino, A. R. Virgilio en España. Ensayo bibliográfico sobre las traducciones de Diego López. Badajoz, 1930.

Influences upon Individual Authors.

Giusso, L. G. BRUNO e la poesia latina. Giornale della Sera (Roma), 8, II, 1948.

Hoonhout, P. Het latijn van Thomas van CELANO, Biograaf van Sint Franciscus. Amsterdam, 1947.

Espinosa Polit, A. Un latinismo en el Quijote. (CERVANTES). RFE, 32, 1948.

Nauwelaerts, M. ERASMUS en de latijnse school van 's-Hertogenbosch. Miscellanea P. J. M. van Gils. Maastricht, 1950.

Mele, E. Las poesías latinas de GARCILASSO de la Vega y su permanencia en Italia. BH, 25, 1924.

Maxwell, J. C. Charles GILDON and the Quarrel of the Ancients and Moderns. RES, N.S., 1, 1950.

Feldman, A. B. GNAPHAEUS in England. MLN, 1952.

Fraenkel, E. The Latin Studies of **HER-MANN** and Wilamowitz. Journal of Roman Studies, 1948.

Mossner, E. C. **HUME** and The Ancient-Modern Controversy, 1725-52: A Study in Creative Scepticism. Texas Studies in English, 28, 1949.

Starnes, D. T. Richard **HUOET**'s Abcedarium: A Study in English-Latin Lexicography. SP, 48, 1951.

Moore, J. R. Dr. **JOHNSON** and Roman History. HLQ, 12, 1949.

Snijders, C. Het latijn der brieven van **LUPUS** van Ferrières, middeleeuws humanist. Amsterdam, 1943.

Verrua, P. Cultori della poesia latina in Ispagna durante il regno di Fernando il Cattolico: note desunte dalle opere di Lucio **MARINEO SICULO**. Adria, 1906.

Carvalho, A. de. Os estudos latinos de Clément **MAROT**. Humanitas, 1, 1947.

Ekfelt, F. E. Latinate Diction in **MILTON**'s English Prose. PQ, 28, 1949.

Oliver, R. P. New Fragments of Latin Authors in **PEROTTI**'s Cornucopiae. TAPhA, 78, 1947.

Paoli, U. E. Il latino del **PETRARCA** e gl'inizi dell'Umanesimo. In: Pensée humaniste et tradition chrétienne (ed. H. Bédarida). Paris, 1950.

Delvaux, G. Les sources de **PLUTARQUE** dans les vies parallèles des Romains. Diss., Bruxelles. RBPh, 25, 1946-47.

Spitzer, L. Zu **PONTANS Latinität**. RF, 63, 1951.

Bar, F. Les épîtres latines de **RAOUL LE TOURTIER** (1065-1114). Paris, 1937.

Atherton, J. S. **SHAKESPEARE**'s Latin, Two Notes. N&Q, 196, 1951.

Meinck, C. Über das örtliche und zeitliche Kolorit in Shakespeares Römerdramen und Ben Jonsons Catilina. Halle, 1910.

Vitale, M. Latinismi e Lombardismi nella polemica cinquecentesca intorno a Gerusalemme Liberata di T. **TASSO**. Convivium, 1950.

Ciaceri, E. La storia romana nel pensiero di Giambattista **VICO**. Rendiconti dell'Accad. d'Italia, 4, 1942-43.

Moll, W. H. Ueber den Einfluss der lateinischen Vagantendichtung auf die Lyrik **WALTERS** von der Vogelweide und die Epigonen im 13. Jahrhundert. Diss., Amsterdam, 1929.

C. ASPECTS OF WESTERN CULTURE

II. LITERARY CURRENTS.

Classicism, Ancient and Modern, Enlightenment, Rationalism, Rococo.

Adams, H. H. & Hathaway, B. (eds). Dramatic Essays of the Neoclassical Age. Columbia U. P., 1950.

Alonso, A. E lideal clásico en la forma poética. Sur, 19, 1950.

Borgerhoff, E. B. O. The Freedom of French Classicism. Princeton U. P., 1950.

Bredvold, L. I. The Rise of English Classicism: Study in Methodology. CL, 2, 1950.

Cassirer, E. The Philosophy of the Enlightenment. Princeton U. P., 1951.

Cornu, A. Rationalisme, classicisme, romantisme allemands. Europe, May, 1948.

Eliot, T. S. What is a Classic? London, 1945.

Hatzfeld, H. Rokoko als literarischer Epochenstil. SP, 33, 1938.

Hornberger, T. The Enlightenment and the American Dream. In: The American Writer and the European Tradition, ed. by Denny & Gilman. Minneapolis, 1950.

Orlov, V. Russkie prosvetiteli 1790-1800-x godov. Moscow, 1950.

Pach, W. Art Must Be Classical. Va. Quart. Rev., 27, 1951.

Pérez Delgado, R. El clasicismo en la literatura española. Leonardo 1 (Barcelona), 1945.

Peyre, H. The Influence of Eighteenth-Century Ideas on the French Revolution. JHI, 10, 1949.

Wolff, H. W. Die Weltanschauung der deutschen Aufklärung in geschichtlicher Entwicklung. Bern, 1949.

Žirmunskij, V. O poézii klassičeskoj i romantičeskoj. In: Voprosy teorii literatury. Leningrad, 1928.

Gautier, R. Deux aspects du style classique: **BOSSUET**, Voltaire. La Rochelle, 1936.

Peltz, Catharine. Thomas **CAMPION**, An Elizabethan Neo-Classicist. MLQ, 11, 1949.

Martins, F. O classicismo do Caristos de Eugenio de **CASTRO**. Humanitas, 2, 1948-49.

Blasi, F. Dal classicismo al secentismo in Ispagna: **GARCILASSO,** Herrera, Góngora. L'Aquila, 1929.

Espino Gutierrez, G. El clasicismo y el romanticismo en la obra de **LOPE DE VEGA.** Bol. Bibl. Menéndez Pelayo, 25, 1949.

Fabre, J. Stanislas-Auguste **PONIATOW-SKI** et l'Europe des lumières. Etude de cosmopolitisme littéraire. Strasbourg, 1952. (Cf. RLC, 1952).

Marzot, G. Un classico della Controriforma: Paolo **SEGNERI.** Palermo, 1950.

Beach, J. W. Rococo: the Poetry of Sacheverell **SITWELL.** Poetry, 74, 1949.

Romanticism.

Pre-Romanticism, Storm and Stress and the Nineteenth Century in General.

General Works.

Auden, W. H. The Enchafèd Flood: Three Critical Essays on the Romantic Spirit. New York, 1950.

Bach, R. Tragik und Grösse der deutschen Romantik. München, 1938.

―――― Deutsche Romantik: ein geistesgeschichtlicher Umriss. Hamburg, 1948.

Barthe, F. de la. Razyskanija v oblasti romantičeskoj poétiki i stilja. Vol. 1: Romantičeskaja poétika vo Francii. Kiev, 1908. 520 p.

Becher, H. S. J. Die Romantik als totale Bewegung. Scholastik, 20-24, 1949.

Béguin, A. L'âme romantique et le rêve: essai sur le romantisme allemand et la poésie française. 2 vols. Marseilles, 1937.

Benda, J. Trois idées romantiques. Paris, 1948.

Benz, R. Lebenswelt der Romantik: Dokumente romantischen Denkens und Seins. München, 1948.

Bochet, H. Le romantisme à Genève. Genève, 1930.

Bowra, C. M. The Romantic Imagination. Harvard U. P., 1949.

Bray, R. Chronologie du romantisme. Paris, 1932.

Brunschwig, H. La crise de l'Etat Prussien à la fin du 18 siècle et la genèse de la mentalité romantique. Paris, 1947.

Camarinha da Silva, M. Sobre a poesia romântica no Brasil. RIA, 14, 1948.

Capek, J. B. Preromantismus nebo Klasicismus? SV, 1948-49, 94-102.

Castro, A. Les grands romantiques espagnols. Paris, n.d.

Charlier, G. Le mouvement romantique en Belgique (1815-50). Liége, 1949.

Clark, M. U. The Cult of Enthusiasm in French Romanticism. Washington, 1950.

Elkuss, S. Zur Beurteilung der Romantik und zur Kritik ihrer Erforschung. Diss., Strassburg. München, 1918.

Galic, L. O religioznoj romantike. RM, 4, 1908, 11-23.

Gandia, E. de. Orígenes del romanticismo y otros ensayos. Buenos Aires, 1946.

Gautier, T. Histoire du romantisme suivie de notices romantiques et d'une étude sur la poésie française (1830-68). Paris, 1927.

Gilman, M. Revival and Revolution in English and French Romantic Poetry. FS, 6, 1950.

Gurevič, L. Nemeckij romantizm i simvolizm našego vremeni. RM, 4, 1914, 102-10.

Havens, R. D. Discontinuity in Literary Development: The Case of English Romanticism. SP, 47, 1950.

Haym, R. Die romantische Schule. Berlin, 1920.

Huch, Ricarda. Die Romantik. Leipzig, 1920.

Huger, Sister M. Die Romantiker in Wien. MDU, 41, 1949.

Hulliger, E. Studien zur Romantik in der Literatur der deutschen Schweiz. Bern, 1941.

Jean-Nesmy, Dom C. Le Romantisme n'existe pas. Témoignages, 20, 1948.

Joachimi, M. Die Weltanschauung der deutschen Romantik. Jena, 1905.

Kassner, R. Das neunzehnte Jahrhundert: Ausdruck und Grösse. Zürich, 1947.

*Kaufman, P. Defining Romanticism: A Survey and a Program. MLN, 40, 1925.

Kogan, P. Romantizm i realizm v evropejskoj literature XIX v. Moscow, 1919.

Lion, F. Romantik als deutsches Schicksal. Stuttgart, 1947.

*Lovejoy, A. O. On the Discrimination of Romanticisms. PMLA, 39, 1924.

Marsan, J. La bataille romantique. Paris, 1931.

Nuffel, R. O. J. van. Il romanticismo e le sue teorie drammatiche. RBPh, 26, 1948.

Ortiz, R. Romantismul italian şi spaniol. Analete Universitatii Libere. Bucarest, 1932.

Pascal, R. The Sturm und Drang Movement. MLR, 1952.

Peckham, M. Toward a Theory of Romanticism. PMLA, 66, 1951.

Peers, E. A. A Short History of the Romantic Movement in Spain. Liverpool, 1949.

Pellissier, G. Le mouvement littéraire au XIXe siècle. Paris, 1890.

Pottle, F. A. The Romantic Imagination Revisited. Yale Rev., 29, 1949.

Raysor, T. M. (ed.). The English Romantic Poets. A Review of Research. New York, 1950. Cf. CL, 4, 1952.

Rehm, W. Experimentum Medietatis: Studien zur Geistes- und Literaturgeschichte des 19. Jahrhunderts. München, 1947.

Rožkov, P. Nužna li nam romantika? Moscow, 1934, 120 p.

Rupprecht, E. Der Aufbruch der romantischen Bewegung. München, 1948.

Sakulin, P. Romantizm i neo-romantizm. VE, 3, 1915, 148-62.

Shimada, K. Before and After Romantic Movements. In: An Introduction to Comparative Literature ed. by Nakajima & Nakano. Tokyo, 1951.

Staiger, E. Deutsche Romantik in Dichtung und Musik. Trivium, 5, 1947.

Steinbüchel, T. (ed.) Romantik: ein Zyklus Tübinger Vorlesungen. Tübingen, 1948.

Strich, F. Europe and the Romantic Movement. GLL, N.S., 2, 1948-49.

Walzel, O. Deutsche Romantik. 2 vols. Leipzig, 1918.

Willoughby, L. A. Modern Romantic Criticism. Festschrift Strich. Bern, 1952.

Zea, L. Del romanticismo al positivismo: dos etapas de pensamiento en Hispanoamérica. México, 1949.

Individual Authors.

Lipmann, H. Georg BÜCHNER und die Romantik. München, 1923.

Herescu, N. I. CATULLO o primero romantico. Coimbra, 1948.

Perus, J. CHATEAUBRIAND et le romantisme. La Pensée, 22, 1949.

Rintelen, F. J. von. Romanticismo, clasicismo y la concepción goetheana del espíritu. GOETHE Festschrift Facultad de Filosofia y Letras, Buenos-Aires, 1949.

Salfinger, T. GOTTHELF und die Romantik. Basel, 1945.

Bland, D. S. GRAY and the Spirit of Romanticism. Cambridge Journal, 2, 1948-49.

Žirmunskij, V. Geijne i romantizm. (HEINE). RM, 5, 1914, 90-116.

Menton, S. HEREDIA, introductor del romanticismo. RIA, 15, 1949.

Thomese, I. A. Romantik und Neuromantik, mit besonderer Berücksichtigung Hugo von HOFMANNSTHALS. Den Haag, 1923.

Wall, B. MANZONI's Novel and His Ideas. Dublin Review, 1952, 28-40. [This author meant by Romanticism an attitude close to what might now be called Realism.]

Gastinel, P. Le romantisme d'Alfred de MUSSET. Paris, 1933.

Held, Mariette. Charles NODIER et le romantisme. Berne-Bienne, 1949.

Žirmunskij, V. Roman o golubom cvetke. (NOVALIS). RM, 3, 1915, 94-101.

Mejlax, B. PUSKIN i russkij romantizm. Moscow, 1937. 296 p.

Seillière, E. SAINTE-BEUVE agent, juge et complice de l'évolution romantique. Paris, 1921.

Borcherdt, H. H. (ed.) SCHILLER und die Romantiker. Briefe und Dokumente. Stuttgart, 1948.

Kiesling, A. Richard WAGNER und die Romantik. Leipzig, 1916.

Veselovskij, A. Poètika romantikov i poètika žukovskogo. In: V. A. ZUKOVSKIJ. Petrograd, 1918.

Later Literary Currents.

Art for Art, Young Europe, Biedermeier, Realism, Naturalism, Symbolism, Impressionism, Expressionism, Modernism, Surrealism, Futurism, Existentialism, etc.

General Works.

Aderaldo Castello, J. Apontamentos para a história do simbolismo no Brasil. Rev. de U. de São Paulo, 1950.

Ahnebrink, L. The Beginning of Naturalism in American Fiction . . . with special Reference to Some European Influence. Harvard U. P., 1950.

Asmus, V. Filosofija i éstetika russkogo simvolizma. LN, 27-28, 1937, 1-53.

Baker, J. E. (ed.). The Reinterpretation of Victorian Literature. Princeton, 1950.

Barré, A. Le Symbolisme. Paris, 1911.

Beck, M. Existentialism versus Naturalism and Idealism. SAQ, 47, 1948.

Becker, G. J. Realism: An Essay in Definition. MLQ, 10, 1949, 184-97.

Belyj, A. Simvolizm. Moscow, 1910.

Berdjaev, N. Dekadentstvo i mističeskij realizm. RM, 6, 1907, 114-23.

Berkovskij, N. Realizm buržuaznogo obščestva i voprosy istorii literatury. Zapadnyj sbornik, 1. Moscow, 1937.

Bietak, W. Das Lebensgefühl des Biedermeier in der österreichischen Dichtung. Wien, 1931.

Blok, A. O sovremennom sostojanii russkogo simvolizma. A, 8, 1910, 21-30.

Bourbousson, E. La littérature existentialiste et son influence. FR, 23, 1950.

Bouvier, E. La bataille réaliste (1844-57). Paris, 1913.

Brjusov, V. Novye tečenija v russkoj poèzii. Futuristy. Akmeizm. Eklektiki. RM, 3, 4, 8, 1913.

——— Zdravogo smysla tartarary. Dialog o futurizme. RM, 3, 1914, 83-95.

Brodskij, N., L'vov-Rogačevskij, V. & Sidorov, N. Literaturnye manifesty ot simvolizma k Oktjabrju. Sbornik materialov. Moscow, 1929. 301 p.

Brunetière, F. Le roman naturaliste. Paris, 1883. 370 p.

Buckley, J. H. The Victorian Temper: A Study in Literary Culture. Harvard U. P., 1951.

Carter, E. The Meaning of, and in, Realism. Antioch Rev., 12, 1952, 78-94. [Realism defended as a method in prose fiction valid as a way of arriving at "meaning"; antirational or nonreal methods attacked.]

Černov, V. Modernizm v russkoj poèzii. VE, 11-12, 1910.

Charpentier, J. L. Sovremennye napravlenija literatury, iskusstva i filosofii vo Francii. A, 7, 1910, 34-56.

——— Le Symbolisme. Paris, 1927.

Cornell, K. The Symbolist Movement. Yale U. P., 1951.

Čudovskij, V. Futurizm i prošloe. A, 6, 1913, 25-30.

Desnickij, V. (ed.) Francuzskij realističeskij roman XIX veka. Moscow, 1932. 234 p. [Stendhal, Balzac, Flaubert, Goncourt, Zola, Daudet.]

Desprez, L. L'évolution naturaliste. Paris, 1884. 374 p.

Dike, D. A. Notes on Local Color and Its Relation to Realism. CE, 14, 1952, 81-88. [Analytical definition of local color and an inquiry into its connection with realism, naturalism, and romanticism. Concludes that local color is distinct from realism in its ignoring of the great continuity of human experience.]

Dinar, A. La croisade symboliste. Paris, 1943.

Dukor, I. Problemy dramaturgii simvolizma. LN, 27-28, 1937, 106-66.

Evlaxov, A. Realizm ili irrealizm? Očerki po teorii xudožestvennogo tvorčestva. 2 vols. Warsaw, 1914, 492, 621 p.

Feigl, H. Naturalism and Humanism. AQ, 1, 1949.

Ferrández Alborz, F. Tres precursores del nuevo realismo literario hispanoamericano. Cuadernos Americanos, 66, 1952, 267-84. [The Argentine Sarmiento, the Uruguayan Acevedo Díaz, and the Ecuadoran Luis A. Martínez.]

Foulquié, P. L'existentialisme. Paris, 1952.

Ghil, R. Sovremennye napravlenija literatury, iskusstva i filosofii vo Francii. A, 6, 1910, 5-24.

Gofman, V. Jazyk simvolistov. LN, 27-28, 1937, 54-105.

Gol'cev, V. Neskol'ko zamečanij o naturalizme v iskusstve. RM, 6, 1894, 53-59.

Gornfeld, A. Novoe iskusstvo i ego ideologija. Boevye otkliki na mirnye temy. Leningrad, 1924, 155-72.

Goškin, G. D. Da razrabotame problemite na socialističeskija realizm v B'lgarskata literatura. FM, 7, 1951, 75-92.

Grünberg, S. Ekspressionizm i posleekspressionizm v germanskoj sovremennoj literature. NoM, 1, 1927, 225-29.

Gumilev, N. Nasledie simvolizma i akmeizm. A, 1, 1913, 42-45.

Huntley, F. L. Zen and the Imagist Poets of Japan. CL, 4, 1952.

Ivanov, V. Zavety simvolizma. A ,8, 1910, 5-20.

Kahn, G. Symbolistes et décadents. Paris, 1902.

——— Les origines du symbolisme. Paris, 1936.

Kallas, V. Na zare našego literaturnogo realizma. RM, 4, 1904, 69-88.

Kluckhohn, P. Biedermeier als literarische Epochenbezeichnung. DVLG, 13, 1935.

Kuhn, H. Encounter with Nothingness: An Essay on Existentialism. Humanist Library, 11. Hinsdale (Ill.), 1949.

Lacher, W. Le réalisme dans le roman contemporain. Genève, 1940. 330 p. [Proust, Gide, Mauriac, Duhamel, Romains, Ramuz, Chateaubriant, Colette, Giraudoux, Bernanos, etc.]

*Levin, H. et al. A Symposium on Realism (in England, France, Germany, Russia and America). CL, 3, 1951.

Lukács, G. Studies in European Realism. London, 1950.

——— Deutsche Realisten des neunzehnten Jahrhunderts. Bern, 1951. 308 p. [The theme uniting individual studies on Kleist, Eichendorff, Keller, Raabe, Fontane, et al. is the contrast between the literary continuity in France and

Russia and its lack (due to different political conditions) in Germany.]

Lunačarskij, A. Neskol'ko slov o germanskom ekspressionizme. Žizn', 1, 1922, 76-82.

——— et al. Iz istorii realizma XIX veka na Zapade. Moscow, 1934, 295 p. [Balzac, Flaubert, Maupassant, Dickens.]

MacAndrew, R. M. Exotic Naturalism in Spanish Poetry. MLR, 26, 1931.

Malaxov, S. Poèzija socialističeskogo realizma. In: Bor'ba za stil'. Sbornik statej, 116-76. Leningrad, 1934.

Manning, C. Socialist Realism and the American Success Novel. SAQ, 48, 1949, 213-19.

Martino, P. Le naturalisme français. Paris, 1945.

Markiewicz, H. O realizmie w literaturze. Szkic informacyjny. Życie literackie, 2-4. [The main features of realism exemplified in novels are: the prime importance of social factors, especially the class position of the hero; the confrontation of the thoughts and experiences of the characters with their objective social function; the social "typicalness," but at the same time concreteness, of the characters and conflicts.]

Millioud, M. Les théories de l'école naturaliste. Lausanne, 1886.

Mokievskij, P. Teorija poznanija filosofov i d'javol'skij splav simvolistov. RuB, 11, 1910, 112-28.

Mokul'skij, S. Francuzkij klassičeskij realism. Zapadnyj sbornik. 1 (ed. by V. Žirmunskij). Moscow, 1937.

Moser, Ruth. L'impressionisme français. Peinture. Littérature. Musique. Genève, 1951.

Osorgin, M. Ital'janskij futurizm. VE, 2, 1914, 339-57.

Piksanov, N. (ed.). Socialističeskij realizm. Bibliografičeskij ukazatel'. Leningrad, 1934. 75 p.

Poggioli, R. Due saggi sul realismo russo. Inventario, 4, 1952, 27-51. [Two essays—on Russian "classical" realism and on Dostoevsky and Western realism—which have appeared previously, the former in CL, 3 (1951), the latter in KR, 14 (1952). They gain from this juxtaposition.]

Red'ko, A. U podnožija afrikanskogo idola. Simvolizm. Akmeizm. Ego-futurizm. RuB, 6-7, 1913.

Rjurikov, B. O nekotoryx voprosax socialističeskogo realizma. NoM, 4, 1952, 222-60. [In the Soviet Union, Socialist

Realism continues to be an object of constant reinterpretation and clarification. The present tendency is to link it up with the 19th-century classical tradition while emphasizing what is new in it. This is a long and authoritative (and in part polemical) exposition of the official view.]

Roy, A. K. Realism of Art and Poetry. Allahabad U. Mag., 23, 1945, 32-35.

Rubio, D. Symbolism and Classicism in Modern Literature; Introduction to the Study of Symbolism in Spanish and Spanish American Literature. Philadelphia, 1923.

Sartre, J. P. L'existentialisme est un humanisme. Paris, 1946.

Serrano Plaja, A. El realismo español. Buenos Aires, 1944.

Sologub, F. Iskusstvo našix dnej. RM, 12, 1915, 35-62.

Souriau, M. Histoire du Parnasse. Paris, 1929.

Swięcicki, J. M. W sieci dekadentyzmu. Przegląd Powszechny, July, 1952, 60-79. [After introductory remarks about literary decadence there follows a comparative analysis of Hesse's Der Steppenwolf and Remarque's Arch of Triumph.]

Torre, A. de la. Naturalism and the Spanish American Novel. BA, 26, 1952, 147-50. [Naturalism may well have been introduced "as a Parisian fashion," but it soon "joined forces with the political, economic, and artistic trends . . . of a social awakening."]

Veksler, I. Tradicii russkoj kritiki 40-60-x godov v bor'be s teoriej čistogo iskusstva. Zv, 2, 1947, 150-62.

Vercman, K. et al. Realism XVIII veka na Zapade. Moscow, 1936. 203 p. [Defoe, Swift, Voltaire, Beaumarchais, Lessing.]

Vipper, R. Simvolizm v čelovečeskoj mysli i tvorčestve. RM, 2, 1905, 98-116.

Vossler, K. Realismus in der spanischen Dichtung der Blütezeit. München, 1926.

Watt, I. Realism and the Novel. Essays in Criticism, 2, 1952, 376-96. [Urges the reinterpretation of traditional views of the novel, especially the view that "the novel is essentially different from poetry, because it is a new literary form which characteristically uses language in a primarily representational, referential, or realistic way."]

Weydt, G. Literarisches Biedermeier. DVLG, 13, 1935.

Wundt, M. Die Philosophie in der Zeit des Biedermeiers. Ibid.

Yoshida, S. Naturalism. In: An Introduction to Comparative Literature ed. by Nakajima & Nakano. Tokyo, 1951.

Žirmunskij, V. Preodolevšie simvolizm. RM, 12, 1916, 25-56.

Individual Authors.

Lukács, G. BALZAC und der französische Realismus. Berlin, 1952. 103 p. [The author sees in the works of Balzac, Stendhal, and Tolstoi the highest accomplishments of the novel of the middle class. The genuine heirs of the achievements of early 19th century French realism are found in Russian and Scandinavian literature.]

Milačić, D. Pobeda Balzakovog realizma. KZ, 1, 1950.

Raymond, M. De BAUDELAIRE au surréalisme. Paris, 1933. 400 p.

Trzynadlowski, J. W. BIELINSKIego koncepja realizmu. PPW, 10, 323-30.

Maslenikov, O. A. The Frenzied Poets: Andrey BIELY and the Russian Symbolists. California U. P., 1951.

Grossman, L. Naturalizm Čexova. (CHEKHOV). VE, 7, 1914, 218-47. And in: Mastera slova. Moscow, 1928, 199-236.

Adams, P. G. CRÈVECOEUR—Realist or Romanticist? FAR, 2, 1949.

Grossman, L. Problema realizma u DOSTOEVSKOGO. VE, 2, 1917, 65-99.

Vinaver, S. Delo T. S. ELIOTa. Njegova postigunća, njegovi problemi, njegova borba protiv dekadenciji. KnN, 28, 1951.

Breunig, L. C. F. S. FLINT, Imagism's Maître d'Ecole. CL, 4, 1952.

Gilman, S. Realism and the Epic in GALDOS' Zaragoza. Festschrift A. M. Huntington. Wellesley, 1952.

Gejman, B. Problemy realizma v rannem tvorčestve Gete. (GOETHE). Zapadnyj sbornik, vol. 1. Moscow, 1937.

Bošković, Maja. Realizam i romantizam u GOGOLjevoj koncepciji folklora. R, 7, 1951, 662-68.

Ioffe, I. Mertvye duši i russkij realizm. UZLU, 87, 1943, 173-203.

Bursow, B. Początki realizmu socjalistycznego. Nowa Kultura, Warsaw, 1. [A survey of the polemics between Gorky and Chekhov concerning realism and Gorky's attitude toward the revolution of 1905.]

Lowrie, W. Johann Georg HAMANN: An Existentialist. Princeton, 1950.

Newton, W. HARDY and the Naturalists: their Use of Physiology. MP, 1951.

Fivian, E. A. Georg KAISER und seine Stellung im Expressionismus. München, 1947.

Lease, B. Realism and Joseph KIRKLAND's Zury. AL, 23, 1952, 464-66. [Re-affirms Kirkland's claim as one of the pioneer American realists and insists that in Zury he plumbed "depths of psychological realism."]

Šibanov, I. P. LESSING na puti k realizmu. IVGPI, 10, 1948.

Short, R. W. MELVILLE as Symbolist. UKCR, 15, 1949.

Vinogradov, I. Put' PUSKINa k realizmu. LN, 16-18, 1934, 49-90.

Dieckmann, H. French Existentialism before SARTRE. FS, 1, 1949.

Bertini, G. Motivi esistenzialistici nella filosofia morale di SENECA. Sophia, 16, 1948.

Richthofen, E. von. VIGNY als philosophisch-dichterischer Wegbereiter des Symbolismus. RF, 63.

Dynnik, V. Romantik naturalizma. (E. ZOLA). NTIPI, 5, 1929, 3-24.

D. THE MODERN WORLD

IV. SPANISH CONTRIBUTIONS

Influences upon Individual Countries.

Ambruzzi, L. La diffusione dello spagnuolo nel mondo. Torino, 1908.

Araujo, F. Influencia de la literatura española en la literatura europea. España moderna, 177 (Madrid), 1903.

BASQUES: see 85 and 707.

Farinelli, A. Más apuntes y divagaciones bibliográficas sobre viajes y viajeros por España y Portugal. Rev. de Archivos, Bibliotecas y Museos, 3, 1901.

——— Aggiunte minime alle note sui viaggi e i viaggiatori nella Spagna e nel Portogallo. Mélanges E. Picot. Paris, 1913.

Foulché-Delbosc, R. Bibliographie des voyages en Espagne et en Portugal. Paris, 1896. (Cf. Farinelli, Rev. critica de historia y literatura españolas, portuguesas y hispano-americanas, 3, 1898.)

Hart, T. Early Histories of Spanish Literature, Bouterwek, Sismondi, Ticknor. Diss., Yale, 1952.

Ors, E. d'. Perspectivas internacionales de la literatura española. Madrid, 1944.

Rubio, D. The Mystic Soul of Spain. New York, 1946.

Aita, A. La influencia española en la literatura argentina. (AMERICA). Atlántida, 12. (Buenos Aires).

Calveiro Couto, A. V. Hispanismo e hispanistas norteamericanos. Cultura Callega, 4. (Habana), 1940.

Cantarell-Dart, J. La influencia espiritual de España en el movimiento literario de América. Rev. del Profesorado, Buenos Aires, 1927 & Antologia, 138, 1929.

Carrizo, J. A. Antecedentes hispano-medievales de la poesía tradicional argentina. Buenos Aires, 1943.

Escosura, P. de la. Apuntes sobre la literatura contemporánea en la América meridional y sus relaciones con la española. Revista Contemporánea, 2 (Madrid).

Lohmann Villena, G. Repertorio de las representaciones teatrales en Lima hasta el siglo XVIII. RFH, 5, 1943.

Leonard, I. A. The 1790 Theater Season of the Mexico City Coliseo. HR, 19, 1951.

Prado, J. El genio de la lengua y de la literatura castellana y sus manifestaciones en la historia intelectual del Perú. Revista Universitaria, 2 (Lima), 1917.

Reyes, A. Los autos sacramentales en España y América. Bol. de la Acad. Argentina de Letras, 5, 1937.

Rubio y Lluch, A. La hispanofobia y la hispanofilia en la poesía colombiana. In his: Estudios Hispanoamericanos. Bilbao, 1923.

Vega, M. A. Españolismo de la literatura de la conquista y de la colonia. Atenea, 53 (Concepción), 1938.

——— El españolismo en la producción literaria de los siglos XVI, XVII y XVIII en Chile. Anales de la Fac. de Filosofía y Educación. U. de Chile, 2, 1941.

Reiffenberg, B. de. La presse espagnole en BELGIQUE. Bibliophile Belge, 1-4, 1845-48.

Araujo, F. La literatura española en DINAMARCA. España Moderna, 125 (Madrid), 1899.

Alpern, H. ENGLISH Translations of Spanish Classics. Hisp., 7, 1924.

Barker, J. W. Influencia de la literatura española en la literatura inglesa. Universidad 23 (Zaragoza), 1946.

Hills, E. C. Dramas españoles traducidos

al inglés. Inter-America, 4 (New York), 1921.

Hume, M. Influencia española sobre la literatura inglesa. España Moderna, 1905, 195-203.

Jones, W. K. Spanish Literature for English Readers. Bull. of Bibliogr. & Dramatic Index, 14 (Boston), 1931.

Krappe, A. H. Spanish Matter in British Chronicles. Anglia, 46, 1934.

Pastor, A. Breve historia del hispanismo inglés. Arbor, 9 (Madrid), 1948.

Underhill, J. G. Caracteres de la influencia española sobre la literatura inglesa. Ateneo, 1 (Madrid), 1906.

Bédarida, H. Le romantisme FRANÇAIS et l'Espagne. Revue de l'U. de Lyon, 4, 1931.

Chastenay, J. Le genre grenadin au théâtre. RH, 8, 1901.

Contamine, E. La literatura española en Francia. España Moderna, 11, 1889.

Elizalde, I. Le Maître de Santiago y el tema español en la literatura francesa contemporánea. RyF, 134, 1949.

Forneaux, M. de. España en las leyendas épicas francesas. Rev. Nacional de Educación (Madrid), 1945.

Llopis y Bofill, M. Influencia de España en la literatura francesa. Ilustración española y americana, 43 (Madrid), 1878.

Magnabal, J. G. Aperçu sur l'étude classique des lettres espagnoles en France. Madrid, 1881.

Picard, G. Le romantisme français et l'Espagne. Hisp., 5, 1922.

Friedwagner, M. Spanisches Drama in Deutschland. (GERMANY). Frankfurt, 1919.

Hinojosa, E. de. Publicaciones alemanas sobre la historia de España. Revista Hispanoamericana, 8 (Madrid), 1882.

Morel-Fatio, A. Les Allemands en Espagne du XV au XVIII siècle. RFE, 9, 1922.

Tiemann, H. La literatura española en Alemania desde el Renacimiento hasta el Romanticismo. Investigación y Progreso, 11 (Madrid), 1940.

Voretzsch, K. Die spanische Sprache und Literatur in der deutschen Romanistik der Frühzeit. Gedenkschrift A. Bonilla y San Martin. Madrid, 1930.

Klempa, S. Hispanismo en la literatura dramática austro-húngara. (In HUNGARIAN). Diss., Pecs, 1922.

Bertini, G. M. Conversazione di due italiani dopo un viaggio in Ispagna (secolo XVIII). (ITALY). Conv., 4, 1932.

Bertoni, G. Catalogo dei codici spagnuoli della Biblioteca Estense in Modena. RF, 20, 1907.

Ceriello, G. R. Poesia femminile religiosa spagnola in Sardegna nel Settecento. BH, 18, 1915.

—— Comedias de Santos a Napoli nel' 600. BH, 22, 1920.

Chiara, B. Tipi, scene, avventure di Italiani in Spagna. Treviso, 1907.

Croce, B. I predicatori italiani del Seicento e il gusto spagnolo. Flegrea & Napoli, 1899.

—— España en la vida italiana durante el Renacimiento. Madrid, 1920. New Italian ed. Bari, 1949.

—— Cultura spagnola in Italia nel Seicento. Critica, 24, 1926.

Fabrizi, N. Gli italiani nelle guerre di Spagna. Risorgimento italiano, 7, 1914.

Farinelli, A. Sonetti spagnoli tradotti in italiano. BH, 16, 1914.

Giardini, F. S. Due umanisti siciliani in Ispagna contemporanei del Colombo e le loro descrizioni della Spagna. Boll. Soc. geografica ital., 12, 1923.

Grassi, C. Sulla dominazione spagnuola in Sicilia. Riv. Tradizioni popolari, 1, 1894.

*Marcu, A. La Spagna ed il Portogallo nella visione dei romantici italiani. Ephemeris Dacoromana, 2 (Roma), 1924.

Mele, E. Sonetti spagnuoli tradotti in italiano. BH, 16, 1914.

Monteverdi, A. Mercanti milanesi in Ispagna. Archivio storico lombardo, 13, 1923.

Morandi, G. B. Un salmo del Cinquecento contro gli spagnuoli e l'impresa di Carlo V nella Provenza. Boll. stor. della Provincia di Novarra, 2, 1908.

Nicolini, F. Aspetti della vita italo-spagnola del seicento. Napoli, 1934.

Rua, G. Poesie contro gli Spagnuoli e in loro favore (1610-25). Festschrift Vittorio Rossi-Teiss. Trento, 1897.

Sorbelli, A. Bibliografia e cultura iberica in Bologna: la Casa degli Spagnuoli. Archiginnasio di Bologna, 30, 1935.

Ugolini, F. A. Avvenimenti, figure e costumi di Spagna in una cronaca italiana del Trecento. In: Italia e Spagna. Firenze, 1941.

Vaganay, H. Les romans de chevalerie italiens d'inspiration espagnole. Essai de Bibliographie. Bibliofilia, 15-16 (Firenze), 1914.

Zaccaria, E. Contributo agli iberismi in Italia. Torino, 1905.

—— L'elemento iberico nella lingua italiana. Bologna, 1927.

Gil, R. Nuestra poesía popular en ORIENTE. In his: Romancero judeo-español. Madrid, 1911.

Retana y Gamboa, W. E. Noticias histo-rico-bibliograficas del teatro en FILIPINAS desde sus orígenes hasta 1898. Madrid, 1909.

Figueiredo, F. de. España en la moderna literatura PORTUGUESA. Estudio, 17 (Barcelona), 1917.

García Peres, D. Catálogo razonado biografico y bibliografico de los escritores portugueses que escribieron en castellano. Madrid, 1890.

Osorio de Oliveira, J. Concepção romântica da Espanha. Lisboa, 1950.

Sousa Viterbo. A litteratura hespanhola em Portugal. Memorias da Academia das Sciencias de Lisboa, 12, 1915.

Anon. Ispanistika v Peterburgskom-Leningradskom Universitete. Bibliografičeskie materialy. (RUSSIA). NBLU, 14-15, 1947, 64-72.

Araujo, F. La literatura española en Rusia. España moderna, 141, 1900.

Mikailof, J. Les lettres espagnoles en Russie. Hisp., 2 (Paris), 1910.

Anon. La literatura española en Suecia. (SWEDEN). Rev. Crít. de Historia y Literatura Españolas, Portuguesas e Hispano-Americanas, 2, 1897.

Hillman, A. Ojeada sobre la literatura española en Suecia. Ibid., 1, 1896.

Kleberg, T. La lengua española en Suecia en el siglo XVIII. Mélanges Karl Michäelsson. Göteborg, 1952, 268-80.

Celestina, Lazarillo and Picaresque Novels.

Espinosa, A. M. El estudiante picaro en el cuento tradicional. Festschrift Menéndez Pidal, 3. Madrid, 1952.

Hollmann, W. Thomas Mann's Felix Krull and Lazarillo. MLN, Nov., 1951.

Lesevič, V. Proisxoždenie sovremennogo romana. 1. Genero picaresco, ego voznikovenie, značenie i rasprostranenie. 2. Picaresque novel v Anglii. Tomas Naš i ego "Zlopolučnyj stranstvovatel" (1594). RM, 11, 1898 & 4, 1901.

Massarani, T. Il romanzo picaresco e i manieristi in Ispagna e in Italia. In: Storia e fisiologia dell' arte di ridere. Milano, 1901.

Mazzei, P. Per la fortuna di due opere spagnuole in Italia. (Celestina). RFE, 9, 1922.

Mele, E. Una traduzione inedita del

Lazarillo de Tormes. Rass. biblio-
grafica della lett. ital., 22, 1914.
———— Un villancico della Celestina popolare in Italia nel Cinquecento. GSLI,
1935.
Praag, J. A., van. La Picara en la literatura española. Spanish Rev., 3, 1936.
Sanvisenti, B. Alcune osservazioni sulla
parola pícaro. BH, 18, 1916.
Seidlin, O. Picaresque Elements in Thomas
Mann's Work. MLQ, 12, 1951.

The Cid

Alonso Cortes, N. El Cid y los Cides. In:
Anotaciones literarias. Valladolid,
1922.
Ambruzzi, L. Il Canzoniere del Cid in
italiano. Meridiano, 15, X, 1938.
Garrone, G. M. Il Ricciardetto di N. Forte-
guerri e il Cid della poesia spagnuola.
RI, 12, 1909.
Momigliano, A. Il Cid di Guillén de Castro
e del Corneille. Riv. del teatro ital.,
7, 1907.
Moreno Garcia, C. El Cid en la literatura
española. Revista Contemporánea, 83
(Madrid), 1891.
Prunaj, G. B. Le tre leggende eterne: Il
Cid, Don Giovanni, Faust. Palermo,
n.d.
Restori, A. Le geste del Cid: antologia
spagnuola. Milano, 1890.
Sorrento, L. Il mio Cid e l'Orlando. RI,
18, 1915.
Zingarelli, N. Per la genesi del poema del
Cid. Alcuni raffronti con la Cronica
General. RIL, 58, 1925.

Cervantes and Don Quijote

Blum, H. Don Quijote dans l'art polonais.
C. R. de l'Acad. Polonaise, 9, 1950.
Cieselska-Borkowska, S. Les traductions
polonaises de Don Quichotte, Sprawozdania Polskiej Akademii Umiejętnosci,
5 (Cracow), 1949. (In Polish.)
Cordasco, F. Smollett and the Translation
of the Don Quixote. MLQ, 13, 1952,
23-26. [Criticism and evaluation of the
most controversial English translation
of Cervantes.]
Fišer, V. Servantes i Don Kixot. RM, 5,
1916, 1-10.
Garrone, M. A. Don Chisciotte nelle prime
commedie spagnuole e nelle ultime
francesi (1605-1910). Fanfulla della
Domenica, 32, 1910.
Greene, T. D. H. Lawrence and the
Quixotic Hero. Sewanee Rev., 59,
1951.
Nava, E. Ancora l'Italia e Cervantes.
Marzocco, 21, 1916.

Rondani, A. A proposito di Sancio Panza
e di Don Abbondio. Don Chisciotte e
certi suoi parenti. Italia moderna, 15,
1905.
Sorrento, L. Cervantes in Italia. Lectura,
4, 1915.
Storoženko, N. Filosofija Don-Kixota. VE,
9, 1895, 307-24.
Szmydtowa, Z. Don Quijote en Pologne
pendant la première moitié du XIXe
siècle. C. R. de l'Académie Polonaise,
2. Cracovie, 1948.

Tirso de Molina and Don Juan

Anon. La historia de Don Juan; su leyenda, su tradición, su vida, su historia
y su dramática. Novela Teatral, 5
(Madrid), 1920.
Agustin, F. Don Juan en el teatro, en la
novela y en la vida. Madrid, 1929.
Castro, A. Don Juan en la literatura española. Buenos Aires, 1924.
Coe, Ada M. Un estudio sobre Tirso tra-
ducido por Millé. Estudios, 6, 1950.
Costanzo, L. Don Giovanni Tenorio nel
teatro spagnuolo e romeno. Napoli,
1939.
Gabrielli, A. Don Giovanni Tenorio. Fan-
fulla della Domenica, 33, 1911.
Giuliano, W. A Spanish Version of the
Authentic Don Juan (Jacinto Grau).
Hisp., 34, 1951.
Lomba de la Pedraja, J. R. La leyenda y
la figura de Don Juan Tenorio en la
literatura española. Murcia, 1920.
Magnabal, J. G. Don Juan et la critique
espagnole. Paris, 1893.
Martuszewski, E. Tirso de Molina. Tw, 4,
1948, 104-12.
Pagano, A. Contributo alla storia del
teatro italo-spagnuolo nel secolo
XVII: Giov. Battista Pasca e Tirso de
Molina. Lett. drammatica, 2, 1908.
Rios, Blanca de los. Don Juan y sus ava-
tares. Rev. Nacional de Educ., 77,
1948.
Rua, F. Don Giovanni attraverso le let-
terature spagnuola e italiana. Torino,
1921.
Said Armesto, V. La leyenda de D. Juan.
Madrid, 1908.
Salomon, M. Don Žuan grafa Alekseja
Tolstogo. Istoriko-literaturnyj etjud.
VE, 10-11, 1907.
Schneider, M. La leyenda de Don Juan,
un mito de Carnaval. Clavileño, 1951.
Sellen, F. El tipo de Don Juan en las
literaturas modernas. Cuba y América,
Dec., 1902.
Simone-Brouwer, F. de. Ancora Don Gio-
vanni. RCLI, 2, 1900.

t'Sertevens, A. La légende de Don Juan. 13th ed. Paris, 1924.

Żygulski, Z. Legenda o Don Juanie w literaturze czterech stuleci. Łodz, 1947.

Other Spanish Authors.

Percopo, E. Giovanni **BOSCÁN** e Luigi Tansillo. RCLI, 17, 1912.

Farinelli, A. Pirandello y **CALDERÓN.** Nación (Buenos Aires), 21, II, 1937.

Gorra, E. Una romanza spagnuola nella poesia popolare e nel teatro: l'Alarcos de F. Schlegel e il dramma religioso di Calderón de la Barca. In: Fra drammi e poemi. Milano, 1900.

Wasserzieher. Goethe's **CLAVIGO** und seine Quelle. Berichte des freien deutschen Hochstifts, 4.

Sanvisenti, B. Pirandello e B. Pérez **GALDÓS.** Convivium, 11, 1939.

Croce, B. I trattatisti italiani del concettismo e Baltasar **GRACIÁN.** Atti Accad. Pontoniana di Napoli, 29, 1899.

———— Virgilio Malvezzi e i suoi rapporti con Gracián, ed Appunti sulla letteratura spagnola e sui costumi in Italia. Atti R. Accad. Scienze morali, 52. Napoli, 1928.

———— Personaggi della storia italo-spagnola: Il duca di Nocera, Francesco Carafa e Baltasar Gracián. Critica, 35, 1937.

Alvar, M. Romances de **LOPE DE VEGA** vivos en la tradición oral Marroqui. RF, 63, 1951.

Caravaglios, B. Amar sin saber a quién di Lope de Vega e La suite du menteur di Corneille. Napoli, 1931.

Cian, V. Una egloga di Lope de Vega nella versione inedita di G. B. Conti. Festschrift Bacci-Del Lungo. Torino, 1895.

Goyri de Menéndez Pidal, Maria. La Difunta Pleiteada; estudio de literatura comparativa. Madrid, 1909.

Navarra, T. Un oscuro imitatore di Lope de Vega: Carlo Celano; un documento della fama di Lope de Vega in Italia. Bari, 1919.

Wilson, E. M. Rule a Wife and Have a Wife (Fletcher) and El sagaz Estacio (Jeronimo de **SALAR BARBADILLO).** RES, 24, 1948, 189-94.

Ferdinandy, M. de. **UNAMUNO** y Portugal. In: Cuadernos de Unamuno. U. de Salamanca, 1951.

Mazzei, P. Per la fortuna di due opere spagnuole in Italia (**VALERA'**s Pepita Jiménez). RFE, 9, 1922.

Spanish Influences upon Individual Authors.

Provenzal, D. La vita e le opere di Ludovico **ADIMARI.** Fonti spagnuole delle tre opere drammatiche. Rocca San Casciano, 1902.

Foulché-Delbosc, R. Madame d'**AULNOY** et l'Espagne. RH, 67, 1926.

Sarrailh, J. Sur quelques histoires espagnoles de **BALZAC.** Festschrift A. M. Huntington. Wellesley, 1952.

Kogan, P. Bomarše i ego geroj. (**BEAUMARCHAIS).** RM, 8, 1899, 107-22.

Rajna, P. I versi spagnuoli di mano di Pietro **BEMBO** e di Lucrezia Borgia. Festschrift Menéndez Pidal. Madrid, 1925.

Laumonier, P. **BRANTOME** et l'Espagne d'après ses Discours sur les dames. BH, 46, 1944.

Churchman, P. H. Lord **BYRON'**s Experiences in the Spanish Peninsula in 1809. BH, 11, 1909.

Legendre, M. **CHATEAUBRIAND** et l'Espagne. Occident, Rev. internat. d'Hispanisme, 1940.

Gobbi, G. Le fonti spagnole del teatro drammatico di G. A. **CICOGNINI.** Biblioteca della Scuola Italiana, 11, 1905 & Roma, 1916.

Verde, R. Studi sull' imitazione spagnuola nel teatro italiano del seicento. G. A. Cicognini. Catania, 1912.

Chasles, P. **CORNEILLE** dans ses rapports avec le drama espagnol. In his: Etudes sur l'Espagne et sur les influences de la littérature espagnole en France et en Italie. Paris, 1847.

Savj-Lopez, P. Precursori spagnuoli di **DANTE.** GD, 4, 1896.

Fitzmaurice-Kelly, J. Un hispanófilo inglés del siglo XVII. (L. **DIGGES).** Festschrift Menéndez Pelayo. Madrid, 1895.

Muñoz Rojas, J. A. Apuntes para un estudio de las relaciones literarias de **DONNE** con España. Festschrift Walter Starkie. Barcelona, 1948.

MacMillan, D. The Sources of **DRYDEN'**s The Indian Emperour. HLQ, 13, 1950.

Merlino, C. P. References to Spanish Literature in **EQUICOLA'**s Natura de amore. MP, 31, 1933.

Bataillon, M. Les sources espagnoles de l'Opus Epistolarum **ERASMI.** BH, 31, 1929.

Bertini, G. M. **FARINELLI** ispanista. Torino, 18, 1938.

Rossi, G. C. Scrittori d'Austria e di Spagna

nella critica di Arturo Farinelli. Convivium, 8, 1936.

García Calderón, V. Lettre ouverte à M. James **FITZMAURICE-KELLY**, hispanisant. Hisp., 5, (Paris), 1922.

Cuccoli, E. M. Antonio **FLAMINIO** e la Spagna. Bologna, 1897.

Messedaglia, L. Echi i riflessi di Spagna nelle Maccheronee **FOLENGHIANE**. GSLI, 126, 1949.

Dam, C. F. A. van. Dos sonetos españoles desconocidos de un poeta portugués (Luis **FRANCO**). Festschrift Menéndez Pidal, 3, 1952.

Olive, A. Saint **FRANÇOIS DE SALES** et les influences espagnoles. Annales Salesiennes, April, 1951.

Martinenche, E. España de Théophile **GAUTIER**. Hisp., 1, 1918.

Guillaume-Reicher, Gilberte. Théophile Gautier et l'Espagne. Paris, n.d.

Gómez de la Serna, J. André **GIDE** y España. Clavileño, May, 1951.

Farinelli, A. **GOETHES** Aufführungen spanischer Dramen in Weimar. Italien. Monatschrift, 2, 1929.

Tinianova, J. Analogías españolas en la obra de **GOGOL**. Literatura Internacional, 4. Moscow, 1945.

Bobio, A. Studi sui drammi spagnoli di Carlo **GOZZI**. Convivium, Sept., 1948.

Chasles, P. D'un théâtre espagnol-vénitien au XVIIIe siècle et de Charles Gozzi. In: Etudes sur l'Espagne et sur les influences de la littérature espagnole en France et en Italie. Paris, 1847.

Gorlich, E. **GRILLPARZER** y el Teatro Español. Ensayos y Estudios, 4, 1942 & Deutsche Zt. f. Spanien, 557, 1943.

Rabanal, M. España en **HORACIO**. Estudio temático. Emerita, 17, 1949.

Blasco-Ibañez, V. Un poeta español romántico: Victor **HUGO**. La Revista (Buenos Aires), Dec., 1927.

Lancaster, H. C. The Genesis of Ruy Blas. MP, 14, 1917.

Martinenche, E. España en las Orientales de Victor Hugo. Revista de América, (Paris), 1913.

Piétri, F. L'Espagne de Victor Hugo. RDM, Aug., 1951-Jan., 1952.

Farinelli, A. Une lettre inédite de Guillaume de **HUMBOLDT** concernant son second voyage en Espagne. RH, 6, 1899.

Bowers, C. G. Las aventuras españolas de W. **IRVING**. Santiago de Chile, 1946.

Place, E. B. Una nota sobre las fuentes españolas de Les Nouvelles de Nicolas **LANCELOT**. RFE, 13, 1926.

Delcombre, R. L'hispanisme de deux parnassiens. **LECONTE DE LISLE** et José-María de Heredia. Hisp., 5 (Paris), 1922.

Manning, C. A. **LERMONTOV** and Spain. RR, 22, 1931.

Monteverdi, A. De **LOLLIS** e la letteratura spagnuola. Nuova Cultura, 7, 1928.

Whitman, Iris L. **LONGFELLOW** and Spain. New York, 1927.

Pitollet, C. Pierre **LOUYS** et l'Espagne. Mercure Universel, Nov. (Lille), 1931.

*Levi, E. Il dramma spagnuolo preludio dei Promessi Sposi. (**MANZONI**). Atti R. Accad. di Archeol. Napoli, 13.

Mele, E. Spagnuolo, spagnolismo e Spagna nei Promessi Sposi. Fanfulla della Domenica, 30, 1908.

Nicolini, F. Don Gonzalo dei Promessi Sposi e la sua discendenza del Gran Capitano. Atti R. Accad. Scienze Morali, 66, Napoli, 1933.

Williams, S. T. Spanish Influences in American Fiction: **MELVILLE** and Others. New Mexico Quart., 22, 1952, 5-14. [Early use of Spanish themes and subject matter by Simms and others, with especial attention to Melville's interest in and use of Spanish material in Benito Cereno.]

Struve, G. Un Russe en Espagne sur les traces de **MÉRIMÉE**. (Sobolevskij). Figaro littéraire, 30, IX, 1930.

Faguet, E. **MOLIERE** et l'Espagne. Temps Présent, 2, VIII, 1913.

Martinenche, E. Histoire de l'influence espagnole sur la littérature française: Molière et le théâtre espagnol. Paris, 1906.

Vezinet, F. Molière, Florian et la littérature espagnole. RHLF, 1907-08 & Paris, 1909.

Loddis, C. de. **MONTAIGNE** e la Spagna. Nuova Cultura, 2, 1923.

Hämel, A. Un gran hispanista aleman que nunca estuvo en España: Ludwig **PFANDL**. Clavileño, Nov., 1951.

Rodríguez, I. **PRUDENCIO**, poeta de la hispanidad. Helmantica, 1, 1950.

Pereverzev, V. **PUSKIN** v bor'be s plutovskim romanom. VPD, 1. Moscow, 1936, 164-88.

Garganta, J. de. Alfonso **REYES** y las letras españolas. U. de Antioquia, Jan., 1951.

Cirot, G. & Laumonier, P. **RONSARD** et les Espagnols. BH, 44, 1942.

Castagnez, H. Hans **SCHLEGEL** und die Renaissance des spanischen Theaters.

Deutsche Zt. f. Spanien (Barcelona), 1944.

Hespelt, E. H. SHELLEY and Spain. PMLA, 38, 1923.

Par, A. SHAKESPEARE y el folklore español. Festschrift D. A. M. Alcover. Palma, 1932.

Peratt, J. D. Spanische Einflüsse bei Shakespeare. Leipzig, n.d.

Oria, J. E. STENDHAL y España. Academia Argentina de Letras, 1944.

Bertrand, J.-J. A. TIECK et le théâtre espagnol. Paris, 1914.

Rosenkranz, J. L. TURGENEV et la littérature espagnole. Slavia, 6, 1927.

Pomès, M. P. VALÉRY y España. Rev. de la U. de Buenos-Aires, July, 1950.

Diez-Canedo, E. La obra de Emilio VERHAEREN y su visión de España. Estudio, 14 (Barcelona), 1916.

Hoepffner, E. L'Espagne dans la vie et l'oeuvre du troubadour Peire VIDAL. In: Etudes littéraires. Paris, 1941.

Mele, E. Giacomo ZANELLA ispanofilo. RI, 10, 1907.

VII. FRENCH CONTRIBUTIONS

Influences upon Individual Countries.

Rogers, C. B. The Spirit of Revolution in 1789: a Study of Public Opinion as Revealed in Political Songs and Other Popular Literature at the Beginning of the French Revolution. Princeton U. P., 1949.

Brown, Esther E. The French Revolution and the AMERICAN Man of Letters. Columbia (Mo.), 1951.

Cohen, H. An Early American Example of French Poetry. MLN, 1952.

Ditchy, J. K. Les Acadiens louisianais. Soc. de Publ. romanes et fr. Genève, 1932.

Poirier, P. Le parler franco-acadien et ses origines. Quebec, 1928.

Sylvestre, G. The Recent Developments of the French-Canadian Novel. UTQ, 21, 1952, 167-78. [An account of the nature, problems, and probabilities for novelists involved in the French culture of Canada.]

Therriault, M. C. La littérature française de la Nouvelle Angleterre. Montréal, 1951.

Dechamps, J. Entre la guerre et la paix: les Iles Britanniques et la Révolution Française (1789-1803). (ENGLAND). Bruxelles, 1949.

Salvan, J. L. Le romantisme français et l'Angleterre victorienne. Paris, 1949.

Bloch, O. La pénétration du français dans les parlers des Vosges méridionales. (GERMANY). Paris, 1921.

Petropoulos, D. La contribution française au développement de la science du folklore en GRECE. BAGB, June, 1951.

Birn, J. The Diffusion of the French Language in POLAND under the Saxon Kings. (In Polish.) Studia z dziejów Kultury. Warsaw, 1949.

Ajzenštok, I. Francuzskie pisateli v ocenkax carskoj cenzury. (RUSSIA). LN, 33-34, 1939, 769-855.

Kareev, N. Kniga o francuzskom kul'turnom vlijanii v Rossii. VE, 9, 1910, 307-12.

Karintsev, N. Quatre cent douze écrivains français édités en U.R.S.S. Etudes Soviétiques (Paris), Dec., 1951.

Kučerov, A. Francuzskaja revoljucija i russkaja literatura XVIII veka. In: Orlov, A. (ed.), XVIII vek. Moscow, 1935, 259-307.

Bréal, A. La culture française en Espagne. (SPAIN). Minerve Française, 2, Oct., 1919.

Riquer, M. de. Los cantares de gesta franceses, sus problemas, su relación con España. Madrid, 1952.

Individual French Authors.

Struve, P. "Neiz'jasnimyj" i "nepostižnyj." Iz etjudov o Puškine i puškinskom slovare. (BAÏF). In: Puškinskij Sbornik, Russkij Naučnyj Institut. Praha, 1929, 259-65. (With a short résumé in French.)

Christophorov, P. Une source d'Ivan Vazov: Le médecin de campagne de BALZAC. Mélanges A. Mazon. Rev. des Etudes Slaves, 27, 1951.

Collon-Bérard, Suzanne. Le dernier voyage de Balzac en Russie. RLC, 24, 1950.

Grossman, L. Bal'zak i Dostoevskij. RM, 1, 1914, 44-45 & In: Tvorčestvo Dostoevskogo. Leningrad, 1928. (Cf. Blinoff in CL, 1951.)

Lapšin, I. Krasnyj kabaček Bal'zaka i Brat'ja Karamazovy Dostoevskogo. VR, 2, 1927, 66-67.

Massant, R. Une contrefaçon belge d'une Fille d'Eve d'Honoré de Balzac. RHLF, 50, 1950.

*Muret, M. Balzac en Allemagne. Journal des Débats, 22, II, 1924.

Ollero, C. Galdós y Balzac. Insula, 15, X, 1952, 9-10. [Despite obvious analogies, the two men reveal in their works wholly antagonistic social views.]

Stafford, J. Samuel Ward's Defense of Balzac's Objective Fiction. AL, 24, 1952, 167-76. [Ward, in his article in the New York Review in 1839, preceded Motley in American criticism of the French realist and offered suggestions toward a critical theory of fiction much in advance of his time and one which pointed toward the later critical "wars" around realism and naturalism.]

Struve, P. Bal'zac kak prorok russkoj revoljucii. RM, 1, 1927, 58-62.

Eliot, T. S. **BAUDELAIRE.** Revue Hommes et Mondes, 7, 1948.

Malkiewicz, M. Asryk et Baudelaire. Bull. de l'Acad. polonaise des Sciences et des Lettres, (Paris), June, 1951.

Bell, M. Pierre **BAYLE** and Moby Dick. PMLA, 66, 1951.

—— Melville and Hawthorne at the Grave of St. John. MLN, 67, 1952, 116-18. [Melville's reference in Moby-Dick to the entombed sleep of St. John comes from Bayle, perhaps through Hawthorne. An addendum to the article above.]

Habicht, R. Henri **BERGSON** und das deutsche Typenlustspiel. Strasbourg, 1935.

Forster, L. Beau Alman et Le Beau Escuyer Gruffy; une source française de Grimmelshausen? (**BRANTOME**). EG, 7, 161-63. [The probable source for Simplicius' Parisian adventures is not Bandello and Bassompiere, but an episode in Brantôme's Recueil des Dames.]

Kozmin, N. Puškin prozaik i francuzskie ostroslovy XVIII v. (**CHAMFORT**, Rivarol). IRJaSl, 1, 1928, 536-58.

*Bem, A. K voprosu o vlijanii Šatobriana na Puškina. (**CHATEAUBRIAND**). PiS, 15, 1911, 146-63.

Komarovič, V. Vtoraja kavkazskaja poèma Puškina. VPD, 6, 1941, 211-34.

Nuñez de Arenas, M. Notas acerca de Chateaubriand en España. RFE, 12, 1925.

Grossman, L. Puškin i Andre Šenje. (**CHÉNIER**). In: Ot Puškina do Bloka. Moscow, 1926.

Dreyer, K. **COMMYNES** and Machiavelli. Symposium, 5, 1951.

Alpatov, M. A. Fustel de **COULANGES** et les historiens russes. Mémoires d'histoire et de philologie, 6 (Moscow), 1949.

Kulczycka-Saloni. La Poupée de B. Prus et l'oeuvre d'Alphonse **DAUDET.** PPL, 1948.

Armitage, A. René **DESCARTES** and the Early Royal Society. Notes & Records of the Royal Society, Oct., 1950.

Bar, A. Descartes en Pologne. Kwartalnik Filosoficzny, 1950. (In Polish.)

Leyden, W. von. Locke and Nicole: their Proofs of the Existence of God and their Attitude toward Descartes. Sophia, 16, 1948.

Struve, P. Ob Aleksandre Djuma-otce. (**DUMAS**). Rossija, 30, 1928.

Duprat, P. Les **ENCYCLOPÉDISTES**, leurs travaux, leurs doctrines et leur influence. Paris, 1866.

Block, H. M. **FLAUBERT,** Yeats and the National Library. MLN, 67, 1952, 55-56. [An incident in Yeats's campaign to spread European culture in Ireland; his help in overcoming moral scruples about Flaubert's works.]

Lebègue, R. Plagiats protestants de poésies de **GARNIER** et de Desportes. BHR, 13, 1951.

Marullo, T. Osservazioni sulle Cantigas di Alfonso X e sui Miracles di **GAUTIER DE COINCY.** AR, 18, 1934.

Bédarida, H. Sur la fortune de J.-M. de Hérédia en Espagne et dans l'Amérique latine. RLC, 11, 1931.

Folkierski, W. Dwa głosy: Wiktora **HUGO** i J. Słowackiego. Życie (London), 22, II, 1952.

Markovitch, M. Victor Hugo en Serbie. RLC, 26, 1952.

Moreau, P. Horizons internationaux de Victor Hugo. Ibid.

Munteano, B. Victor Hugo en Roumanie. Ibid.

Nuñez, E. Victor Hugo en el Perú. Mar del Sur (Lima), March, 1952.

Orrok, D. H. Hemingway, Hugo, and Revelation. MLN, 66, 1951.

Parker, A. & Peers, E. The Influence of Victor Hugo on Poetry and Prose Fiction. MLR, 28, 1933.

Rosselet, Jeanne. First Reactions to Les Misérables in the United States. MLN, 67, 1952, 39-43. [Pros and cons in extracts from the New York Tribune, New England and Southern journals, reflecting moral principles and issues, as well as literary praise or condemnation.]

Roudomino, M. Victor Hugo et les lecteurs soviétiques. Etudes soviétiques (Paris), Feb., 1952.

Ruffini, M. L'influsso di Victor Hugo e

Alfred de Musset sul poeta romeno Alexandra Macedonski. Convivium, 1948.

Zaleski, Z. L. Victor Hugo et la Pologne. RLC, 1952.

Tomaševskij, B. Puškin i Lafonten. (LA-FONTAINE). VPD, 3. Moscow, 1937, 215-54.

Kielski, B. Jocelyn de LAMARTINE et En Suisse de Słowacki. PPL, 1948.

Surina, N. Tjutčev i Lamartin. In: Poètika. Leningrad, 1927.

—— Russkij Lamartin. In: Russkaja poèzija XIX veka. Leningrad, 1929, 299-335.

Nekrasov, A. K voprosu o literaturnyx istočnikax Kavkazskogo plennika Puškina (X. de MAISTRE). Festschrift Orlov. Leningrad, 1934, 153-63.

Entwistle, W. J. The Spanish MANDE-VILLES. MLR, 17, 1922.

Mondor, H. MALLARMÉ et Rodenbach. L'Immagine, 2, 1948.

Modzalevskij, L. Dva pis'ma Merime k Sobolevskomu. (MÉRIMÉE). LN, 16-18, 1934, 758-70.

Mongault, H. Mérimée, Beyle et quelques Russes. MF, 1, III, 1928.

Parturier, M. Une amitié littéraire: Prosper Mérimée et Ivan Tourgueniev. Paris, 1952.

Struve, P. Sobolevskij i Merime. Rossija, 31, 1928.

Vinogradov, A. Merime v pis'max k Sobolevskomu. Moscow, 1928.

—— Merime i Turgenev (pis'ma P. Merime k I. S. Turgenevu). LG, 10, VI, 1929.

—— Merime i ego russkie druz'ja. In: Merime v pis'max k Dubenskoj. Moscow, 1937. 244 p.

Camargo, J. O MOLIERE brasileiro. (Martins Pena). Dionysos, 1, 1950.

McClain, W. H. Kleist and Molière as Comic Writers. GR, 24, 1949.

Rulin, P. Russkie perevody Mol'jera v XVIII v. IRJaSl, 1, 1928, 221-44.

Tomaševskij, B. Malen'kie tragedii Puškina i Mol'er. VPD, 1. Moscow, 1936, 115-33.

Veselovskij, A. Al'cest i Čackij. Otryvok iz etjuda o Mizantrope. (Molière and Griboedov). VE, 3, 1881, 91-112.

Butakova, V. Puškin i Monten'. (MON-TAIGNE). VPD, 3. Moscow, 1937, 203-14.

Marenduzzo, E. José Cadalso e le Cartas Marruecas. (MONTESQUIEU). Napoli, 1934.

*Pypin, A. Ekaterina II i Montesk'e. VE, 5, 1903, 272-300.

Savioz, R. Montesquieu et le philosophe genevois Charles Bonnet. Rev. des Sciences humaines, 1950.

Izmajlov, N. Strofy o NAPOLEONE i Bajrone v stixotvorenii K morju. VPD, 6, 1941, 21-29.

Strich, F. Goethe und Napoleon. Horen, 5, 1928-29.

Struve, P. Šarl' Nod'e i Puškin. (NO-DIER). Rossija, 5, 1927.

Neveux, J. PASCAL et le piétiste allemand J. H. Reitz. RLC, 26, 1952.

Varia. Anketa o Pruste. (PROUST). Čisla, 1, 1930, 272-78.

Pellegrini, C. Emilio Castelar e Edgar QUINET. Fanfulla della Domenica, 27, 1915.

Neri, F. La dubbia Fortuna del RABE-LAIS in Italia. In: Letteratura e Leggende. Torino, 1951.

Veselovskij, A. Rable i ego roman. VE, 3, 1878, 128-200.

Vinja, V. Rabelais dans la traduction de Vinaver. Republica (Zagreb), 1951.

Casnati, F. Alfieri, RACINE e la Doppia tristizia di Giocasta. Vita e Pensiero, 32, 1949.

Anon. Les traductions polonaises des oeuvres d'Ernest RENAN. Bull. de l'Acad. polonaise des Sciences & des Lettres. Paris, June, 1951.

Samazueilh, G. (ed.). Strauss, Richard & ROLLAND, Romain: Correspondance et Fragments de Journal, Paris, 1951. 243 p. [Extends over period 1899 to 1924 and reveals extent of assistance given Strauss by the novelist-critic, as well as their friendship and frequent similarity of views.]

Varia. Romain Rolland et la Belgique. Hommages, textes, souvenirs. Bruxelles, 1950.

López de Meneses, A. Pliegos sueltos románticos: Pablo y Virginia, Atala y Corina en España. (B. de SAINT-PIERRE). BH, 1950.

*Furrer, P. Der Einfluss SAINTE-BEUVES auf die Kritik Matthew Arnolds. Wetzikon, 1920.

Karenin, V. Gercen, Bakunin i Zorž Zand. (G. SAND). RM, 3, 1910, 47-64.

Grossman, L. STENDAL' i Tolstoj. Batalizm i psixologija ras v literature XIX veka. RM, 6, 1916, 32-51 & In: Mastera slova. Moscow, 1928, 71-96.

Pichois, C. Stendhal et A. von Reumont. Le Divar, Oct., 1951.

Kogan, P. Russkij učenyj školy Tena. (**TAINE** and Shakhov). RM, 12, 1897, 79-88.

Cesare, R. de. Alfred de **VIGNY** e l'Italia. Contributo bibliografico alla fortuna del Vigny in Italia. Studi Urbinati, 25 (Milano), 1951.

Petroni, L. Les interprétations italiennes d'Alfred de Vigny. RLC, 26, 1952.

Davidson, F. **VOLTAIRE** and Hawthorne's The Christmas Banquet. Boston Publ. Libr. Quart., 3, 1951.

Grossman, L. Russkij Kandid. K voprosu o vlijanii Vol'tera na Dostoevskogo. VE, 5, 1914, 192-203.

Kadlubovskij, A. K voprosu o vlijanii Vol'tera na Puškina. PiS, 5, 1907, 1-29.

*Schilling, B. N. Conservative England and the Case against Voltaire. New York, 1950.

Aixengol'c, M. Romany Lurd, Rim, Pariž E. Zolja i ix sud'ba v Rossii, (**ZOLA**). LN, 33-34, 1939, 457-590.

French Influences upon Individual Authors.

Durden, R. F. Joel **BARLOW** in the French Revolution. William & Mary Quart., 8, 1951.

Grossman, L. **BRJUSOV** i francuzskie simvolisty. In: Mastera slova. Moscow, 1928, 261-69.

Moore, J. R. **DEFOE**, Steele, and the Demolition of Dunkirk. HLQ, 13, 1950.

Komarowitsch, W. Die Brüder Karamasoff. In: Die Urgestalt der Brüder Karamasoff. (**DOSTOEVSKI**). München, 1929.

Horsman, E. A. **DRYDEN**'s French Borrowings. RES, N.S., 1, 1950.

GOR'KIJ, M. O tom kak ja učilsja pisat'. In: O Literature. Moscow, 1933.

Polonskij, L. Genrix Gejne v Pariže. (**HEINE**). VE, 11, 1869, 190-246.

Stojunin, V. Knjaz' Antiox **KANTEMIR** v Pariže. VE, 8-9, 1880.

Tynjanov, J. Francuzskie otnošenija V. K. **KJUXELBEKERA**. LN, 33-34, 1939, 331-78.

Stewart, C. O. **LOWELL** and France. Nashville, 1951.

Fucilla, J. G. La traduzione del Cinque Maggio di Ramón de Palma y Romay. (**MANZONI**). GSLI, 128, 1951.

Gasparini, M. Traducciones españolas del Cinco de Mayo de Alejandro Manzoni. Roma, 1948.

Tramer, F. Alfred **MEISSNERS** Bezie-

hungen zu Paris und Heinrich Heine. RLC, 26, 1952.

Collet, G. P. George **MOORE** et la France. Ibid.

Hilton, R. A Spanish Francophile: Emilia **PARDO-BAZÁN**. Ibid. 241-49. [The novelist's admiration for France from the point of view of religion, of the moral qualities of Paris, of criticism, science, painting, feminism.]

Kovalevskij, M. Novye dannye o prebyvanii Petra v Pariže. (**PETER THE GREAT**). RM, 1, 1884, 104-60.

Kovarskij, N. **POLEŽAEV** i francuzskaja poèzija. In: Russkaja poèzija XIX veka. Leningrad, 1929, 142-75.

Struve, P. **PUŠKIN** i francuzskie romantiki. Rossija, 1, 1927.

Tomaševskij, B. Zametki i Puškine. PiS, 28, 1917, 56-72.

*——— Puškin i romany francuzskix romantikov (K risunkam Puškina). LN, 16-18, 1934, 947-60.

Dieckmann, Liselotte. Rainer Maria **RILKE**'s French Poems. MLQ, 12, 1951.

Sanchez, L. A. Nicanor della **ROCCA DE VERGALÓ**, un precursor olvidado. Rev. de las Indias, Jan., 1951.

Markiewicz, Z. The Dramas of Juliusz **SLOWACKI** in the Years 1832-43 and French Theatre. (In Polish.) Słowacki Centenary Volume. London, 1951.

Struve, G. S. A. **SOBOLEVSKIJ** v Pariže: Stranica iz istorii russko-francuzskix soprikosnovenij sto let tomu nazad. RiSl, 30, XI, 1929.

Gukovskij, G. O **SUMAROKOV**skoj tragedii. In: Poètika. Sbornik statej. Leningrad, 1926, 67-80.

Teerink, H. A Source-Book for A Tale of a Tub from **SWIFT**'s Own Library. Irish Book Lover, Oct., 1949.

Kyrieleis, R. Moritz August von **THUEM-MEL**s Roman Reise in die Mittäglichen Provinzen von Frankreich. Marburg, 1908.

Ejxenbaum, B. Molodoj **TOLSTOJ**. Petrograd, 1922.

Vengerova, Z. Parižskij arxiv A. I. **URU-SOVA**. LN, 33-34, 1939, 591-616.

Todd, F. M. **WORDSWORTH**, Helen Maria Williams and France. MLR, 43, 1948.

VIII. ENGLISH CONTRIBUTIONS
Shakespeare

Bejblik, A. Deux notes sur Shakespeare en **BOHÈME**. (In Czech.) Listy filologické, 1951.

Strnad, M. Quelques remarques sur Shakespeare en Bohème. (In Czech.) SV, 1949.

Filipović, D. Shakespeare chez les CROATES au XIX siècle. (In Croat.) SIR, 1949.

Hergesić, I. Shakespeare en Croatie. (In Croat.) HK, 1949.

Manchester, P. T. Macbeth in the Hands of FRENCH and Spanish Translators. MLJ, 16, 1931.

Luethi, H. J. Das deutsche Hamletbild seit Goethe. (GERMANY). Bern, 1951.

Crinò, A. M. In margine alle traduzioni shakesperiane. (ITALY). GSLI, 1949.

Galletti, A. Shakespeare e i suoi nuovi traduttori. NAnt, 1948.

Aksjonov, I. Šekspir. (RUSSIA). Moscow, 1937. 365 p.

Anixt, A. Shakespeare in Russia. SL, 4-5, 1946.

Bojadžijev, G. N. et al. Šekspirovskij sbornik. Moscow, 1947. [Shakespeare symposium. Articles and extensive bibliographical material.]

Juzovskij, J. Šekspir i sovetskaja scena. SZ47, 19-40.

––––– Šekspir i sovetskij teatr. DN, 14, 1947.

Morozov, M. Sovetskoe šekspirovedenie i teatr. SZ47, 5-18.

Smirnov, A. Sovremennoe sostojanie šekspirologii v Zapadnoj Evrope i v SŠA. VLU, 7, 1947, 158-65.

Trengutt, S. Shakespeare au théâtre de Leningrad. Nowa Kultura (Warsaw), 1951.

Uzin, V. Šekspir mertvyji Šekspir živoj. SZ47, 105-22. [Shakespeare studies in the West and in the USSR, particularly in respect to the social background of Elizabethan England and Sh's audience.]

Vetrinskij, C. Šekspir v Rossii. RM, 10, 1916, 50-79.

Zagorskij, M. Šekspir v Rossii. SZ47, 57-104.

Moravec, D. Les SLOVÈNES et Shakespeare. SIR, 1949.

Michaelis de Vasconcellos, Carolina. Romeo and Juliet in SPAIN. Bibliothèque Universelle, 7, XI, 1874.

Fridlender, G. M. BELINSKI et Shakespeare. (In Russian.) In: Belinski, Institut de Philologie de Leningrad, 1949.

Gates, W. B. COOPER's Indebtedness to Shakespeare. PMLA, 67, 1952, 716-31. [The novelist borrowed extensively from Shakespeare for plot and incident, and was also influenced by the playwright in his characterization.]

Oppel, H. Das Shakespeare - Bild GOETHEs. Mainz, 1949.

Levaillant, M. Quand Shakespeare à Jersey parle à Victor HUGO. RLC, 26, 1952.

Guille, Frances V. François-Victor Hugo et son temps. Paris, 1950.

Krumpelmann, J. T. KLEIST's Krug and Shakespeare's Measure for Measure. GR, 26, 1951.

Böhtlingk, A. LESSING und Shakespeare. In: Shakespeare und unsere Klassiker. Leipzig, 1909.

Olson, C. MELVILLE et Shakespeare. Temps Modernes, 7, 1951.

Vogelback, A. L. Shakespeare and Melville's Benito Cereno. MLN, 67, 1952, 113-16. [An interesting, if not especially original, suggestion that Babo in Melville's story is modeled directly on Iago in Shakespeare's Othello.]

Jakubovič, D. Perevod PUŠKINA iz Šekspira. Zven'ja, 4, 1936, 144-48.

Batjuškov, F. Šekspir i TOLSTOJ. VE, 5, 1916, 33-45.

Kin, V. Gamletizm i nigilizm v tvorčestve TURGENEVa. LiM, 6, 1929, 71-106.

Babler, O. F. Shakespeare's Tempest as an Opera. (Hugo WOLF). N&Q, 196, 1951.

Other English Authors.

Lowe, R. L. A Note on ARNOLD in America. AL, 23, 1951.

Cross, T. P. A Note on Sohrab and Rustrum in Ireland. Journal of Celtic Studies, 1, 1950.

Kynaston-Snell, H. F. Jean Baudoin et les Essais de BACON en France jusqu'au XVIII siècle. Paris, 1939.

Stein, W. B. A Possible Source of Hawthorne's English Romance. MLN, 67, 1952, 52-55. [BARHAM's Ingoldsby Legends may hold the material used by Hawthorne in his last abortive efforts at fiction.]

Bejblik, A. L'influence de BEAUMONT et Fletcher (The Maid's Tragedy) sur Julius Zeyer. (In Czech.) Casopis pro moderni filologii, 1949.

Pypin, A. Russkie otnošenija Bentama. (BENTHAM). VE, 2-4, 1869.

Weisinger, Nina L. José Joaquín de Mora's Indebtedness to William BLAKE. BHS, 28, 1951.

Greer, Louise. BROWNING and America. Chapel Hill, 1952.

────── Richard Henry Wilde to Elizabeth Barrett Browning: An Unpublished Sonnet. Festschrift J. S. Wilson. Charlottesville (Va.), 1951.

Povarnin, S. Russkij Pelam A. S. Puškina. Pamjati Puškina. U. of St. Petersburg, 1900, 329-50. [**BULWER-LYTTON's** Pelham as a possible source and stimulus of Pushkin's unfinished novel.]

Gabričevskij, A. Strannik Puškina i ego otnošenie k anglijskomu podlinniku. (**BUNYAN**). PiS, 17-18, 40-48.

Sann, Auguste. Bunyan in Deutschland. Studien zur literarischen Wechselbeziehung zwischen England und dem deutschen Pietismus. Giessen, 1951.

Copeland, T. W. **BURKE**, Paine, and Jefferson. In: Our Eminent Friend Edmund Burke. Yale U. P., 1949.

Hennig, J. Early English Translations of Goethe's Essays on **BYRON**. MLR, 44, 1949.

Ivanov, V. Bajronizm kak sobytie v žizni russkogo duxa. RM, 5, 1916, 93-97.

Klučevskij, V. Evgenij Onegin i ego predki. (Pushkin). RM, 2, 1887, 291-306.

Petrov, D. Russkaja nauka i Bajron. Annaly, 3, 1923, 256-57.

Pujals, E. Espronceda y Lord Byron. Madrid, 1951.

Šipovskij, V. Puškin, Bajron i Šatobrian. St. Petersburg, 1889.

*Spasowicz, W. Bajronizm u Puškina i Lermontova. VE, 3-4, 1888.

Šuvalov, S. Lermontov—perevodčik Bajrona. In: Sem' poetov. Moscow, 1927.

Vinogradov, A. Bajron. Moscow, 1936. 304 p.

Žirmunskij, V. Bajronizm Puškina kak istoriko-literaturnaja problema. In: Puškinist 4. Petrograd, 1923.

Duncan-Jones, E. E. **CAREW** and Guez de Balzac. MLR, 1951.

Jakubovič, D. Zametka ob Ančare. (**COLERIDGE**). LN, 16-18, 1934, 869-74.

Štejn, S. Puškin i Kol'ridž (K voprosu o proisxoždenii stixotvorenija Ančar). Zveno, 193, 1926.

Jakovlev, N. Poslednij literaturnyj sobesednik Puškina. (Barry **CORNWALL**). PiS, 28, 1917, 5-28.

Jacob, G. **DEFOE** und Robinson. Archiv, 186, 1949.

DE QUINCEY: See Quincey.

Fiedler, L. A. William Faulkner: An American **DICKENS**. Commentary, 10, 1951.

Katkov, G. Steerforth and Stavrogin. SEER, 27. [The theme of Dostoevskij's Possessed, as far as Stavrogin is concerned, was built up from reminiscences of reading Dickens' David Copperfield. James Steerford as prototype for Stavrogin.]

Weniger, E. Wilhelm Raabe und die Bildung. Sammlung, 7, 1952, 521-30. [The author sees the reason for Raabe's lack of popularity in the fact that his work is rooted in the cosmopolitan culture of the 18th and early 19th centuries. Raabe had little contact with the world of his own time; Dickens and Turgenjev are the only non-German novelists with whom he was acquainted.]

Rust, J. D. Henry Rowe Schoolcraft and George **ELIOT**. Michigan Hist., 24, 1950.

*Gallup, D. A Bibliographical Check-list of the Writings of T. S. **ELIOT** including . . . Translations of his Work into Foreign Languages. New Haven, 1947.

Lebois, A. T. S. Eliot, Les Imagistes et Jean de Boschère. RLC, 26, 1952.

Helsztynski, S. Od **FIELDING**a do Steinbecka. Warsaw, 1948. 255 p.

Longhurst, J. E. Fielding and Swift in Mexico. MLJ, 36, 1952, 186-87. [Two interesting opinions drawn from the files of the Mexican Inquisition on the merits of Swift and Fielding.]

González Lanuza, E. & Canto, P. Dos puntos de vista sobre El fin de la aventura. Sur, 213-14, 1952, 100-13. [Graham **GREENE's** The End of the Affair (Spanish transl. Buenos Aires, 1952) elicits unreserved praise from both critics for style, characterization, and treatment of theme.]

Thielmann, L. J. Thomas **HOBBES** dans l'Encyclopédie. RHLF, July, 1951.

Merlan, P. From **HUME** to Hamann. Personalist, 32, 1951.

Grossman, L. Kto byl umnyj afej? (Puškin and Dr. **HUTCHINSON**). VPD, 6, 1941, 414-19.

Struve, G. Marginalia Pushkiniana. MLN, 1950.

Scott, A. L. A Protest against the **JAMES** Vogue. CE, 13, 1952, 194-201. [James's novels, lacking in narrative power and convincing characterization, are not "liked" and should not be inflicted on students.]

Renucci, P. Une source de Dante, le

Policraticus de **JEAN DE SALIS-BURY**. Diss., Paris, 1951.

Lubbers-van der Brugge, C. J. M. **JOHNSON** and Baretti. Some Aspects of Eighteenth-Century Literary Life in England and Italy. Groningen, 1951.

Quinlan, M. J. Dr. Franklin Meets Dr. Johnson. Penn. Mag. of Hist. & Biogr., 73, 1949.

Sewall, R. B. Dr. Johnson, Rousseau, and Reform. Festschrift B. Tinker. Yale U. P., 1949.

Cordasco, F. The first American Edition of **JUNIUS**. N&Q, 194, 1949.

Perry, M. **KEATS** in Georgia. Georgia Review, 1947.

Borowy, W. O Asie Dygasinskiego. Studia i Rozprawy. Warsaw, 1952, 219-26. [Deals with Dygasinski's novel and its relation to **KIPLING**; lays bare its weaknesses, its schematism and inconsistencies.]

Rice, H. C. Rudyard Kipling in New England. Brattleboro, (Vt.), 1951.

Weld, W. E. Rudyard Kipling, l'illustre écrivain: a Study of the Fame and Fortunes of Rudyard Kipling in France. Diss., Columbia U., 1951.

Setschkareff, V. Ch. R. **MATURIN's** Roman Melmoth, the Wanderer und Dostojevskij. ZSP, 21, 1951, 99-106. [Dostoevsky, who not only read but admired Maturin's novel, is shown to have drawn upon the latter, compositionally and thematically as well as ideologically. Some of the parallels are very striking.]

Patten, H. van. Icelandic Translations of **MAUGHAM**. PBSA, 45, 1951.

Briet, Suzanne. L'Areopagitica de **MILTON**. Histoire d'une traduction. (Mirabeau). RLC, 26, 1952.

Alekseev, M. Dostoevskij i kniga de-Kvinsi. (De **QUINCEY**). Učenye Zapiski Vyssej Skoly, Odessa, 1922.

Jakubovič, D. Predislovie k Povestjam Belkina i povestvovatel'nye priemy Val'ter Skotta. (**SCOTT**). In: Puškin v mirovoj literature. Leningrad, 1926.

——— Reminiscencii iz Val'ter Skotta v Povestjax Belkina. Puškin i ego sovremenniki, 37. Leningrad, 1928, 110-18.

———Rol' Francii v znakomstve Rossii s romanami Val'ter Skotta. JaiL, 1928, 137-84.

*——— Iz zametok o Puškine i Val'ter Skotte. Puškin i ego sovremenniki, 35-39. Leningrad, 1930, 122-40.

——— Lermontov i Val'ter Skott. IAN, 3, 1935, 243-72.

——— Kapitanskaja dočka i romany Val'ter Skotta. VPD, 4-5, 1939, 165-97.

Šamič, B. Thomas Mann on G. B. **SHAW**. (In Serbian). B, 4, 1951.

Wright, Nathalia. A Note on Melville's Use of **SPENSER**: Hautia and the Bower of Bliss. AL, 24, 1952, 83-85. [An interesting comparison of passages in Melville's Mardi with relevant passages in The Faerie Queen.]

Binni, W. **STERNE** e Foscolo. Spettatore Italiano, 1, 1948.

Boys, R. C. Tristram Shandy and the Conventional Novel. Papers of Michigan Acad., 37, 1952, 423-36. [Deals in part with Sterne's influence on the Continent.]

Elsoffer-Kamins, Louise. Un imitateur original de Jonathan **SWIFT**: l'Abbé Coyer et ses Bagatelles morales (1754). RLC, 23, 1949.

Alekseev, M. Sibirskaja ssylka i anglijskij poèt. (**SWINBURNE**). Sibirskie Ogni, Novosibirsk, 4, 1928, 182-93.

Brinnin, J. M. Dylan **THOMAS** in America. Vassar Alumnae Mag., 37, 1951.

Gifford, H. Puškin's Feast in the Time of the Plague and Its Original (John **WILSON's** The City of the Plague). ASEER, 8.

Cossio, J. M. de. Un dato de la fortuna de las Noches de **YOUNG** en España. Bol. de la Biblioteca Menéndez Pelayo, 5, Santander, 1923.

Templeman, W. D. Additions to the Checklist of Young's Night-Thoughts in America. PBSA, 43, 1949.

English Influences upon Individual Authors.

Reboul, P. Les Anglais de **BALZAC**. Rev. des Sciences Humaines, Jan., 1950.

Simon, J. Jacques-Emile **BLANCHE** et l'Angleterre. RLC, 26, 1952.

Lebègue, R. **CORNEILLE** connaissait-il le théâtre anglais? Rev. d'hist. du théâtre, 1950.

Baluxatyj, S. **GOR'KIJ** i anglijskaja kul'tura. UZLU, 87, 1943, 92-122.

Stojunin, V. Knjaz' Antiox **KANTEMIR** v Londone. VE, 1-2, 1867.

Grégoire, H. Les sources rythmiques écossaises du Borodino de M. J. **LERMONTOV**. Mélanges André Mazon. Rev. des Etudes Slaves, 27, 1951.

Croce, B. Un letterato italiano in Inghilterra, Vincenzio **MARTINELLI**. Quaderni della Critica, 4, 1948.

Goddard, N. G. **MAUPASSANT** and the English. FS, 6, 1952, 35-40. [Examines Maupassant's superficial readings, acquaintances, including Swinburne, his visit to England, his reasons for dislike of the English and the caricature of them in his work.]

Young, M. L. M. Jean des **MOUSTIERS**, dit Le Fresse and his Account of Scotland (1538). Ibid.

Bogoslovskij, M. Petr Velikij v Anglii v 1698 g. (**PETER THE GREAT**). In: Gedenkschrift A. N. Savin. Moscow, 1926, 393-434.

Alekseev, M. Neskol'ko anglijskix knig biblioteki A. S. **PUŠKIN**a. NBLU, 6, 1946, 27-32.

Morozov, P. Puškin i anglijskaja poèzija. A, 1, 1917, 44-52.

Gautier, J. M. Les Immémoriaux de Victor **SEGALEN** et leurs sources anglaises. RLC, 26, 1952.

Struve, G. A Russian Traveller in Scotland in 1828: Alexander **TURGENEV**. Blackwood's Mag., Nov., 1945.

Beer, G. R. de. **VOLTAIRE** F. R. S. (Fellow of the Royal Society). Notes and Records of the Royal Society of London, Oct., 1950.

*Fenger, H. Voltaire et le théâtre anglais. Orbis litterarum, 7, 1949.

Flower, D. (ed.). Voltaire's England. London, 1950.

Thaler, A. **WHITTIER** and the English Poets. NEQ, 1951.

XI. AMERICAN CONTRIBUTIONS

Generalities, Inter-American Relations
[See also Indians (111, 709, 772), Negroes (129, 710, 774), and American Types (161)]

Anderson, I. E. Raconteurs of the Conquest. Américas, 3, 1951.

Arias-Larreta, A. Literaturas aborigines: Azteca, Incaica, Maya-Quiche. Los Angeles, 1951.

Geist, S. Fictitious Americans. Hudson Rev., 5, 1952, 199-211. [Interesting analysis of James' Daisy Miller, Dos Passos' J. Ward Morehouse etc. as instances of American fictional characterization.]

Reid, J. T. El americanismo en la literatura americana. Quito, 1943.

Rippy, J. F. Literary Yankeephobia in Hispanic America. Journal of Inter-

nat. Relations, 12, (Worcester, Mass.), 1922.

Vazquez-Arjona, C. Spanish and Spanish-American Influences on Bret Harte. RH, 76, 1929.

Influences upon Individual Countries.

Astre, G. A. L'apport américain au roman contemporain. (**EUROPE**). Age Nouveau, 68.

Miller, P. Europe's Faith in American Fiction. AM, 188, 1951.

Russell, L. The Impact of America on European Culture. Boston, 1951.

Arrowsmith, W. Letter from **ENGLAND**. Hudson Rev., 4, 1951.

Arban, D. Romans américains, lecteurs **FRANÇAIS**. Preuves, March, 1952.

Arnavon, C. Les Lettres américaines devant la critique française (1887-1917). Paris, 1951.

Chinard, G. (ed.). Oderahi, histoire américaine. Paris, 1950.

Isopescu, C. Un roman français du XVIIIe siècle sur le Canada. Rev. de Culture européenne (Paris), July, 1951.

Julien, C., Herval, R. & Beauchesne, T. Les Français en Amérique pendant la première moitié du XVIe siècle. Paris, 1946.

Miłosz, C. Wprowadzenie w Amerikanów. (**POLAND**). Tw, 4, 1949, 10-37.

Isopescu, C. Letteratura americana in **ROMANIA**. Osservatore romano, 15, II, 1952.

Hoffman, A. M. The American Villain on the Soviet Stage. **RUSSIAN** Rev., 10, 1951.

Makogonenko, G. Rossija i amerikanskaja revoljucija. NBLU, 8, 1946, 14-19.

Mendel'son, M. Sovremennaja amerikanskaja literatura. Moscow, 1947.

Manchester, P. T. A Bibliography and Critique of the **SPANISH** Translations from the Poetry of the United States. George Peabody College for Teachers Contributions to Education, 41. Nashville (Tenn.), 1927.

Osborne, R. E. La literatura hispanoamericana en España. Cuadernos Americanos, 10, 1951.

Speratti Pinero, E. S. Los americanismos en Tirano Banderas. Filologia (Buenos Aires), Sept., 1950.

Individual American Authors.

Stevenson, J. W. The Literary Reputation of Stephen **CRANE**. SAQ, 51, 1952,

286-300. [Traces the undulations of opinions and analyzes the basis for Crane's position as a writer of fiction.]

Jovanović, Z. Američka Tragedija T. Drajzera. (DREISER). Ml, 11-12, 1950.

Aldridge, A. O. EDWARDS and Hutcheson. Harvard Theol. Rev., 44, 1951.

T. S. ELIOT: See English Literature.

Minnick, W. C. Matthew Arnold on EMERSON. Quarterly Journal of Speech, 37, 1951.

Olsson, K. A. Fredrika Bremer and Ralph Waldo Emerson. Swedish Pioneer Hist. Quart., 2, 1951.

Thompson, F. T. Emerson and Etienne Geoffroy St. Hillaire. Symposium, 5, 1951.

Hoffman, F. J. & Vickery, Olga W. (eds.). William FAULKNER: Two Decades of Criticism. East Lansing (Mich.), 1952, 280 p. [A valuable sheaf of critical essays on Faulkner from a number of viewpoints.]

Holmes, C. S. FITZGERALD: the American Theme. Pacific Spectator, 6, 1952, 243-52. [An interesting analysis of the writer's interpretation of American life as well as of his relation to European thought and literature.]

Aldridge, A. O. Jacques Barbeu-Dubourg, a French Disciple of Benjamin FRANKLIN. PAPS, 95, 1951.

Alekseev, M. Puškin i brazil'skij poet. (T. GONZAGA). NBLU, 14-15, 1947, 54-61.

Prezzolini, G. HEMINGWAY e l'Italia. Idea, 24, IX, 1950.

Henry JAMES: See also English Literature.

Murray, D. M. Henry James and the English Reviewers, 1882-90. AL, 24, 1952, 1-20. [An account of James' reception in English periodical criticism in his early career, with emphasis upon the British reaction both against the upstart American and against realism as opposed to romance in the eighties.]

Sackville-West, E. James: An American in Europe. SRL, 34, 1951.

Rice, H. C. JEFFERSON in Europe a Century and a Half Later. Princeton Library Chronicle, 12, 1951.

Kozlovskij, V. Imperator Aleksandr I i Džefferson. RM, 10, 1910, 79-95.

Fatur, B. Američka literatura in Sinclair LEWIS. NS, 7-8, 1951, 638-62.

Smith, H. (ed.). From Main Street to Stockholm: Leters of Sinclair Lewis.

New York, 1951. 207 p. [They reveal him as a thoroughly serious professional in his attitude toward the writing of his novels.]

Kojić, B. Maxime Gorki sur Jack LONDON. (In Croat.) HK, 1950.

Canby, H. S. Turn East, Turn West: MARK TWAIN and Henry James. New York, 1951.

Clemens, C. Bernard Shaw and Mark Twain. N&Q, 196, 1951.

—— Mark Twain Is Entertained by Edward VII. Hobbies (March), 1951.

Herzl, T. Mark Twain in Paris. Mark Twain Quart., 9, 1951.

Aničkov, E. Bodler i Edgar Po. (Baudelaire & POE). Sovremennyj Mir, 2, 1909.

Hyslop, L. & F. E. Baudelaire on Poe. Critical Papers. State College (Pa.), 1951.

Kühnelt, H. H. Deutsche Erzähler im Gefolge von Edgar Allan Poe. RLM, 1951, 457-65. [The traces of Poe in German literature from Spielhagen to Ewers, Strobl, and Kubin in his book Die andere Seite.]

Nisbet, Ada B. New Light on the Dickens-Poe Relationship. NCF, 5, 1951.

Quinn, P. F. Poe's Imaginary Voyage. Hudson Rev., 4, 1952, 562-85. [A valuable study of Poe's Arthur Gordon Pym with special emphasis on its significance for the influence of Poe in France and as a text revealing his characteristic artistic methods and meanings.]

Thompson, F. J. Ezra (POUND) at Dublin. UTQ, 21, 1951.

Frenz, H. (ed.). WHITMAN and Rolleston: A Correspondence. With an Introduction and Notes. Indiana U. P., 1951.

Pongs, H. Walt Whitman und Stefan George. CL, 4, 1952.

Wood, F. Three Poems on Whitman. (Lorca et al.). Ibid.

American Influences upon Individual Authors.

Leonard, I. A. Mateo ALEMÁN en Méjico. Bol. del Inst. Caro y Cuervo, 5, 1951.

Flanagan, J. T. An Early Novel of the American Revolution (by R. H. d'AUBERTEUIL). N. Y. Hist., 32, 1951.

Gautier, J. M. L'exotisme américain dans l'oeuvre de CHATEAUBRIAND. Etude de vocabulaire. Manchester U. P., 1951, 65 p. [Demonstrates that Chateaubriand's sources for exotic local color and vocabulary are mainly eighteenth century travel books. Examines names of flora and fauna, place names, etc. and analyzes author's purposes in choice of terms.]

Martino, P. Le voyage de Chateaubriand en Amérique. Essai de mise au point. RHLF, 1952, 149-64. [Juxtaposition of Chateaubriand's own texts, recent scholarship, maps etc. to show that Chateaubriand never went far from the Great Lakes, certainly not further south than Pittsburgh, and suggesting the desire of making his fortune as a motive for his trip. An important contribution to the investigations begun by Bédier.]

Feder, E. **GOETHES** Liebe zu Brasilien. Ijui (Brazil), 1950.

Surkow, E. Maxim **GORKIS** Pamphlete über Amerika. SL, 7, 1949.

Moore, E. R. José Maria **HEREDIA** in New York, 1824-25. Symposium, 5, 1951.

Pountintsev, V. A. **HERTZEN** sur l'Amérique. (In Russian). IAN,OLJA, 9, 1950.

Bjalyj, G. **KOROLENKO** i Amerika. UZLU, 87, 1943, 141-51. [Echoes of his visit to America in his work.]

KOVALEVSKY, M. American Impressions. Russian Rev., 10, 1951.

Guillemin, H. **LAMARTINE** et les U.S.A. MF, 305, 1949.

Parra-Pérez, C. Emil **LUDWIG** y su Biografía de Bolívar. Rev. nacional de Cultura (Caracas), 1951.

Politzer, H. America in the later writings of Thomas **MANN.** MLF, 37, 1952, 91--100. [Examines the importance of America for Thomas Mann from Royal Highness to Dr. Faustus; he perceives reflexes of recent political events in a number of details in the Joseph books.]

Varese, C. Scrittori d'oggi. NAnt, 87, 1952, 200-07. [Contains remarks on Cesare **PAVESE** and American literature. Brings out the cultural activity of Pavese in fostering an interest in American literature and stresses the effect of American fiction on him.]

Carter, E. **TAINE** and American Realism. RLC, 26, 1952.

Beloff, M. **TOCQUEVILLE** and the Americans. Fortnightly, 17, 1951.

Thorp, W. & Drinker, H. S. Two Addresses Delivered to Members of the Grolier Club: I. **TROLLOPE's** Amer-

ica. II. The Lawyers of Anthony Trollope. New York, 1950.

XII. SCANDINAVIAN CONTRIBUTIONS
By P. M. Mitchell
University of Kansas

BIBLIOGRAPHIES. GENERALITIES INTERSCANDINAVIAN RELATIONS.

Hermannsson, H. Bibliography of the Eddas. (Islandica 13), Ithaca, 1920.

———, Bibliography of the Sagas of the Kings of Norway and Related Sagas and Tales. (ibid 3 & 26), 1910, 1937.

———, Bibliography of the Icelandic Sagas and Minor Tales. (ibid 1 & 24), 1908, 1935.

———, Bibliography of the Mythical-Heroic Sages. (ibid 5 & 26), 1912, 1937.

Svensk litteraturhistorisk bibliografi 1900-1935. Uppsala, 1939-50. 522 p.

Afzelius, N. Sverige i utländsk och utlandet i svensk Litteratur. En bibliografisk Översikt. Biblioteksbladet. 15, 1930, 45-64.

Bredsdorff, E. Danish Literature in English Translation . . A Bibliography. Copenhagen, 1950. 198 p.

Pettersen, H. Norge og Nordmænd i Udlandets Literatur. Beskrivende Katalog over Bøger og Tidsskriftsartikler om norske Forhold. (Bibiotheca norvegica, 3) Christiania, 1908-17.

Generalities.

Enquête sur l'influence des lettres scandinaves. Revue blanche 12, 1897, 153-66 [i.a. R. de Gourmont, G. Lecomte, S. Mallarmé, O. Mirbeau, M. Prévost, E. Verhaeren, E. Zola].

Brandes, G. Skandinavischer Einfluss. Nord und Süd, 37, vol. 144, 23-27. [General remarks].

Lemaître, J. Les Contemporains. Études et Portraits littéraires. 6. Ser. Paris, n.d. [Pp. 225-70, De l'Influence récente des Littératures du Nord].

Barnason, C. F. The Revival of Old Norse Literature 1600-1750. Harvard Summaries of Theses . . . 1936, 362-66.

Blanck, A. Den nordiska renässansen i sjuttonhundratalets litteratur. Stockholm, 1911. 452 p.

Körner, J. Die Renaissance des germanischen Altertums. Eine literarhistorische Skizze. ZDU, 27, 1913, 1-29.

Raumer, R. von. Geschichte der germanischen Philologie vorzugweise in

Deutschland. München, 1870. 743 p. [On the Germanic renaissance].

'an Tieghem, P. La mythologie et l'ancienne poésie scandinaves dans la littérature européenne au XVIIIe siècle. Edda 11, 185-207; 12, 122-37, 290-306; 13, 38-65.

———, Le Préromantisme I. Paris, 1924.

Benson A. The Beginning of AMERICAn Interest in Scandinavian Literature. SS, 8, 1924, 133-141.

White, G. Scandinavian Themes in American Fiction. Diss., Philadelphia, 1937. 231 p.

Paulson, A. The Norwegian-American Reaction to Ibsen and Bjørnson 1850-1900. Diss., Iowa, 1933. Typescript. 245 p.

Wilt, N. & Naeseth, H. Two Early Norwegian Dramatic Societies in Chicago. Norwegian - American Studies and Records, 10, 1938, 44-75.

Alexis, J. La littérature suédoise d'Amérique. Paris, 1930.

Benson, A. & Hedin, N. (eds.). Swedes in America 1638-1938. New Haven, 1938.

Naeseth, H. The Swedish Theatre of Chicago 1868-1950. Rock Island, 1951. (Augustana Hist. Society Pub., 12.)

Kenstrom, A. The Earliest Swedish Imprints in the United States. Papers Bibliogr Society of America, 39, 1945, 181-91.

Bibliografie česko-skandinásko-nizozemská. Catalogue des traditions tchèques du danois, de l'islandais, de norvégien, suédois, hollandais et de la langue flammande. (CZECHOSLOVAKIA). Praha, 1932. 32 p.

Allen, R. Old Icelandic Sources in the English Novel. (ENGLAND). Philadelphia, 1933. 121 p.

Blenner-Hassett, R. Two Old-Norse Motifs in Lawman's Brut. Studia Neophilologica 21, 1949, 211-15.

Bugge, S. The Norse Lay of Wayland (Völundarkvitha) and its Relation to English Tradition. Saga-Book of Viking Club, 2, 1900, 271-312.

Craigie, W. The Northern Element in English Literature. Toronto, 1933. 135 p.

Dietz, H. Nordischer Mythus in der englischen Literatur. NM, 10, 1939, 305-19.

Farley, F. E. Scandinavian Influence in the English Romantic Movement. HSPhL, 9, 1903.

Herford, C. Norse Myth in English Poetry. BRL, 5, 1918, 75-100.

Jerrold, C. The Balder Myth and Some English Poets. Saga-Book of Viking Club, 3, 1904, 94-116.

Krappe, A. A Viking Legend in England. Anglia 56, 1932, 432-35.

Leach, H. G. Angevin Britain and Scandinavia. Cambridge, Mass., 1921.

Lindsay, J. The Norse Hero in the English 18th Century. Norseman, 4, 1946, 332-40.

Litzenberg, K. The Victorians and the Vikings: A Bibliographical Essay. Michigan Contributions in Modern Philology, 3, 1947. 27 p.

Nordby, C. The Influence of Old Norse Literature upon English Literature. New York, 1901. (Columbia U. Germanic Studies 1), 78 p.

Paris, G. La Poésie du Moyen Age. 2. Ser. Paris, 1895. [Pp. 45-74, L'Esprit normand en Angleterre].

Seaton, E .Literary Relations of England and Scandinavia in the Seventeenth Century. Oxford, 1935. 384 p. 20 pl.

Smith, A. The Early Literary Relations of England and Scandinavia. Saga-Book of Viking Society, 11, 1934, 215-232.

Stedman, D. Some Points of Resemblance between Beowolf and the Grettla (or Grettis Saga). Saga-Book of Viking Society, 8, 1913, 6-28.

Stefánsson, J. Oldnordisk Indvirkning på engelsk Literatur i det attende og nittende århundrede. Nordisk Tidskrift, 1891, 488-503.

Tuschke, L. "Fair Janet" und "Kong Valdemar og hans Søster." Ein Beitrag zur Frage der Beziehungen zwischen englisch - schottischen und skandinavischen Volksballaden. Berlin, 1940.

Wright, H. Studies in Anglo-Scandinavian Literary Relations. Bangor, 1919, 157 p.

Christophersen, P. Early Anglo-Danish Literary Relations. Norseman, 3, 1945, 363-73.

Downs, B. Anglo-Danish Literary Relations 1867-1900. MLR, 39, 262-79.

Lukman, N. British and Danish Traditions. Classica et Mediaevalia, 6, 1944, 72-109.

Nielsen, L. Ældre dansk Litteratur i engelske Biblioteker. NTBB, 15, 1928, 203-16.

Mead, W. Anglo-Finnish Cultural Relations. Norseman, 6, 1948, 376-87.

Burchardt, C. Norwegian Life and Literature. English Accounts and Views especially in the 19th Century. Oxford, 1920. 230 p.

Downs, B. Anglo-Norwegian Literary Relations 1876-1900. MLR 47, 1952, 449-94.

——, Norse Literary Visitors to Britain. Norseman 6, 1948, 421-25.

Haugen, E. Norges litteraere profil i den engelsktalende verden. Vinduet, 6, 1949, 473-79.

Mortensen, J. (ed.). Sverige i England. Göteborg, 1923. [Pp. 291-96, Svensk litteratur.]

Karsten, T. Die alten nordischen und germanischen Völkerbeziehungen FINNLANDS im Lichte der neueren Forschung (Bidrag till Kännedom af Finlands Natur och Folk Utgifne af finska Vetenskabs-Societeten, 88), Helsingfors, 1946. 14 p.

Beck, T. Northern Antiquities in French Learning and Literature 1755-1855. A Study in Preromantic Ideas, 2 vols. (FRANCE). New York, 1934-35.

—— Ragnar Lodbrok's Swan Song in the French Romantic Movement. RR, 22, 1931, 218-22.

Carstensen, R. Skandinavisch-romanische Wechselbeziehungen, dargestellt am Beispiel des Lebenswerkes Kristoffer Nyrops. NM, 10, 1939, 365-80.

Castrén, G. Norden i den franska litteraturen. Helsingfors, 1910. 270 p.

Davison, Mother St. G. The Scandinavian Movement in the Contemporary French Theatre. Fordham U. Diss., 16, 1949, 156-60.

Heeren, A. Ueber den Einfluss der Normannen auf die französische Sprache und Litteratur. Göttingen, 1789. 32 p.

Maury, L. L'Imagination scandinave. Paris, 1929. [Pp. 356-67: Le Nord dans la littérature française.]

——, Les Scandinaves et nous. MF, 301, 1947, 440-53, 676-89.

Pinot, V. Le Nord dans la littérature française. Revue scandinave, 2, 1911, 110-24.

Jessen, F. de. Bibliographie de la littérature française relative au Danemark. Paris, 1924. 322 p.

Jóhannesson, A. Menningarsamband Frakku og Islendinga. Reykjavík, 1943.

Blanck, A. La Suède et la littérature française des origines à nos jours. Paris, 1924.

Garling-Palmér, S. Vår litteratur inför fransk publik och kritik. Varia 10, 1907, 451-61.

Batka, R. Altnordische Stoffe und Studien in Deutschland. (GERMANY). Euphorion 2, Suppl. 1896, 1-70, and 6, 1899, 66-83.

Bertram, E. Norden und deutsche Romantik. Deutsch-Nordisches Jb., 1927, 61-79.

Boor, H. de. Deutschland und der germanische Norden. Das deutsche Buch 5, 1925, 353-57.

Ehrmann, E. Die bardische Lyrik im achtzehnten Jahrhundert. Diss., Halle, 1892.

Garin, P. Die Skandinaven in der deutschen Literatur. Die Zukunft, 27, 1899, 554-62.

Gerhardt, M. & Hubatsch, D. Deutschland und Skandinavien im Wandel der Jahrhunderte. Bonn, 1950. 482 p.

Golther, W. Die Edda in deutscher Nachbildung. ZVL, 1892, 275-304.

Grimm, W. Über die Entstehung der altdeutschen Poesie und ihr Verhältnis zu der Nordischen. 1808. Repr. in Kleinere Schriften, 1, 1881, 92-170.

Günther, I. Die Einwirkung des skandinavischen Romans auf den deutschen Naturalismus. Diss. (Nordische Studien 14) Greifswald, 1934, 158 p. [Bibliography, 134-158.]

Herrmann, P. Island in der modernen deutschen Dichtung. Mitteilungen der Islandfreunde, 7, 1920-21.

Lawson, M. Nordic Subjects in Popular Annals of the Romantic Period. GR 11, 1939, 229-45.

Magon, L. Deutschland und Skandinavien in ihren geistigen Wechselbeziehungen. In: Deutschland und die Kultur der Ostsee . . ed. G. Schreiber. Münster, 1927, 40-126.

Michael, F. Nordische Erzähler in Deutschland. Das deutsche Buch 1, 1921, 4-7.

Mitchell, P. M. Old Norse-Icelandic Literature in Germany 1789-1849. With a Critical Bibliography. Diss., typescript. Urbana, Ill., 1942. 249 p.

Oppel, H. Studien zur Auffassung des Nordischen in der Goethezeit. Halle 1944. 243 p.

Pertz, S. Das Wort "Nordisch." Seine Geschichte bis zur Jahrhundertwende. Dresden, 1939. 72 p.

Petersen, C. Deutschland und der Norden in ihren geschichtlich-kulturellen Beziehungen. In: Deutschland und der Norden. Stuttgart, 1935, 30-52.

——, Deutscher und nordischer Geist. Ihre Wechselwirkungen im Verlauf

der Geschichte (Schleswig-Holstein-
ische Universitäts-Ges. 38) Breslau,
1937. 170 p.
Puschnig, A. Die Ragnar Lodbrokssage in
der deutschen Literatur. Jahresbericht
Oberrealschule Laibach, 1910.
Roos, C. Germania. København 1938. [Pp.
80-95: Drømmen om Norden i tysk
Aandsliv.]
Strauss und Torney, L. von. Nordische
Literatur und deutsches Geistesleben.
Schleswig-holsteinische Zs. f. Kunst &
Literatur, I, 1906, 371-80, 408-14.
Strich, F. Mythologie in der deutschen
Literatur von Klopstock bis Wagner.
Halle, 1910.
Wrangel, E. Tysklands litteratur under
1700 talet före Klopstock och dess
förhållande till den svenska. Sam-
laren, 22, 1901, 47-64.
Zwiegespräch zwischen den Völkern.
Deutschland und der Norden. Herausg.
von der Nordischen Ges. Lübeck, 1940.
[Der erste Teil . . . geschichtlicher
Überblick aus Briefen und Lebens-
beschreibungen. Der zweite Teil . . .
Gegenwärtiges.]
Grossmann, S. Dansk Digtning i Tyskland.
Tilskueren, 1917, 542-48.
Magon, L. Ein Jahrhundert geistiger und
literarischer Beziehungen zwischen
Deutschland und Skandinavien 1750-
1850. Vol. 1: Die Klopstockzeit in
Dänemark. Dortmund, 1926. 565 p.
Nielsen, L. Ældre dansk Litteratur i tyske
Biblioteker. NTBB, 9, 1922, 203-25.
Beyer, H. Sammenhang og brytning mel-
lom tysk och norsk åndsliv. Samtiden,
61, 1952, 225-44.
Meyen, F. Die deutschen Übersetzungen
norwegischer Schönliteratur, 1730-
1941. Oslo, 1942. 198 p.
Alker, E. Schweden in der deutschen Dich-
tung. WM, 1926, 398-400.
Berg, R. G. Svenskt i Blätter für lit-
erarische Unterhaltung, 1827-45. In:
Studier tillägnade G. Bernstrom.
Stockholm, 1927. 7-32.
Schröder, E. Deutsch-schwedische und
schwedisch-deutsche Kulturbeziehun-
gen in alter und neuer Zeit. Mitteilungen Universitätsbund Göttingen, 1922.
20 p.
Backman, C. P., & Leffler, B. Ungern i
kultur och historie. (HUNGARY).
Stockholm, 1924. [Pp. 83-86, Svensk
litteratur i Ungern.]
Leyen, F. von der. Utgardaloke in IR-
LAND. Beiträge z. Gesch. d. dt.
Sprache & Lit., 33, 1907, 382-91.

Grimble, I. The King of Norway in Gaelic
Folk Lore. Norseman, 8, 1950, 225-30.
Boer-den Hoed, P. De studie van de scan-
dinavische invloeden op de neder-
landsche litteratuur. (N E T H E R-
LANDS). NP, 36, 1952, 234-40.
Rosman, H. Svensk litteratur i Holland.
Ord och Bild, 12, 1903, 229-32.
Buceta, E. Más sobre Noruega, símbolo
de la oscuridad. (PORTUGAL). RFE,
7, 1920, 378-81.
Campos Ferreira Lima, H. de. Portugal
e a Suecia. Revista da historia 13,
1925, 208-21.
Belaiew, N. Eymundar Saga and Icelandic Research in RUSSIA. Saga-
Book of Viking Society, 11, 1934, 93-
99.
Briem, B. Alt-Skandinavien in der
neueren russischen wissenschaftlichen
Literatur (1918-28). Acta philol.
scandinavica, 5, 1930, 211-36.
Lindquist, R. Sverige och svenskarna i
den ryska folkpoesien. Ord och Bild,
38, 1929, 383-86.
Schlauch, M. Scandinavian Influence on
the Slovo. In: Russian Epic Studies,
ed. Jakobson & Simmons (Memoirs
of American Folklore Society 42)
Philadelphia 1947, 99-124.

Interscandinavian Relations.

a. General.

Afzelius, N. Svenska skrifter rörande
Island. Gåva till Islands Allting . . .
1930. (Kungl. Bibliotekets Handlinger
42) Uppsala, 1930.
Andersson, O. Den svenska folkvisan i
Finland. Nordisk Kultur IX, A.
Folkesvisor. Utgjeven av K. Liestøl,
1931. 55-60.
Benson, A. The Old Norse Element in
Swedish Romanticism. New York,
1914, 192 p.
Helgason, J. Finland and Iceland. Le
Nord, 2, 1939, 455-58.
Elovson, H. Studier i brytningarna i
nordisk litteratur omkring 1890. Edda,
36, 1936, 369-449.
Halvorsen, E. Bjørnsons forhold til den
norrøne litteratur. Edda, 51, 1951,
211-19.
Klockhoff, O. Studier över 1600-talets
svenska dramatik i Sverige och Fin-
land. In: Festskrift H. Pipping. Helsingfors, 1925. 267-90.
Lidén, A. Den norska strömningen i
svensk litteratur under 1800-talet.
Uppsala, 1926. 311 p.

Nielsen, L. Ældre dansk Litteratur i Norge. NTBB, 10, 1923, 155-66.
———, Ældre dansk Litteratur i Sverige. Ibid, 13, 1926, 72-86.
Nilsson, A. Tre fornnordiska gestalter. Helge, Frithiof och Kung Fjalar. Lund, 1928, 415 p.
Paasche, F. Finnland und Norwegen. Le Nord, 2, 1939, 448-54.
Söderhjelm, W. Minna Canth. Några ord om norskt inflytande i finsk litteratur. In: Til Gerhard Gran 9. Dec. 1916, 284-304.
Steffen, R. Den norska kämpavisan och dess genljud i svensk litteratur. Nordisk Tidskrift, 1924, 19-32.
Wallén, E. Nordisk mytologi i svensk Romantik. Stockholm, 1918. 152 p.

b. Individual Authors, General Relations.

Heimer, A. Den danska sagodiktaren i Sverige och bland svenskar. (H. C. ANDERSEN). Stockholm, 1925. 205 p.
Birket-Smith, F. BELLMAN og Danmark. Ord och Bild, 37, 1928, 289-306, 357-71.
Schoning, O. Bellmans Digtning og dens Indflydelse i Danmark. (Studier fra Sprog og Oldtidsforskning, 63) København, 1904. 60 p.
Salokas, E. Bellmanin runous Soumessa. In: Kirjallisuudentutkijain seuran vuosikirja. Helsinki, 1929, 23-181.
Brandes, E. BJØRNSON og den danske Scene. In: Bjørnstjerne Bjørnson. Festskrift. København, 1902, 15-28.
Bull, F. Bjørnson og Norden. Nordens Kalendar 1933, 34-38.
Hirn, Y. Björnson och Finland. ibid. 18-24.
Söderhjelm, W. Björnson i Finland. In: Bjørnson Festskrift. København, 1902, 107-19. [Extended in his: Profiler ur finskt Kulturliv, 1913.]
Key, E. Björnson och Sverige. ibid. 41-69. (Also in E. Key, Verk och Människor, 1910, 229-69.)
Bull, F. Bjørnson og Sverige. In: Bjørnson Studier, Kristiania, 1911 (Smaaskrifter fra det litt. Seminar 7-13.) 171-281.
Knudsen, B. Signalfeiden. ibid. 319-351. [Bjørnson in Denmark.]
Landquist, J. Björnson och Sverige. Nordens Kalendar 1933, 25-33.
Stolpe, S. Björnson och Sverige. Bonniers litt. magasin, 1, 1932, 62-68.
Leijonhufvud, S. Ett bidrag till belysning af Sveriges litterära beröring med Danmark vid slutet af sextonhundra-

talet. Samlaren 19, 1898, 112-17. [BORDING's poetry in Sweden.]
Ahlenius, H. Georg BRANDES i svensk litteratur till och med 1890. Hans ställning och inflytande. Stockholm 1932. 418 p.
Linder, S. Georg Brandes och Norge. Ord och Bild, 15, 1941, 164-70.
Castrén, G. Frans Michael FRANZÉN i Finland. Helsingfors, 1902. 377 p.
Thesen, R. Arne GARBORG og Sverige. Ord och Bild 15, 1941, 220-28.
Kyrre, H. M. GOLDSCHMIDT og Norge. Edda, 1921, 276-91.
Lindbæk, S. P. A. HEIBERG og Norge. Edda, 34, 1934, 87-104.
Wildhagen, F. Verner v. HEIDENSTAM og Norge. Ord och Bild 15, 1941, 31-36.
Tarkianen, V. HOLBERG i Finland. Edda 31, 1931, 60-80.
Ehrencron-Müller, H. Jeppe paa Bjerget i Sverrig. Edda 30, 1930, 667-79.
Warburg, K. Holberg i Sverige jämte meddelanden om hans svenske öfversättare. Göteborg, 1884. 102 p.
Svedfelt, T. Alexander KIELLAND och det svenska åttitalet. Edda 31, 1931, 287-312.
Beyer, H. Søren KIERKEGAARDS betydning for norsk aandsliv. Edda, 19, 1923, 1-143.
Erichsen, V. Søren Kierkegaards betyding for norsk aandsliv. Edda 19, 1923, 209-429.
Hansen, H. Søren Kierkegaard og Sverige. Nordisk Tidskrift, 1946, 52-59.
Henriksen, Aa. Methods and Results of Kierkegaard Studies in Scandinavia. Copenhagen, 1951. 160 p.
Kabell, Aa. Kierkegaardstudiet i Norden. København, 1948. 329 p.
Oppel, H. Die Nachwirkung Kierkegaards in der nordischen Dichtung. Nordische Rundschau, 9, 1936-38, 145-57.
Pineau, L. Soeren Kierkegaard et la Norvège. RG, 28, 1927, 209-214. [Criticism of H. Beyer, Sören Kierkegaard og Norge, 1924.]
Sjöstedt, N. Søren Kierkegaard och svensk Litteratur från Fredrika Bremer till Hjalmar Söderberg. Göteborg, 1950. 418 p.
Nörregaard, G. Christian MOLBECH og Sverige. Nordisk Tidskrift, 17, 1941, 253-63.
Clausen, J. RUNEBERG og Danmark. In: J. L. Runebergs Hundraårsminne. Skrifter utgivna af Svenska Littera-

tursällskapet i Finland 62.) Helsingfors, 1904. 125-34.

Wrangel, E. Runeberg och Sverige. ibid. 55-110.

c. Individual Authors, Individual Relations.

Bo, A. **ÅKJÆR** og Fröding. Danske Studier 1949-50, 78-84.

Børge, V. August Strindberg og H. C. **ANDERSEN**. København, 1931. 146 p.

Krohn, H. Georg Brandes och Ernst **AHLGREN**. Nya Argus 20, 1927, 51-54.

Linder, S. Ernst Ahlgren och Georg Brandes. Samlaren, N.F. 16, 1935, 57-89.

Paludan, J. Lyksalighedens Ö. **ATTERBOM** og Paludan-Müller. Nordisk Tidskrift, 1900, 173-205.

Thesen, R. Bjørnstjerne **BJØRNSON** og Georg Brandes. Edda 38, 1939, 1-40.

Frisch, P. Gustaf Fröding og hans Bjørnsonbillede. Edda 51, 1951, 4-30.

Paludan, J. Geijer og **GRUNDTVIG**. Edda, 1923, 99-117.

Anker, Ø. Bjørnson og Grundtvig inntil 1872. Edda 32, 1932, 273-338.

Schneider, H. Henrik **IBSEN** und Knut Hamsun. D&V, 42, 1942, 1-14.

Aster, E. von. Ibsen und Strindberg. München 1921. 129 p.

Bühler, C. Strindberg und Ibsen. NSp. 31, 1923, 146-53.

Linder, S. Ibsen och Strindberg. Samlaren NF 13, 1932, 52-105.

Petersen, C. Gustav Fröding—Søren **KIERKEGAARD**. Kirke og kultur, 38, 1931, 203-15.

La Chesnais, P. Ibsen disciple de Kierkegaard. Edda 34, 1934, 355-410.

Möhring, W. Ibsen und Kierkegaard. Berlin (Palaestra 160) 1928. 187 p.

Sturtevant, A. **OEHLENSCHLÄGER** and Tegnér's 'Frithiofssaga.' SS, 6, 1920-21, 134-58.

Bæhrendtz, N. Viktor **RYDBERG** och Bjørnstjerne Bjørnson. Edda, 42, 1942, 1-55.

Krogvig, A. August **STRINDBERG** og Björnstjerne Björnson. In: Böker og mennesker. Kristiania, 1919, 150-74.

Sylwan, O. O. P. **STURZEN-BECKER** och Christian Winther. In: Til Gerhard Gran 9. XII. 1916, Kristiania 1916, 215-18.

Bull, F. **TEGNÉR** og Wergeland. ibid. 105-34.

Böök, F. Undset och Tegnér. Kirke og Kultur 33, 1926, 55-61.

Beyer, H. Sigrid **UNDSET** und Selma Lagerlöf. GRM, 20, 1932, 20-27.

IBSEN

General Studies

Dresdner, A. Ibsen als Norweger und Europäer. Jena 1907. 105 p.

Wais, K. Henrik Ibsens Wirkung in Spanien, Frankreich, Italien. Braunschweig, 1933. 84 p. [Four essays previously published.]

Andersen, Annette. Ibsen in **AMERICA**. SS, 14, 1935-37, 63-109, 115-155.

Fife, R. H. & Anstensen, A. Henrik Ibsen on the American Stage. ASR, 16, 1928, 218-28.

Haugen, E. Ibsen i Amerika. En ukjent førsteopførelse og et Ibsenbrev. Edda, 35, 1935, 553-59.

Zucker, A. Southern Critics of 1903 on Ibsen's Ghosts. PQ, 19, 1940, 392-99.

Domet, A. Arabischer Brief. (Ibsen und das arabische Drama). (**ARABIA**). Die Literatur, 1928, 540-43.

Archer, W. Ibsen and English Criticism. (**ENGLAND**). Fortnightly Rev. 46, 1889, 30-37.

————, The Mausoleum of Ibsen. ibid. 54. 1893, 77-91.

Burchardt, C. Ibsen and England. Norseman, 5, 1947, 149-56.

Decker, C. Ibsen's Literary Reputation and Victorian Taste. SP 32, 1935, 632-45.

Downs, B. Ibsen and his British Admirers. Norseman, 6, 1948, 259-62.

Filon, A. Le théâtre anglais contemporain. Ibsen à Londres. Le drame de demain. RDM, 132, 1895, 178-200.

Franc, M. Ibsen in England. Boston, 1919. 195 p.

Huber, R. Ibsens Bedeutung für das englische Drama. Diss., Marburg, 1914. 87 p.

Irvine, W. Shaw's Quintessence of Ibsenism. SAQ, 46, 1947, 252-62.

Qvamme, B. Ibsen og det engelske Teater. Edda, 42, 1942, 113-21.

Shaw, G. B. The Quintessence of Ibsenism. London, 1891.

Stefánsson, J. Henrik Ibsen i England. Nordisk Tidskrift, 1891, 31-39.

Toledano, D. Ibsen en Angleterre. Revue scandinave, 2, 1911, 597-602.

Söderhjelm, W. Ibsen på finska teatern. (**FINLAND**). In: Henrik Ibsen, Festskrift. Bergen 1898, 246-54.

Brandes, G. Henrik Ibsen en **FRANCE**. Cosmopolis, 5, 1897, 112-24.

Darthèze, A. Ibsen et les acteurs français. Revue d'Art dramatique, 13, 1898, 27-35.

Destrez, F. Ibsen et la Critique française. ibid. 36-45.

Lorde, A. de. Bibliographie. ibid. 68-71, 234-35. [On Ibsen in France.]

Lugné-Poe, A. M. Le théâtre d'Ibsen en France. ibid. 15-20.

Lundeberg, O. Ibsen in France. SS, 8, 1924, 93-107.

Mähly, J. Ibsen in Frankreich. Gegenwart 46, 1894, 38-40.

Reque, A. Trois auteurs dramatiques scandinaves Ibsen, Björnson, Strindberg devant la critique française 1889-1901. Paris 1930. 228 p.

Swanson, C. Ibsen and the Comédie-française. SS, 19, 1946-47, 70-78.

———, An Ibsen Theater in Paris: Lugné-Poe and the Théâtre de l'Oeuvre. SS, 17, 1942-43, 133-39.

Tissot, E. Petite histoire du courant Ibsenien en France. La Quinzaine, 41, 1901, 1-23.

Behrendsohn, W. Henrik Ibsen und die deutsche Geisteswelt. (GERMANY.) Deutsch-Nordisches Jb. 1928, 1-13.

Berg, L. Henrik Ibsen. Köln, 1901. [Pp. 32-39, Ibsen in Deutschland.]

Ellehauge, M. Ibsens Indflydelse paa de moderne tysk-østrigske Dramatikere. Tilskueren, 45, 1928, 131-44.

Eller, W. Ibsen in Germany, 1870-1900. Boston, 1918. 203 p. [Bibliography 193-97.]

Fischer, E. Ibsen und das Dritte Reich. NSR, 12, 1940, 755-63.

Jacobsohn, S. Ibsen und Berlin. Schaubühne 7. VI. 1906, 654-60.

Litzmann, B. Ibsens Dramen, 1877-1900. Ein Beitrag zur Geschichte des deutschen Dramas im 19. Jahrhundert. Hamburg 1901, 176 p.

Meyer, E. Was bedeutet Ibsens Lebenswerk für das deutsche Volk und für die deutsche dramatische Literatur? Deutsche Monatsschrift f. d. gesamte Leben d. Gegenwart, 6, 1906, 190-204.

Schmidt, F. Ibsen's Influence upon German Literature. PL 17, 1906, 112-18.

Thalmann, M. Henrik Ibsen, ein Erlebnis der Deutschen. Marburg 1928. 66 p.

Varia. Henrik Ibsen, Gedenkblätter zum 75. Geburtstag. Bühne & Welt 5, 1903, 497-528.

Wais, K. Henrik Ibsen und das Problem des Vergangenen im Zusammenhang der gleichzeitigen Geistesgeschichte. Stuttgart 1931. 281 p.

Wihan, J. Henrik Ibsen und das deutsche Geistesleben. Reichenberg i. B. 1925, 73 p.

Wolff, E. Die deutsche Ibsen-Litteratur (1872-1902). Bühne & Welt, 5, 1903, 566-70, 605-10.

Anon. Enrico Ibsen. (ITALY). Marzocco 22, XI. 1906.

Gara, E. Fortuna del Ibsen in Italia. Libri del giorno, 11, 1928, 139-42.

Prieto, M. Ibsen und PORTUGAL. Edda, 28, 1928, 129-135.

Krag, E. Ibsen i Russland. (RUSSIA). Edda, 28, 1928, 72-95.

Gregersen, H. Ibsen and SPAIN. A Study in Comparative Drama. Harvard U. P., 1936, 209 p.

———, Visiting Italian Interpreters of Ibsen in Barcelona and Madrid. HR, 3, 1935, 166-69.

Grol, M. Ibsen na Beogradskoj pozornici. (SERBIA). SKG, 47, 1936, 121-34.

Influences upon Individual Authors.

Krijn, S. Ernst AHLGREN en Brand. NP 26, 1941, 141-52.

Kalischer, S. Ibsen und BRAHM. Deutsche Theater Zs. 2, 23, 24, 26, 29, 1909.

Prampolini, G. CROCE e Ibsen. Rassegna d'Italia, 1, 1946, 223-25.

Vries, J. de. Ibsen en de CUREL. Onze Eeuw, 24, 1924, 250-69.

Gregersen, H. Ibsen and ECHEGARAY. HR 1, 1933, 338-40.

Kennedy, R. The Indebtedness of Echegary to Ibsen. Sewanee Rev. 34, 1926, 402-415.

Kirsch, E. Ibsens Peer Gynt und Dietrich ECKARTS freie Übertragung. ZDU, 53, 1939, 429-37.

Klenze, H. von. Paul ERNST and Hendrick Ibsen. GR, 16, 1941, 134-45.

Maynial, E. Ibsen et FOGAZZARO. RLC, 4, 1924, 92-108.

Kröner, J. Die Technik des realistischen Dramas bei Ibsen und GALSWORTHY (Diss. München; Beiträge zur engl. Philol. 28) Leipzig 1935, 113 p.

Feise, E. HAUPTMANNS Einsame Menschen und Ibsens Rosmersholm. GR, 10, 1935, 145-65.

Gunvaldsen, K. The Master Builder and Die Versunkene Glocke. MDU, 33, 1941, 153-62.

Bucks, D. & Nethercot, A. Ibsen and HERNE's Margaret Fleming. AL, 17, 1946, 311-33.

Kenner, H. JOYCE and Ibsen's Naturalism. Sewanee Rev. 59, 1951, 75-96.

MacLeod, V. The Influence of Ibsen on Joyce. PMLA, 60, 1945, 879-98; 62, 1947, 573-80.

Arestad, S. The Iceman Cometh and The Wild Duck. (O'NEILL). SS, 20, 1948, 1-11.

Küther, H. Arthur Wing PINERO und sein Verhältnis zu Henrik Ibsen. Diss., Münster, 1937. 67 p.

Julmont, C. Ibsen jugé par PIRANDELLO. L'Age Nouveau, 57, 1951, 121-22.

Lamm, M. Ibsen och SHAW. Edda, 47, 1947, 130-40.

Lavrin, J. Ibsen and Shaw. In his: Studies in European Literature. London 1929, 80-98.

Tveterås, H. Ibsen og SNOILSKY. In: Norvegica; Minneskrift. Oslo, 1933, 119-71.

Jürgensen, H. Henrik Ibsens Einfluss auf Hermann SUDERMANN. Diss., Lausanne, 1903. 85 p.

Zucker, A. The Ibsenian Villain in Sudermann's Heimat. GR, 3, 1928, 208-17.

Setterquist, J. Ibsen and SYNGE. Studia Neophilologica 24, 1952, 68-154.

Lamm, M. Ibsen och TJEKOV. Edda 47, 1947, 119-29.

Barnes, T. YEATS, Synge, Ibsen and Strindberg. Scrutiny 5, 1936, 257-62.

STRINDBERG

Ellehauge, M. Ekko fra Strindberg i Verdensteatret. Edda 31, 1931, 313-27.

Herzog, W. Strindberg und unsere Zeit. Forum, 1, 1914, 65-69.

Jacobsen, H. Strindbergs Verdensry. Tilskueren 41, 1924, 338-49, 402-11.

Robertson, J. Essays and Addresses on Literature. London 1935. [Pp. 255-71: Strindberg's Position in European Literature.]

Gassner, J. Strindberg in AMERICA. Theatre Arts, 33, 1949, 49-52.

Gustafson, A. Some Early English and American Strindberg Criticism. In: Festschrift G. T. Flom. Urbana, Ill. 1942, 106-24.

Rapp, E. Strindberg Bibliography. Strindberg's Reception in England and America. SS, 23, 1951, 1-22, 49-59, 109-37.

Anon. Strindberg in ENGLAND. TLS 30. I. 1930, 65-66.

Dahlström, C. The Parisian Reception of Strindberg's Plays. (FRANCE). SS, 19, 1947, 195-207.

————, Strindberg's 'Fadren' and the Théâtre Libre. MLN, 59, 1944, 567-68.

Gravier, M. Strindberg et le théâtre çais contemporain. LM, 1949, 282-91. See also A. Reque under Ibsen, above.

Burkhard, A. August Strindberg and Modern GERMAN Drama. GQ, 6, 1933, 163-74.

Gravier, M. Strindberg et le théâtre naturaliste allemand. EG, 2-4, 1947-48.

————, Strindberg et le théâtre moderne: L'Allemagne. Lyon, 1949, 185 p.

Marcus, C. Strindberg och den tyska vetenskapen. Nordisk Tidskrift, 1924, 435-41.

Sternberg, K. Unsere Zeit und August Strindberg. Glocke 6, 1920-21, 1176-84.

Wiese, L. Strindberg und die junge Generation. Köln, 1921. 16 p.

Wright, H. Rupert BROOKE och Strindberg. Forum, 6, 1919, 164-66.

Cohn, A. HAUPTMANN und Strindberg. Glocke, 7, 1921, 988-90.

Lavrin, J. HUYSMANS and Strindberg. In his: Studies in European Literature. London 1929, 118-30.

Haywood, I. Strindberg's Influence on Eugene O'NEILL. PL 39, 1928, 596-604.

Gravier, M. Strindberg et WEDEKIND. EG, 3, 1948, 309-318.

Marcuse, L. Theologie des Eros, Strindberg und Wedekind. Blätter des dt. Theaters, 94, 1923, 1-5.

SWEDENBORG

Hotson, C. Early Influence of Swedenborg in Europe. New-Church Review 37, 1930, 16-34.

Lamm, M. Swedenborg en Angleterre. (ENGLAND). Revue Bleue, 1936, 118-22.

Viatte, A. Les Swedenborgiens en FRANCE de 1820 à 1830. RLC, 11, 1931, 416-50.

Benz, E. Immanuel Swedenborg als geistiger Wegbahner des deutschen Idealismus und der deutschen Romantik. (GERMANY). DVLG, 19, 1941, 1-32.

Bernheim, P. BALZAC und Swedenborg. (Romanische Studien, 16) Berlin, 1914. 123 p.

Wright, T. Balzac and Swedenborg. New-Church Review 3, 1896, 481-503.

Schorer, M. Swedenborg and BLAKE. MP, 36, 1938, 157-78.

Hotson, C. EMERSON and the Swedenborgians. SP, 27, 1930, 517-45.

————, Emerson's Biographical Sources for "Swedenborg." SP, 26, 1929, 23-46.

Torbert, J. Emerson and Swedenborg. Texas Review, 2, 1917, 313-26.

Hotson, C. Swedenborg's Influence in America to 1830. (FRENEAU). New-Church Review, 37, 1930, 188-207.

Nugent, C. The Influence of Swedenborg upon GOETHE. ibid. 7, 1900, 541-47.

Peebles, W. Swedenborg's Influence upon Goethe. GR, 8, 1933, 147-56.

Morris, M. Swedenborg in Faust. Euphorion, 6, 1899, 491-510.

Schlieper, H. Emanuel Swedenborgs System der Naturphilosophie besonders in seiner Beziehung zu Goethe-Herderschen Anschauungen. Diss., Berlin, 1901. 48 p.

Schuchard, G. The Last Scene in Goethe's Faust. PMLA, 64, 1949, 417-44.

Ahlberg, A. KANT och Swedenborg. Nordisk Tidskrift, 1919. 386-98.

Benz, E. Swedenborg und LAVATER. Zs. f. Kirchengeschichte 57, 1938, 153-216.

Silver, E. MAETERLINCK and Swedenborg. New-Church Review 12, 1905, 416-22.

OTHER SCANDINAVIAN AUTHORS

Bredsdorff, E. H. C. ANDERSEN og Charles Dickens, København, 1951. 151 p.

Drachmann, A. E. B. Browning and Hans Andersen. Edda 33, 1933, 494-502.

Hersholt, J. (ed.) H. C. Andersen og Horace E. Scudder. En Brevveksling. Efterskrift af H. Topsøe-Jensen. København, 1948. 207 p.

Porterfield, A. BOJER'S Conquest of America. Bookman 58, 1923-24, 287-94.

Larson, H. & Haugen, E. BJÖRNSON and America. SS, 13, 1933, 1-12.

Sturtevant, A. Bjørnson and America. In: Bjørnson-Studier (Smaaskrifter fra det litt. Seminar 7-13) Kristiania, 1911, 99-113.

Kodicek, J. Bjørnson and Czechoslovakia. Norseman 3, 1945, 265-67.

Rytter, O. Bjørnson and Czechoslovakia. Norseman 2, 1944, 63-67.

See also A. Reque under Ibsen above. (France).

Eeden, W. van. Bjørnson og Nederland. Edda 51, 1951, 268-80.

Sawicki, S. Björnstjerne Björnson und Polen. Edda 32, 1932, 413-22.

Kara-Murza, S. Bjørnson på den russiske scene. Edda 34, 1934, 168-74.

Benson, A. Mark Twain's Contacts with Scandinavia. (BLICHER.) SS 14, 1935-37, 159-67.

Haugen, E. Georg BRANDES and his American Translators. JEGP 37, 1938, 462-87.

Rouveyse, A. Souvenirs de mon commerce. George Brandes parmi nous. MF, 194, 1927, 568-88.

Anon. Frederika BREMER och Amiel. Hertha, 11, 1924, 27-28.

Benson, A. The Essays on Frederika Bremer in the North American Review. PMLA 41, 1926, 747-55.

Krumm, G. Gustaf FRÖDINGS Verbindungen mit der deutschen Literatur. (Nordische Studien 16) Greifswald 1934, 195 p.

Behrendsohn, W. Knut HAMSUNS Aufnahme in Deutschland. Deutsch-Nordisches Jb., 1929, 85-92.

Ferwerda, S. HOLBERG en Holland. Zutphen 1939, 270 p.

Roos, C. Det 18. Aarhundredes tyske Oversættelser af Holbergs Komedier, deres Oprindelse, Karakter og Skæbne. Kjøbenhavn 1922. 284 p.

————, Holberg und die deutsche Komödie. Deutsch-Nordisches Jb., 1928, 27-40.

Stender-Petersen, A. Holberg og den russiske Komedie i det 18de Århundrede. Holberg Aarbog, 1923-25.

Baer, Lydia. Rilke and Jens Peter JACOBSEN. PMLA, 54, 1939, 900-32, 1133-80.

————, A Study of Ernst Wiechert with Special Reference to Jens Peter Jacobsen and Rilke. MLQ 5, 1944, 469-80.

di San Lazzaro, C. Die Aufzeichnungen des Malte Laurids Brigge von R. M. Rilke in Vergleich mit Jacobsens Niels Lyhne und A. Gides Nourritures Terrestres. GRM, 29, 1941, 106-17.

Alexander, I. La philosophie existentialiste en France. Ses sources et ses problèmes fondamentaux. (KIERKEGAARD.) FS, 1, 1947, 95-114.

Bohlin, T. Sören Kierkegaard und das religiöse Denken der Gegenwart. München, 1923. 178 p.

Brachfeld, O. Kierkegaard en Allemagne. Revue d'Allemagne, 6, 1932, 596-603.

Chestov, L. Kierkegaard et la philosophie existentielle. Traduit du russe. Paris 1936. 384 p.

Hohlenberg, J. Jean-Paul Sartre og hans

forhold til Kierkegaard. Samtiden 1947, 310-22.

Jancke, R. Rilke-Kierkegaard. D&V, 39, 1938, 314-29.

Johnson, H. Kierkegaard and Sartre. ASR, 35, 1947, 220-25.

Löwith, K. Kierkegaard und Nietzsche. DVLG, 11, 1933, 43-66. [A comparison.]

Lowrie, W. 'Existence' as Understood by Kierkegaard and/or Sartre. Sewanee Review, 53, 1950, 379-401.

Lunding, E. Adalbert Stifter. Mit einem Anhang (133-50) über Kierkegaard und die existentielle Literaturwissenschaft. Aarhus 1946.

Moore, W. Recent Studies of Kierkegaard. Journal of Theol. Studies, 40, 1939, 225-31.

Mustard, H. Sören Kierkegaard in German Literary Periodicals, 1860-1930. GR, 26, 1951, 83-101.

Mutius, G. von. Kierkegaard und das heutige Deutschland. Deutsch-Nordisches Jb., 1925, 1-13.

Oppel, H. Kierkegaard und die existentielle Literaturwissenschaft. D&V, 38, 1937, 18-29.

Rougemont, D. de et al. Kierkegaard. [Special number of] Foi et Vie, 64, 1934, 601-720. [Articles by Torsten Bohlin, Jean Wahl, Paul Tisseau; selections from Kierkegaard and reviews.]

Rougemont, D. de. Kierkegaard en France. NRF, 46, 1936, 971-76.

Sjestov, L. Kierkegaard og Dostojevski. Gads danske Magasin 1943, 358-78.

Steere, D. Kierkegaard in English. Journal of Religion 24, 1944, 271-78.

Wahl, J. Heidegger et Kierkegaard. Recherches philosophiques 2, 1932-33, 349-70.

Egidy, E. von. Selma LAGERLÖF und Ricarda Huch. Kunstwart 41, 1927-28, 283-90, 351-59.

Jolivet, A. La Winterballade de Gerhart Hauptmann et Herr Arnes peningar de Selma Lagerlöf. In: Mélanges C. Andler. Strasbourg, 1924, 163-70.

Eeden, W. van. Lidt om Jonas LIE og Nederland. Edda 52, 1952, 347-48.

Croce, B. Il Corregio dell' OEHLENSCHLAEGER e Olinto dal Borgo. Critica 26, 1928, 216-20.

Stewart, W. Oehlenschlæger's Relation to German Romanticism. SS, 2, 1914, 1-24.

Eigenbrodt, W. RUNEBERG in Deutschland. In J. L. Runebergs Hundra-

årsmine (Skrifter utgifna af Svenska Litteratursällskapet i Finland 62) Helsingfors, 1904. 111-124.

Söderhjelm, W. Profiler ur finskt kultur liv. Helsingfors, 1913. [Pp. 1-71: Runeberg inför utlandet.]

Waenerberg, T. J. L. Runebergs dikter på holländska. Förhandlinger och uppsatser utg. av Svenska Litteratursällskapet i Finland, 16, 1903, 113-27.

Appelmann, A. The Relation of Longfellow's Evangeline to TEGNÉR's Frithiofs Saga. SS 2, 1914-15, 165-80.

———, Longfellow's Evangeline und Tegner's Frithiof-Saga. Anglia, 49, 1925, 153-72.

Balakian, A. The two Axels. FR, 17, 1943, 18-22. [On Tegnér and Villiers de l'Isle-Adam.]

Benson, A. A List of English Translations of the Frithiofs Saga. GR, 1, 1926, 142-67.

Gravier, M. Tegnér et la France. Aubier 1943, 162 p. [Pp. 123-133, Tegnér en France.]

Nordell, O. Concerning English Translations from the Swedish Poem Frithiof's Saga: A Critique. SS 13, 1933-35, 53-66.

Swan, G. The English Versions of Tegnér's Axel, A Bibliographic Sketch. SS, 1, 1911-14, 179-84.

Thorstenberg, E. The Skeleton in Armour and the Frithiof Saga. MLN, 25, 1910, 189-92.

SCANDINAVIAN INFLUENCES UPON INDIVIDUAL AUTHORS

Gülzow, E. Ernst Moritz ARNDT in Schweden. Greifswald 1920. 28p.

Petersen, R. Fire Livsbilleder. København, 1894. [Pp. 141-185: Moritz Arndt og hans Forhold til Danmark.]

Wolfram, R. Ernst Moritz Arndt in Dänemark. Deutsch-Nordische Zs., 2, 1929, 125-30.

———, Ernst Moritz Arndt und Schweden. (Forschungen zur neueren Literaturgeschichte, 65) Weimar, 1933. 232p.

Wolters, F. Ernst Moritz Arndt und der Norden. Deutsch-Nordische Zs., 2, 1929, 5-15.

Rasmussen, E. BLAKEs revolusjonære forkynnerperiode. Edda 23, 1938, 290-331.

Hustvedt, S. George BORROW and his Danish Ballads. JEGP, 22, 1923, 262-70.

Wright, H. George Borrow's Translations from the Scandinavian Languages. Edda 16, 1921, 137-45.

——, DEFOE's Writings on Sweden. RES, 16, 1940, 25-32.

Diederichs, N. Eugen DIEDERICHS und sein Verhältnis zum Norden. Deutsch-Nordisches Jb., 1931, 130-35.

Benson, A. The Sources of William DUNLAP's Ella, A Norwegian Tale. SS, 19, 1946, 136-43.

Reuschel, K. Theodor FONTANEs nordische Balladen und Bilder. Festschrift Eugen Mogk, Halle, 1924, pp. 335-49.

Krejči, J. Nordische Stoffe bei FOUQUÉ. Vierteljahrsschrift für Litteraturgeschichte, 6, 1893, 553-70.

Hirsch, J. Fouqués Held des Nordens. Seine Quellen und seine Komposition. Berlin 1910, 74p.

Pfau, W. Das Altnordische bei GERSTENBERG. Vierteljahrsschrift für Litteraturgeschichte, 2, 1889, 161-95.

Döring, P. Der nordische Dichterkreis und die Schleswiger Litteraturbriefe. Sonderburg, 1880. 60p.

Petersens, H. Robert Pearse GILLIES, Foreign Quarterly Review och den svenska litteraturen. Samlaren, 14, 1933, 55-106.

Schwarz, I. Friedrich David GRÄTER. Ein Beitrag zur Geschichte der germanischen Philologie und zur Geschichte der deutsch-nordischen Beziehungen. Diss., Greifswald, 1935.

Vetterlund, F. Drag ur Amalie v. HELVIGS litterära förbindelser med Sverige. Nordisk Tidskrift, 1903, 27-37.

Kirby, W. William HERBERT and his Scandinavian Poetry. Saga-Book of Viking Club, 7, 1911, 206-19.

Paasche, F. HERDER og den norröne Digtning. Maal og Minne 2, 1910, 121-38.

Nyrop, K. Autor d'une poésie de Victor HUGO. In: Mélanges Baldensperger II, 1930, 141-150. [On Hugo's "Après la bataille" in Légende des Siècles.]

Pées, S. L'origine de la couleur locale scandinave dans le "Han d'Islande" de Victor Hugo. RLC, 9, 1929, 261-84.

Scheel, W. KLOPSTOCKs Kenntniss des germanischen Alterthums. Vierteljahrsschrift für Litteraturgeschichte, 6, 1893, 186-212.

Eggli, E. Note sur la source scandinave de l'Épée d'Angantyr de LECONTE DE LISLE. CLS, 1, 1941.

Vianey, J. Les sources de Leconte de Lisle. (Publ. de la Société des Langues Romanes, 21) Montpellier, 1907.

Hilen, A. LONGFELLOW and Scandinavia. A Study of the Poet's Relationship with the Northern Languages and Literatures. New Haven, 1947.

Leighly, J. Inaccuracies in Longfellow's Translation of Tegnér's Nattvardsbarnen. SS, 21, 1949, 170-80.

Nyland, W. Kalevala as a Reputed Source of Longfellow's Song of Hiawatha. AL, 22, 1950, 1-20.

Osborn, C. & S. Schoolcraft-Longfellow-Hiawatha. Lancaster, Pa. 1942, 697p.

Swan, M. Professor Longfellow, Scandinavian Book Buyer. Harvard Library Bull. 4, 1950, 359-73.

Burkhard, A. Thomas MANN's Indebtedness to Scandinavia. PMLA, 45, 1930.

Marcus, C. Thomas Mann und das Nordische. Deutsch-Nordisches Jb., 1930, 88-103.

Maury, L. Xavier MARMIER en Scandinavie. MF, 309, 1950, 353-55.

Wiehe, E. Gottlieb MOHNIKE als Vermittler und Übersetzer nordischer Literatur. (Nordische Studien, 15) Greifswald 1934. 123p.

Anderson, K. Scandinavian Elements in the Works of William MORRIS. Diss., Harvard, 1942.

Blöndal, S. William Morris und Island. Nordische Rundschau, 5, 1932, 160-70.

Hoare, D. The Works of Morris and of Yeats in Relation to Early Saga Literature. Cambridge, 1937. 179p.

Litzenberg, K. William Morris and Scandinavian Literature: A Bibliographical Essay. SS, 13, 1935, 93-105.

——, William Morris as Critic of Old Norse Literature. Edda 40, 1940, 301-20.

——, Allusions to the Elder Edda in the Non-Norse Poems of William Morris. SS, 14, 1935, 17-24.

——, William Morris and the Heimskringla. ibid., 33-39.

——, William Morris and the Burning of Njál. ibid., 40-41.

Benson, A. Scandinavian References in the Works of POE. JEGP, 40, 1941, 73-90.

Batho, E. Sir Walter SCOTT and the Sagas; Some Notes. MLR, 24, 1929, 409-15.

Lieder, P. Scott and Scandinavian Literature; the Influence of Bartholin and

Others. Smith Coll. Studies in Modern Languages, 2, 1920-21, 8-57.

Wright, H. SOUTHEY's Relations with Finland and Scandinavia. MLR, 27, 1932, 149-67.

Wagner, H. TASSO und die nordische Heldensage. Euphorion 6, 1899, 1-18.

Benson, A. Bayard TAYLOR's Interest in the Scandinavian North. SS, 7, 1925, 165-84.

———, Scandinavian Influence in the Writings of THOREAU. SS, 16, 1940-41, 241-56.

Moestue, W. UHLANDs nordische Studien. Berlin, 1902, 63p.

Golther, W. Die sagengeschichtlichen Grundlagen der Ringdichtung Richard WAGNERs. Charlottenburg, 1902.

Giese, A. Die Beziehungen Friedrich W. WEBERs zur nordischen Dichtung, (Nordische Studien 12) Braunschweig, 1930.

Unwerth, W. von. Christian WEISEs Dramen Regnerus und Ulvilda nebst einer Abhandlung zur deutschen und schwedischen Literaturgeschichte. Breslau, 1914, 296 p.

Trube, H. Friedrich G. WETZELs Leben und Werk mit besonderer Berücksichtigung seiner Lyrik. Berlin, 1928.

Allen, G. Walt WHITMAN's Long Journey Motif. JEGP, 38, 1939, 76-95.

Benson, A. Walt Whitman's Interest in Swedish Writers. JEGP, 31, 1932, 332-45.

Hartman, H. WORDSWORTH's Lapland Night. RES, 14, 1938, 189-93.

XIII. EAST-EUROPEAN CONTRIBUTIONS
By Thomas G. Winner
Duke University

GENERALITIES AND INTER-SLAVIC RELATIONS

Slavism in General.

Anon. K voprosu o slavjanskoj idee. Brat'ja Čexi. VE, 11, 1877, 429-43.

———, Po povodu našej perevodnoj literatury o Slavjanstvu. VE, 6, 1877, 859-66.

———, Davnost' slavjanskoj idei v russkom obščestve. VE, 5, 1878, 283-316.

Pogodin, A. Pričiny i celi novejšego slavjanskogo dviženija. VE, 1, 1909, 249-65.

Pypin, A. Iz istorii panslavizma. VE, 9, 1893, 267-313.

———, Literaturnyj panslavizm. VE, 6-9, 1879.

———, Obzor russkix izučenij slavjanstva. VE, 4-6, 1899.

———, Panslavizm v prošlom i nastojaščem. VE, 9-12, 1878.

———, Russkoe slavjanovedenie v XIX veke. VE, 7-9, 1889.

Spasowicz, W. Pol'skie fantazii na slavjanofil'skuju temu. VE, 8, 1872, 738-58.

Trubetzkoy, N. The Common Slavic Element in Russian Culture. New York, 1950.

Inter-Slavic Relations Among Countries.

Auézov, M. Tradicii russkogo realizma i kazaxskaja literatura. DN, 2, 1949.

Bučar, V. Sui rapporti culturali bulgarosloveni. Bulgaria, (Roma), 1942.

Fischer, G. Russian Studies in Czechoslovakia. AB, 6, 1949.

Goleniščev-Kutuzov, I. Russkaja kul'tura i Jugoslavija. Čisla, 2-3, 1930.

Harkins, W. E. The Russian Folk Epos in Czech Literature, 1800-1900. New York, 1951.

Hlobenko, M. The Ukraine in Russian Fiction. (In Ukrainian.) Enciklopedija Ukrainoznavstva, Munich-New York, 1950.

Jakóbiec, Marian. Literatura rosyjska wsród Polaków w okresie pozytywizmu. Wróčław, Inst. badań literackich, 1950.

Lev. Ukraino-Polish Relations in Polish Literary Works. (In Ukrainian.) Enciklopedija Ukrainoznavstva, Munich-New York, 1950.

Magnuszewski, J. Stosunki literackie polsko-czeskie w końcu XIX i na początku XX wieku. Wróčław, 1951, 199 p.

Manning, C. A. The Soviet Interpretation of Ukrainian Literature. UQ, 7, 1951.

Mašinskij, S. Russko-ukrainskie literaturnye svjazy. NoM, 2, 1952, 269-73.

Mìček, E. Early Russian Influence on Czech Language and Literature. AB, 8, 1951.

Muqanov, S. Kazaxskaja sovetskaja literatura posle postanovlenija CK VKP(b) ot 14 avgusta 1946 goda o žurnalax "Zvezda" i "Leningrad." LG, 18. XII, 1948.

Nalepinskij, T. Duša Pol'ši. Opyt irracional'nogo issledovanija. VE, 10, 1909.

Oliva, R. Polish Literature in Czech translation. (A bibliography), PZ, 7, 1951. (In Polish.)

Parry, A. Spread of the Russian Language in the USSR's Satellite Countries of Europe and Asia. AB, 8, 1951.

Pypin, A. Epizod iz literaturnyx otnošenij malorussko-pol'skix. VE, 2-3, 1886.

———, Pervye sluxi o serbskoj narodnoj poézii. VE, 12, 1876, 689-743.

———, Pol'skij vopros v russkoj literature. VE, 2-11, 1880.

Struve, P. Obščerusskaja kul'tura i ukrainskij partikuljarizm. RM, 1, 1911.

Szyjkowski, Marian. Polish Influence on the Czech Renaissance. (In Czech.) Prague, 1948.

———, Czeskie odrodzenie w XIX wieku. Warszawa, 1948.

Xačapuridze, G. Cultural Relations Between Russia and Georgia During the First Half of the Nineteenth Century (In Russian). Voprosy istorii, Moscow, 5-6, 1946.

Živanović, D. Srbi i poljska književnost. (1800-1871). Beograd, 1941, 276 p.

Inter-Slavic Relations Among Individual Authors.

Hepner, B. P. **BAKOUNINE** et le Panslavisme révolutionnaire. Paris, 1950.

Szyjkowski, Marian. Otokar **BREZINA** a J. Słowacki. SV, 1948.

Charques, R. D. **DOSTOEVSKY** and the Slavic Idea. Fortnightly, April, 1951.

Tureček, O. Tschechische Literatur und Dostojewski. WSJ, 1950.

Efimenko, A. Nacional'naja dvojstvennost' v tvorčestve **GOGOL**ja. VE, 7, 1902. [Russian and Ukrainian characteristics in Gogol's work.]

German, F. Gogol i Mickiewicz. DJ, 30, III. 1952.

Manning, C. Gogol and Ukraine. UQ, 4, 1950.

Taufer, J. Nikolaj Vasiljevič Gogol. Praha-Brno, 1952. [Some material on Gogol's influence on Havliček-Borovský.]

Zaxarov, L. Gogolj i Nušič. K, 6, 1951.

Běhounek, V. České vydání spisů Maxima Gorkého. (**GORKIJ**) NoZ, 6, 1951.

Kadlec, J. Maxim Gorkij v Československu. Praha, 1951, 53 p.

Karakostov, S. Maksim Gorki i b'lgarskata literatura. Vlijanie i vr'zki. Sofia, 1947, 152 p.

Georgiev, E. Slavjanska pis'mennost do **KIRILLA** i Mefodija. Sofia, 1952, 96 p.

Szyjkowski, Marian. **KRASINSKI** in Czech Literature. Sprawozdania Polskiej Akademii Umejętnosci. Kraków, 50, 1949.

Czerniatowicz, J. **MAJAKOVSKIJ** in Poland (In Polish). Warszawa, 1950.

Moldavskij, D. Majakovskij i poézija Sovetskogo Vostoka. Zv, 4, 1949, 165-70.

Neumann, S. Vliv Majakovského na čєské básnictví. SloP, 36, 1950.

Šejxzade. Majakovskij i uzbekskaja sovetskaja literatura. LG, 14, IV. 1940.

Aronson, M. Konrad Wallenrod i Poltava. (**MICKIEWICZ** & Puškin). VPD, 2, 1936.

Berkov, P. N. Genij pol'skoj poézii Adam Mickevič. IAN-OLJA, 2, 1949.

Brailovskij, S. K istorii russko-pol'skix literaturnyx otnošenii. Mickevič i Puškin. PiS, 7, 1908, 79-109.

Černobaev, V. Stoletie tret'ej časti Dziadów Mickeviča (1832-1932). In Festschrift Orlov, Leningrad, 1934.

Fiszman, S. Mickiewicz w Rosji. Z archiwów, museów, bibliotek Moskwy i Leningradu. Warszawa, 1949.

Frančić, V. Mickiewicz in Croat and Serb translations. (In Polish). PS, 1, 1949.

Gomolicki, L. Mickiewicz' Diary on His Visit to Russia 1824-29. (In Polish). Warszawa, 1949.

Jacimirskij, A. Mickevič i Puškin v novom osveščenii. VE, 10, 1907, 739-51.

Szyjkowski, Marian. Mickiewicz' Travels to Prague. (In Polish). PZ, 1950.

Weintraub, W. Mickiewicz and Bakunin. SEER, 28, 1949-50.

Zwyjkowski, M. New Translations of Miczkiewicz into Czech. (In Czech). SV, 2, 1949.

Popov, N., (ed.) Pis'ma k M.P. **POGODINU** iz slavjanskix zemel'. Moscow, 1880.

Anon. Izdanija proizvedenii **PUŠKIN**a na jazykax narodov SSSR (po dannym vsesojuznoj knižnoj palaty). DN, 3, 1949.

Badalić, J. Puškin in Croat Literature (In Croat). R, 5, 1949.

Banjać, D. Two Serbian Translations of Puškin's Boris Godunov. (In Serbian). K, 5, 1950.

Barac, A. Mažuranić prema Puškinu. SlR, 3, 1950.

Brtan, R. Puškin a Slováci. SloP, June, 1949.

———, Puškin v Slovakii. Slavyane, 3, (Moscow), 1949.

Burian, V. Puškin a česká proza. In Dolanský: Puškin u nás. Praha, 1949.

Dolanský, J. Čím nám byl Puškin. Nož, 5, 1949, 58-68.

———. (ed.) Puškin u nás. 1799-1949. Praha, 1949.

Francev, V. Puškin i pol'skoe vosstanie

1830 i 1831 g. Opyt istoričekogo kommentarija k stixotvorenijam Klevetnikam Rossii i Borodinskaja godovščina. In: Puškinskij Sbornik. Russkij Naučnyj Institut, Praha, 1929, 65-208. (With a short French résumé).

Grund, A. Puškin and Czech Verse. (In Czech). In: Dolanský: Puškin u nás. Praha, 1949.

Krejčí, J. The Czech Illustrators of Puškin. (In Czech). ibid.

Lednicki, W. Some Doubt about the Identity of Pushkin's Polonophil. SEER, 30.

Nikol'skij, S. Evgenij Onegin v pol'skom perevode. RM, 12, 1905, 86-92.

Pražák, A. Puškin a Fr. Táborský. In Dolanský: Puškin u nás. Praha, 1949.

Procházková, H. Puškin v Čechách do 1860. ibid.

Spasowicz, W. Puškin i Mickevič u pamjatnika Petra Velikogo. VE, 4, 1887, 743-93.

Toporowski, M. Puszkin w Polsce. Warszawa, 1950. [Bibliography of translations, critical articles, etc.]

Zakrzewski, B. Puškin in Polish Poetry (In Polish). PZ, 5, 1949, also DJ, 6, 1950.

Zołkiewski, S. Puszkin a my. Warszawa, 1949.

Damiani, E. SLOWACKI in Bulgaria. (In Polish). Słowacki Centenary Volume, London, 1951.

Magnuszewski, J. Słowacki in the Translation of the Czech poet F. Hallas. (In Polish). PZ, 7, 1951.

Lednicki, W. Russian Themes in Słowacki's Writings. (In Polish). Słowacki Centenary Volume, London, 1951.

Anon. Serbo-Croat Translations of TOLSTOY's Work (In Croat). VNFH, 31, III. 1950.

Korabljov, V. Lev Tolstoj i slavjanstvo. In: Festschrift Orlov, Leningrad, 1934, 413-21.

Mráz, A. L. Tolstoj a Slováci. SlPo, 66, 1950.

Anon. Serbskij perevod TURGENEVskoj Novi. VE, 12, 1877, 874-77.

Nikol'skij, J. Turgenev i pisateli Ukrainy. RM, 7, 1914, 99-117.

Spasowicz, W. Knjaz' Petr Andrejevič VJAZEMSKIJ i ego pol'skie otnošenija i znakomstva. RM, 1, 1890, 51-82.

Petré, F. Začatek korespondence med VRAZOM in Šafařikom. SlR, 4, 1951.

MINOR SLAVIC AND DANUBIAN COUNTRIES

Leo, M. La BULGARIE et son peuple sous la domination Ottomane, tels que les ont vus les voyageurs Anglo-Saxons (1586-1878). Sofia, 1949.

Mixajlov, G. Greek Epigrams from Bulgarian Lands. (In Bulgarian with a German résumé). U. of Sofia, Faculty of Hist. & Philol., 1943-44.

Primov, B. Geoffroi de Villehardouin, la quatrième croisade et la Bulgarie. Ann. de l'U. de Sofia, 1949.

Turdeanu, E. La littérature bulgare du XIVe siècle et sa diffusion dans les pays Roumains. Paris, 1947.

Mann, S. E. Literary Borderland: Reflections on Modern CZECH Poetry. SEER, 30.

Birgas, G. French Travellers in HUNGARY. (In Hungarian). Szeged, 1948.

Gáldi, L. Petöfi and Eminescu. ASEER, 7, 1948, 171-79.

Karl, L. Magyarország a spaniol nemzeti és a Francia Klasszikus drámában. Budapest, 1911.

Remenyi, J. Hungarian Publications in English. ASEER, 6, 16-17.

Szigethy, V. de. H. F. Amiel traducteur, son européanisme. Ses relations avec la Hongrie. Szeged, 1929.

Tronchon, H. Les débuts de la littérature hongroise en France. REH, 1925.

Balys, J. LITHUANIAN Folk Songs in the United States. JIFM, 3, 1951.

Bersano Begey, M. & M. La POLONIA in Italia. Saggio bibliografico, 1799-1948. Torino, 1949.

Matić, T. Un écho de la polonophilie allemande en Croatie. RLC, 26, 1952.

Wolff, Z. Eighteenth Century Poland as seen by Italian Travellers. (In Polish). Studia dziejów kultury. Warszawa, 1949.

Cioranescu, A. La ROUMANIE dans la nouvelle littérature provençale. CL, 2, 1950.

Isopescu, C. Letteratura romena in Occidente. Osservatore Romano, 11, II. 1949.

———, Philaret Chasles e i Romeni. ibid. 19. II. 1950.

———, As primeiras notícás estrangeiras sôbre a vida literária na Romênia. (French résumé). Revista de Historia, São Paulo, 8, 1951.

———, Les origines de l'enseignement du Roumain en France. LM, 4, 1950.

Roque-Ferrier, A. La Roumanie dans les

littératures de la France. RLR, 20, 1881.
Dobriansky, L. E. **UCRAINICA** in American and Foreign Periodicals. UQ, 7, 1951.
Sichinsky, V. A French Description of Ukraine 300 Years Ago. ibid. 6, 1950.
Borgeaud, W. Les Illyriens en Grèce. Etude linguistique et mythologique. **(YUGOSLAVIA)**. Genève, 1943.
Mojasević, M. The Serbian Folktale in German Translation (1815-1819). (In Serbo-Croat with German résumé). Beograd, 1950.
Salvini, L. Italijani o slovenski kulturi. SlR, 4, 1951. [A bibliography.]

RUSSIAN INFLUENCES

Alpatov, M. The Russian Impact on Art. New York, 1950.
Mendel'son, M. Sila pravdy. K voprosu o vlijanii klassičeskoj russkoj i sovetskoj literatury na amerikanskuju. **(AMERICA)**. Znamja, 1, (Moscow), 1948.
Tverskoj, P. Amerikanskij ženskij klub o russkix pisateljax. VE, 3, 1896.
Deržavin, K. Russkaja povest' v argentinskoj dramaturgii. **(ARGENTINA)**. NBLU, 14-15, 1947.
Schanzer, O. Parallels between Spanish-American and Russian Novellistic Themes. Hisp, 35, 1952. [Influence of Russian Literature on some Spanish-American novelists.]
Gleason, J. H. Genesis of Russophobia in Great Britain. **(ENGLAND)**. Harvard U. P., 1950.
Phelps, G. Russian Realism and English Fiction. Cambridge Journal, 3, 1950.
Zvavic, I. Russkaja kniga v Anglii. PiR, 6, 1923.
Berkov, P. Izučenie russkoj literatury vo Francii. **(FRANCE)**. LN, 33-35, 1939.
Chamberlain, J. L. Notes on Russian Influences on the Nineteenth Century French novel. MLJ, 33, 1949.
Gal'perin-Kaminskij, E. Russovedenie vo Francii. RM, 9, 1894.
Hemmings, F. W. J. The Russian Novel in France (1884-1914), Oxford U. P., 1950.
Lortholary, A. Le Mirage russe en France au xviiie siècle. Paris, 1951. [A full analysis of the legend in eighteenth century France of an enlightened, tolerant and culturally advanced Russia, fostered primarily by Voltaire, who sought a foil to oppose to Charles XII and Frederick II, and by the

blandishments of Catherine the Great.]
Vengerova, Z. Russkij roman vo Francii. VE, 2, 1899.
Weidlé, W. "Tolstoievski" et l'occident. C, Aug. 1948.
Tal'skij, M. Russkaja poézija v nemeckix perevodax **(GERMANY)**. RM, 11, 1901.
Zalkind-Alenina, E. Nemeckie pisateli o Sovetskoj Rossii. Čisla, 7-8, 1933.
Messina, G. L. Le traduzioni del Russo nel 1920-1943. **(ITALY)**. Belfagor, Nov. 1949.
Švyrov, A. Russkie tečenje v japonskoj literature. **(JAPAN)**. Čisla, 2-3, 1930.
Benediktov, M. Russkaja kul'tura v **PALESTINE**. Čisla, 1, 1930.
Berkov, P. Pervaja istorija russkoj literatury na portugal'skom jazyke. **(PORTUGAL)**. In: Festschrift Orlov. Leningrad, 1934.
Deržavin, K. Russkaja literatura v Ispanii. **(SPAIN)**. NBLU, 14-15, 1947.
Lesevič, V. Vzgljady ispanskoj kritiki na russkuju žizn' i russkij roman. RM, 10, 1888.

DOSTOEVSKI

Morand, P. L'Europe russe annoncée par Dostoievsky. Genève, 1948.
Siller, F. Legenda o Dostoevskom v zapadno-evropejskoj literaturnoj kritike. LiM, 5, 1928.
Hemmings, F. W. Dostoievski in Disguise. The 1888 **FRENCH** Version of the Brothers Karamazov, FS, July, 1950.
Hoentsch, A. Dostojewski in Deutschland. **(GERMANY)**. Ho, 41, 1948-49.
Guarnieri Ortolani, A. M. V. Saggio sulla fortuna di Dostoevskij in **ITALIA**. Padova, 1947.
Rodriguez Beteta, V. Dostoyevski en España. **(SPAIN)**. La Prensa, (Buenos Aires), 17, V. 1936.
Curnier, P. A. **GIDE**, Dostoievski, et les problèmes du roman contemporain. L'Information littéraire, Nov.-Dec. 1950.
Struve, G. Novye varianty šigaljovščiny: O romanax Zamjatina, Xaksli i Orvella. Nžu, 30, 1952. [A comparative study of three "anti-utopian" novels: Zamyatin's We, **HUXLEY**'s Brave New World and Orwell's Nineteen Eighty Four. All three are related to Dostoevsky's Legend of the Grand Inquisitor and The Possessed.]

Kranz, G. **JÜNGER** und Dostojewski. Neuphilologische Zs., 4, 1952. [Although Ernst Jünger was influenced mainly by French and English writers and was even repelled, both ethically and aesthetically, by Russian literature, he felt gradually more and more drawn toward Dostoevsky. The change in Jünger's attitude to D. is traced, and the influence of Stavrogin and Prince Myshkin on his own characters shown.]

Starobinski, J. **KAFKA** et Dostoievski. CS, 304, 1950.

Tramer, B. Dostojevskij a **NIETSCHE.** Sla, 1950.

Turrian, M. Dostojewskij und **FRANZ WERFEL.** Vom östlichen zum westlichen Denken. Bern, 1950.

PUSHKIN.

Anon. Puškin in Foreign Literature (In Russian). In: Berkov, P. N. & Lavrov, V. M. Bibliografija Puškina. Moscow, 1949.

*Alekseev, M. Puškin na Zapade. VPD, 3, 1937.

Dietrich. Puschkins Weltgeltung. NW, 4, 1949.

Lukacs, G. Puschkins Platz in der Weltliteratur. Sinn & Form, 1, 1952, 150-81.

Tverskoj, P. Puškinskoe prazdnestvo v Kalifornii. (**AMERICA.**) VE, 9, 1899, 333-43.

Glinka, S. Angličanin o Puškine zimoju 1829-30 gg. (**ENGLAND.**) PiS, 31-32, 1927, 105-10.

Struve, G. Puškin in Early English Criticism. 1821-38. ASEER, 8, 1949, 296-314.

Kaz'menko, K. O vlijanii A. S. Puškina na francuzskuju literaturu. (**FRANCE.**) In: Puškinskij sbornik. Stavropol, 1949, 79-84.

L'vov, L. Sto let smerti Puškina. Parižskie otkliki v 1937 godu. Paris, 1937.

Trubicyn, N. O russkix narodnyx pesnjax, perevedennyx Puškinym na francuzskij jazyk. Pamjati Puškina. U. of St. Petersburg, 1900, 351-88.

Anon. Puschkins Werke in deutscher Sprache. (**GERMANY.**) BDB, 116, 1949.

Behrsing, S. Wie übersetzt man Puschkin? Neue Welt, 10, 1949.

Kaiser, B. Puschkin und Deutschland NG, 3, 1949.

Ščogolev, P. Sud'ba odnogo nemeckogo perevoda Klevetnikam Rossii. PiS, 7, 1908, 60-64.

Mizutani, K. A. S. Puškin i Nippon. (**JAPAN.**) In: Rossija i Puškin. Harbin, 1937, 81-83.

Van den Veen, H. R. S. Poesjkin in **NEDERLAND.** LT, 150, June, 1949.

Niscov, L. Le centenaire de la mort de Pouchkine dans les périodiques **ROUMAINS.** Sla, 18, 1947-48.

Alekseev, M. Neskol'ko dannyx o Puškine i Batjuškove. IAN, OLJA, 4, 1949. [ANTON **DIETRICH** as translator of Russian poets and intermediary between German and Russian literature.]

Kazanskij, B. Razgovor s angličaninom. VPD, 1936. [Captain C. Colville FRANKLAND, an English traveller, and Puškin.]

Čebyšev, A. Prosper **MERIME.** K ego znakomstvu s Puškinym i russkoj literaturoj. PiS, 23-24, 1916.

Schroeder, H. Puškin's Cygany und Mérimée's Carmen. ZSP, 21, 1952, 307-19. [Tends to discredit the widely accepted notion that M's Carmen was stimulated, if not directly influenced, by P's Cygany, but admits the similarity between the two works, "which bespeak stronger than any direct connection, the spiritual affinity between the two great writers."]

Grossman, L. Pikovaja dama i novella Renje. In: Ot Puškina do Bloka. Moscow, 1926. [Henri de **RÉGNIER.**]

Bazankur, O. Perevodčik Puškina-Ričči. VPD, 6, 1941. (Translators: Conte Miniato **RICCI.**)

TOLSTOI.

Suxotina-Tolstaja, T. Druz'ja i gosti Jasnoj Poljany. VE, 11, 1904, 5-35. Also: RM, 11, 1914, 74-82.

Lindstrom, Thaïs S. Tolstoï en **FRANCE** (1886-1910.) Paris, 1952, 172 p. [A valuable study of Tolstoy's fortunes in France. Divided into two parts, the first dealing with the French criticism of, and attitude toward, Tolstoy, and the second with personal contacts of French scholars, writers, pacifists and journalists with Tolstoy.]

Kjuner, N. L. N. Tolstoj v japonskoj literature. (**JAPAN.**) Vestnik Azii, Harbin, 1922.

Gordlevskij, V. Tolstoj v Turcii. (**TURKEY.**) Vostok, 5, 1925, 208-12.

Šifman, A. Lev Tolstoj o kolonial'nom razboe. IAN, OLJA, 11, 1952, 509-26.

[T. as a fighter against imperialism, who influenced Anatole **FRANCE**, R. Rolland, G. B. Shaw and others.]
Nag, Kalidas. Tolstoy and **GANDHI**. Patna, 1950.
Popov, N. Jasnaja Poljana i ostrov Kaprera (Iz vospominanij garibal'dijca). RM, 1, 1905, 61-67. [**GARIBALDI.**]
Budd, L. J. William Dean **HOWELLS'** Debt to Tolstoy. ASEER, 9, 1950.
Ejxenbaum, B. Tolstoj i Pol' de Kok. (Paul de **KOCK.**) In: Zapadnyj sbornik, 1, Moscow, 1937.
Mohašević, M. Jedan pogled na Buddenbrokove i Anu Kareninu. [Thomas **MANN.**] NJK, 1-2, 1951, 29-37.
Rusanov, N. Anglijskij biograf Tolstogo. RuB, 12, 1910, 92-124.

TURGENEV.

Alekseev, M. Turgenev — propagandist russkoj literatury na Zapade. In: Meilax, B. (ed.) Trudy Otdela novoj russkoj literatury. Akademija Nauk SSSR. Institut literatury. Moscow, 1948, 324.
Percov, P. O Turgeneve russkaja i innostrannaja kritika (1818-1918). Moscow, 1918.
Anon. Čerty iz parižskoj žizni I. S. Turgeneva. (**FRANCE.**) RM, 11, 1883, 311-28.
Gut'jar, N. Iv. S. Turgenev vo Francii: 1847-50. VE, 11, 1902, 94-136.
Kleman, M. Zapiski oxotnika i francuzskaja publicistika 1854 goda. In: Festschrift Orlov. Leningrad, 1934, 305-14.
Mazon, A. Manuscripts parisiens d'Ivan Tourguénev. Notices et extraits. Paris, 1930.
Anon. Pis'ma Turgeneva k ego nemeckim druz'jam. (**GERMANY.**) VE, 3-6, 1909.
Carter, A. E. Tourgeneff's New Year's Greeting to **FLAUBERT.** MLN, 64, 1949.
Donskaja, S. Anatol' Frans i Turgenev. (Anatole **FRANCE**). NBLU, 4, 1945, 36-38.
Strémooukhoff, D. Lettres de Tourguénev à Victor **HUGO.** Rev. des Etudes Slaves. 27, 1951.
Dunbar, V. R. The Problem in Roderick Hudson (**JAMES**). MLN, 1952.
Anon. Kritika russkix pisatelei v Germanii. VE, 12, 1868, 909-16. (Julius **SCHMIDT.**)
Gutjar, N. Ivan Sergeevič Turgenev i semejstvo **VIARDO-GARSIA.** VE, 8, 1908, 417-460.

OTHER SLAVIC AUTHORS.

Grigor'jan, K. V. **BRJUSOV** i armjanskaja poézija. IAN, OLJA, 3, 1948, 251-56.
Anon. R. M. Ril'ke po povodu "Mitinoj ljubvi." RM, 1, 1927, 54-56. (**BUNIN.**)
Geršenzon, M. Iz perepiski **ČAADAEV**a 1845 g. Po povodu stat'i v žurnale Le Semeur: Un sermon à Moscou. VE, 12, 1900, 465-76.
Heifetz, Anna. **CHEKHOV** in English: A List of Works By and About Him. BNYPL, 53.
Wilson, E. Seeing Chekhov Plain. New Yorker, 22, XI, 1952, 180-98. [A review essay, controversial but suggestive, prompted by two recent English books on Chekhov (Ronald Hingley and David Magarshak), criticizing some accepted Anglo-Saxon views on C., including those of Virginia Woolf and Somerset Maugham, and attempting to place C. against the Russian social and cultural background of his time. C. is said to be "much more limited and local than Tolstoy and Dostoevsky.]
Alekseev, M. Amerikano-russkie literaturnye zametki: A. G. **EVSTAF'EV**—russko-amerikanskij pisatel' načala XIX veka. NBLU, 8, 1946.
Anon. Les traductions françaises des comédies d'Aleksander **FREDRO.** Bul. de l'Acad. Polonaise des Sciences et des Lettres, Centre Polonais de Paris. June, 1951.
Pierre, A. A propos d'un centenaire: **GOGOL** et Mérimée. Le Monde, 4, III. 1952.
Borovik, E. & Rumjancev, J. A. M. **GOR'KIJ** i progressivnye pisateli Indii. Znamja, 3, (Moscow), 1952, 176-179.
Fedorenko, N. Nasledie M. Gor'kogo i sovetskaja literatura v Kitae. In: Gor'kovskie čtenija: 1949-50. Moscow, Akademija Nauk SSSR, 1951. [Emphasizes the influence of Gorkij and other Soviet writers on present-day Chinese literature.]
Messina, G. L. Gorkij in Italia. ICS, 31, 1948.
Schumskij, A. Wie sehen fortschrittliche deutsche Schriftsteller Maxim Gorki? NW, 3, 1949.
Gamazov, M. Gore ot uma v tureckom perevode. (**GRIBOEDOV**). VE, 1, 1886, 430-50.
Kamenev, J. Samyj ostroumnyj protivnik Gercena. VE, 4, 1914, 118-60. (**HERZEN** and Reinhold Solger.]

Mendelson, N. Gercen-Prudon-Tolstoj. LN, 15, 1934, 282-86. [Herzen's and Tolstoj's relations and meetings with Proudhon.]

IGOR: See 111 & 709.

Wagner, A. M. Undivine Comedy: Zygmund **KRASINSKI** and German Expressionism. ASEER, 6, 1947, 18-19.

Zygulski, Z. Krasiński i Hebbel. Pamiętnik Literacki, Lwów, 1947.

Anon. Anglijskij perevod **LERMONTOV**skogo Demona. VE, 10, 1875, 884-88.

Mitropan, P. Prvi perevodi Ljermontova na srpskom. B, 4, 1951, 576-82.

Chiavazza, B. The Fate of **MICKIEWICZ** in Italy. (In Polish.) SAU, 50, 1949.

Hahn, W. Translations of Mickiewicz' work into Latin and Greek. Me, 1951.

Karenin, V. Adam Mickevič i Georges Sand. VE, 5, 1907.

Mikusinski, L. German Opinions on Mickiewicz. (In Polish.) PZ, 5, 1949. Also DJ, 6, 1950.

Miłosz, C. Mickiewicz and Modern Poetry. ASEER, 7, 1948.

Zakrzewski, B. Mickiewicz w Berlinie. PZ, 3-4, 1949.

Levin, Ju. **NEKRASOV** v Anglii i Amerike. (Kritiko - bibliografičeskie zametki). NBLU, 16-17, 1947. (Reception of N. and translations of his work in England and USA.)

Anon. L'oeuvre de Jules **SLOWACKI** en France. Bull. de l'Acad. polonaise des Sciences et des Lettres. Centre polonais de Paris. June, 1951.

Andreis, E. de Traduzioni e scritti su Slowacki. Słowacki Centenary Volume, London, 1951.

Folejewski, Z. Słowacki in Scandinavian Countries. (In Polish.) ibid.

Folkierski, W. Wierny towarzysz twórczej myśli: Alfred de Vigny. ibid.

———, Dwa glosy: Viktora Hugo i J. Słowackiego. Zycie, London, 22. II. 1952.

Marković, Z. Život i pjesnički rad Juliusa Slowackoga. HK, 3, 1950.

EAST-EUROPEAN INFLUENCES UPON INDIVIDUAL AUTHORS.

Collon-Bérard, Suzanne. Le dernier voyage de **BALZAC** en Russie. RLC, 24, 1950.

Zaleski, Z. L. Les opinions de Balzac sur les Polonais et la Russie. Tęki historyczne, 4, (London), 1950.

———. Réalités et fictions polonaises dans l'oeuvre de Balzac. RLC, 24, 1950.

———, Balzak między Polską a Rosją. London, 1953.

Berkov, P. Dominik Blekford i russkaja literatura. NBLU, 8, 1946, 12-14. (**BLACKFORD.**)

Azadovskij, M. Poéma Šamisso o dekabriste A. Bestuževe. (**CHAMISSO.**) Sibirskie Ogni, 3, (Novosibirsk), 1926, 148-57.

Morf, G. The Polish Heritage of Joseph **CONRAD.** London, 1930.

Kohler, Phyllis P. Journey for Our Time: The Journals of the Marquis de **CUSTINE.** New York, 1951.

Kulczycka-Saloni, Janina. Z dziejów **DICKENS**a w Polce: Emancypantki a Bleak House. Łódz, 1947.

Korzon, K. Polonais dans l'Encyclopédie de **DIDEROT.** Pamiętnik Literacki, 1950.

Pichois, C. La Russie en 1839 jugée par un Allemand. (Varnhagen von **ENSE**). RLC, 26, 1952.

Messer, R. Ruský vliv na **FONTANE** i Rilke. SV, 1, 1948.

Blankenagel, J. C. Gustav **FREYTAG** on the Menace of Russia. MLN, 65, 1950.

Markiewicz, Z. Les personnages polonais chez **GOBINEAU.** C. R. de la Société Historique et Littéraire Polonaise de Paris, 1951.

Zaleski, Z. L. Victor **HUGO** et la cause de la Pologne. RLC, 24, 1952.

Anon. Aleksander fon Gumbol'dt v Rossii i poslednie ego trudy. (Alexander von **HUMBOLDT.**) VE, 7, 1871, 1-57.

Danilov, V. Sborniki pesen XVII stoletija—Ričarda Džemsa i P. A. Kvašnina. (Richard **JAMES.**) TODRL, 2, 1935, 165-80.

Alekseev, M. Amerikano-russkie literaturnye zametki: Stixotvornaja antologija Longfello o Rossii. (**LONGFELLOW**). NBLU, 8, 1946, 22-28.

Malkiewicz- Strzalkowa, M. La question des sources dans la tragi-comédie de **LOPE DE VEGA** El Rey Sin Reyno. (La Pologne dans le théâtre espagnol). PAU-AN, 3, 1950.

Vernet, J. Las fuentes de El Gran Duque de Moscovia. Cuad. de Lit. 5, 1950, 13-15.

Savin, A. Žosef de Mestr. Očerk ego političeskix idej. (De **MAISTRE.**) VE, 2, 1900, 715-45.

Markiewicz, Z. Le monde polonais dans l'oeuvre et la vie de Prosper **MÉRIMÉE.** C. R. de l'Académie Polonaise, Cracow, 4, 1948.

Struve, G. Russkie temy v novoizdannoj

perepiske Merimée. RiSl, 19, X. 1929.
Coleman, Marion Moore. A Yale Man
Studies Russian; James Gates PERCI-
VAL (1795-1856) and Russian in New
Haven a Century Ago. Russian Rev.,
8, 1949.
Kotljarevskij, N. Šekspir i staraja Rossija.
skoj Rusi XVII v. (QUEVEDO).
NBLU, 14-15, 1947, 23-25.
Anon. Russkie pesni v anglijskom pere-
vode g. Ral'stona. (English transla-
tors: W. RALSTON.) VE, 4, 1872.
Ilkova, Z. RILKE a Russko. CMF, 32.

Starr, W. T. Romain ROLLAND and Rus-
sia. RR, 40, 1949.
Kotljarevskij, N. Šekspir i staraja Rossija.
(SHAKESPEARE). VE, 5, 1916, 23-
31.
Platonova, N. Vol'ter v rabote nad Istoriej
Rossii pri Petre Velikom. (VOL-
TAIRE.) LN, 33-34, 1939, 1-24.
Alekseev, M. Russkij jazyk u nemeckogo
poéta XIV veka. (Oswald von WOL-
KENSTEIN.) In: Festschrift Orlov.
Leningrad, 1934, 557-72.